HARDY'S

TESS OF THE D'URBERVILLES

ALKA SAXENA
SUDHIR DIXIT

ATLANTIC PUBLISHERS AND DISTRIBUTORS

Published by
ATLANTIC PUBLISHERS AND DISTRIBUTORS
B-2, Vishal Enclave, Opp. Rajouri Garden, New Delhi-27
Phones : 5413460, 5429987

Sales Office
4215/1, Ansari Road, Darya Ganj, New Delhi-02
Phones : 3273880, 3285873, 3280451
Fax : 91-11-3285873
e-mail : info@atlanticbooks.com
web site : www.atlanticbooks.com

ISBN 81-7156-970-6

Typeset at
APD Computer Graphics, Delhi
Printed in India at
Mehra Offset Press, Delhi

PREFACE

Tess of the d'urbervilles (1891), Hardy's 'tragic masterpiece, deals with the story of Tess, a simple country girl whose misfortunes begin after the chance discovery of her being a descendant of a noble, yet extinct family. The subtitle of a 'pure woman' affixed to a woman who was seduced and who murdered her seducer created a great uproar and controversy. However, its popularity has immensely increased since then.

This book is a full-length study on the various issues presented in this novel and aims at solving the difficulties the novel presents to the Indian students. The novel is studied and analysed from various angles and its relation with other works of Hardy is deftly analysed. We hope this book will be extremely useful for the students.

ALKA SAXENA
SUDHIR DIXIT

CONTENTS

1

Thomas Hardy : His Life and Works

[June 2, 1840 — Jan. 11, 1928]

Hardy, eminent novelist and poet of the late Victorian era, was born close to Edgon Heath, immortalised in his novel *The Return of the Native*, in Dorset near Dorchester. The son of a stonemason, Hardy had music and architecture in his blood from his father's side. His mother came from a family of yeoman farmers and Hardy inherited the bookish tastes from his mother. The lush beautiful region of the Southern England, which Hardy named Wessex, forms the background of his literary works. No other region has been so immortalised in English fiction. In all his works characters have been taken from the Wessex countryside. A critic has rightly observed that 'In Wessex, the legendary kingdom bequeathed by Alfred, where almost all his scenes are laid, Hardy was king.'

Taken for a still birth, he was revived by the keen admonition of a vigilant nurse. Hardy was a precocious child and could read before he learnt to talk. He studied in four schools from 1848 to 1856 and studied French with a private tutor. At sixteen he was apprenticed to a local ecclesiastical architect who was also a classical scholar and incurred in Hardy a love of Greek. In 1862 Hardy was sent to Sir Arthur Bloomfield an eminent architect. In 1863 he won the national competition for essay on the application of coloured bricks and terra cotta to modern architecture. Hardy was a practising architect upto 1873. In 1874, he married Lavinia Gifford, a vicar's sister-in-law. Meanwhile he wrote poetry, which, however, couldn't be published.

In 1867, Hardy wrote his first novel *The Poor Man and the Lady* which was rejected by George Meredith and Hardy destroyed its manuscript. His next work was *Desperate Remedies*. It had a melodramatic plot and the critical opinion was also not favourable. Hardy decided to give up writing but couldn't do so and the very next year published *Under the Greenwood Tree*. Next came *A Pair of Blue Eyes*. *Far From the Madding Crowd* was Hardy's first financially successful novel. Hardy, convinced of his success as a novelist, decided to marry and settle in the outskirts of London. For the next nine years they lived in London. In 1880, Hardy fell seriously ill with a series of internal haemorrhages. In 1883, for health reasons Hardy shifted to Dorchester and in 1885 built a house called Maxgate. With a few months spent in London, and a few on the continent Hardy spent the rest of his life in Dorchester. Till 1896 Hardy continued producing a novel every year or two but the uproar over *Tess of the d'Urbervilles* and *Jude the Obscure* finally drove him to give up fiction writing and he turned wholly to poetry.

The Trumpet Major [1880], *The Woodlanders* 1887], *Tess of the d'Urbervilles* [1891] and *Jude the Obscure* [1896] were other novels published by Hardy. *Tess of the d'Urbervilles* had to be greatly changed in the serial version owing to the taste of the public; Hardy had realised its unconventional aspect and kept the original pages intact for the single volume publication. The charges of 'infidelity' and 'obscurity' were received by him with mild humour but the criticism of *Jude the Obscure* made him renounce novel writing for ever.

The Well Beloved, serialised in 1892, was published as a book in 1897. Now he took to poetry and many works including the three volume verse drama '*The Dynasts*' were written. He achieved wide acclaim both as a poet and as a novelist. In 1910 he received the Order of Merit and the freedom of the City of Dorchester. Honorary degrees were conferred upon him by Oxford, Cambridge, Bristol and St. Andrew's. The Royal Society of literature awarded him the gold medal. He became the honorary fellow of the Royal Institute of British Architect.

In 1912 Hardy's first wife Lavinia died and he married his secretary Florence Digdale in 1914 at the age of 74. The 14 years of married life that he spent with her were extremely happy. Both of his marriages were childless.

Hardy died in 1928 on Jan. 11. He was cremated and buried in the Poet's corner in Westminster Abbey, his heart was, however, removed and buried in his first wife's grave, near Dorchester. He wished to be remembered as a poet but his reputation as a novelist far outweighs his merits as a poet. *Tess* and *Jude*, the two novels that created an uproar in the late Victorian era, are now acclaimed as his masterpieces and are a prized collection of the library of every student of literature.

Hardy's Literary Works

Critics have classified Hardy's fictional works according to two nomenclatures.

(i)	Novels of Character and Environment	(i)	Pastoral Tragedies
(ii)	Romances and Fantasies	(ii)	Pastoral Romances
(iii)	Novels of Ingenuity	(iii)	Pastoral Comedies
		(iv)	Pastoral Extravaganza

Poetic Collections

[i] Wessex Poems [1898]
[ii] Poems of Past and Present [1901]
[iii] The Dynasts [1903,1906,1908]
[iv] Time's Laughing Stocks [1909]
[v] Satires of circumstances [1914]
[vi] Selected poems [1916]
[vii] Moments of Vision [1917]
[viii] Late Lyrics and Earlier
[ix] The Famous tragedy of the Queen of Cornwall [1923]
[x] The.........shadows
[xi] Winter words [1928] {published posthumously}

Collection of Short Stories

I. The Wessex Tales [1883]

II. A Group of Noble Dames [1891]
III. Life's Little Ironies [1894]
IV. A Changed Man [1913]
V. A Few Trusted Characters

HARDY HAS HIMSELF FAVOURED THIS CLASSIFICATION

I. *Novels of Characters & Environment*

1. Under the Greenwood Tree 1872
2. Far from the Madding Crowd 1874
3. Return of the Native 1878
4. The Mayor of Casterbridge 1886
5. The Woodlanders 1887
6. Tess of the d'Urbervilles 1891
7. Jude the Obscure 1895

II. *Romances & Fantasies*

1. A Pair of Blue Eyes 1873
2. The Trumpet Major 1880
3. Two on a Tower 1882
4. The Well-Beloved 1897

III. *Novels of Ingenuity*

1. Desperate Remedies 1871
2. The Hand of Ethelberta 1876
3. A Laodicean 1881

OTHER CLASSIFICATION OF HARDY'S NOVELS

I. *Pastoral tragedies*

1. Return of the Native 1878
2. The Mayor of Casterbridge 1886
3. Tess of the d'Urbervilles 1891
4. Jude the Obscure 1895

II. *Pastoral Comedies*

1. The Hand of Ethelberta 1875
2. A Laodicean 1881
3. Two on a Tower 1881

III. *Pastoral Romances*

1.	Under the Greenwood Tree	1872
2.	Far From the Madding Crowd	1874
3.	A Pair of Blue Eyes	1873
4.	The Trumpet Major	1880
5.	The Woodlanders	1887

IV. *Pastoral Extravaganza*

1.	The Well Beloved	1897

Lascelles Abercrombie divides Hardy's chief novels into dramas and epics. In the dramatic novels like *Far from the Madding Crowd, The Return of the Native* and *The Mayor of Casterbridge* the essence of the plot lies in the interaction of a number of different lives. In the epic novels like *Tess of the d'Urbervilles* and *Jude the Obscure*, we see the unfolding of the tragic life of a single character.

2

Hardy as a Tragic Novelist

1. The Only Tragic Novelist

"The true index of Hardy's stature is that he is almost the only tragic novelist in our literature and that when we consider him we have ultimately to do so in relation to Shakespeare and Webster and to the Greek dramatists," asserts Walter Allen. No other English novelist has traversed the tragic paths so consistently and so convincingly. His temperament is as tragic as was Matthew Arnold's and his tragic vision is so broad that it bears comparison with Shakespeare's tragic art. Other novelists have written one or two great tragic novels, but Hardy produced great tragic novels one after another. He was so convinced of the righteousness of his tragic art, that he boldly wrote his great masterpieces when the public was not yet ready to receive and appreciate his tragedies. When he found it too hot to write in the tragic mode, he chose to lay down his tragic pen and did not compromise with his tragic art. His four great tragic novels are, *The Return of the Native*, [the earliest great tragedy, which has, however, been given a happy ending on the publisher's request], *The Mayor of Casterbridge, Tess of the D'Urbervilles* and *Jude the Obscure.*

2. Tragic Vision Influenced by Drama

David Cecil writes, "To achieve tragic intensity he turned to tragedy for a model; and to find true tragedy in English letters he had to go back to writers who lived before the novel was invented. Tess differs from a Dickens heroine. She is not more like Anna Karenina, however. She is more like the Duchess of Malfi."

Hardy had no predecessors in the field of the true tragic novel and this is why he had to go to the tragic drama for inspiration and for imitation. He went to Greek dramatists Aeschylus and Sophocles for lessons. It must be kept in mind that Hardy studied the Greek dramatists in Greek itself. Routh says, 'Hardy had trained his mind on Greek literature, and,...he was especially impressed by Sophocles.' The Greek drama is rooted in a pagan religion, where gods intervene in human life and affect human actions. In Greek plays, destiny plays a more important role than the actions of the hero. In *Oedipus Rex*, his magnum opus, Sophocles did not hold Oedipus responsible for incest, but held the destiny or gods responsible for his misfortune. In the play, even before Oedipus was born, it had been foretold that he would murder his father and marry his mother Jocasta. The Greek drama strongly believed in determinism and Hardy found this determinism or the supremacy of destiny congenial to his taste.

Although Aristotle lays down the dictum that human actions should be the root cause of tragedy, the fact remains that when gods intervene, human actions cannot be unaffected. Gods can even affect or disturb the thinking process of a person, as is evidenced in the Greek play *Ajax*. Hardy also takes lessons from Elizabethan, or to be more precise Jacobean, drama. In Jacobean drama the average plot was constructed on and around a bizarre love-story, spiced with adultery and mismatched marriages. Significantly enough, Hardy's plots are also normally constructed around a love-or-marriage story. In *The Return of the Native* we find two instances of frustrated love [in the love-affair of Wildeve-Eustacia] as well as mismatched marriages [two mismatched marriages of Wildeve-Thomasin and Eustacia-Clym]. In *Tess of the D'Urbervilles*, we find Tess's seduction, unhappy marriage, Alec's murder and Tess's final hanging — which are Jacobean in spirit. In *Jude the Obscure*, Father Little Time hangs himself and his two younger brothers 'Done because we are too menny.' Beside this macabre episode, there are two mismatched marriages [of Sue-Phillotson and Jude-Arabella] as well as adultery [Sue-Jude]. In *The Mayor of Casterbridge* also pre-marital sex features in Lucetta-Henchard relationship besides adultery in Susan-Newson living together without marriage. The plot of a Hardy novel is hardly the plot of a Victorian novel; it is rather the plot of an Elizabethan drama. David Cecil avers, 'So far from being the first of the modern school of novelists, Hardy is the last representative of the tradition and spirit of the Elizabethan drama.'

3. Concept of Tragedy in Hardy and Before

In Aristotelian tragedy, the cause of the tragedy was hamartia and the result was cathartic, brought about by the reversal of the situation. In Shakespearean tragedy the tragic hero was high-ranked and he suffered due to some tragic flaw. In the last moments of a Shakespearean tragedy, there was the restoration of order and peace, along with the sense of tragic waste.

Hardy's concept of tragedy is radically different from Aristotelian as well as Shakespearean tragedy. His characters are no exalted personages, they rather belong to the low-class. Henchard in *The Mayor of Casterbridge* at the beginning is a hay-trusser; Clym in *The Return of the Native* is reduced to the status of a furze-cutter in the middle of the novel; Jude becomes a common mason and Tess a common labourer. However, in Hardy 'tragic flaw' is conspicuous by its absence. There is no tragic flaw in Jude or Tess; they suffer not due to their actions. As the source of their tragedy is outside them, so they need not have 'tragic flaw' within them. In Shakespeare *'Character is Destiny,'* but in Hardy '*Destiny is Character*'. Character is not responsible for the tragedy of a Hardy hero or heroine. Tess does not choose to be seduced, she acts for the best but the worst befalls her. She is more sinned against than sinning because she suffers from no fault of hers, but owing to circumstances beyond her control.

Cross comments on Hardy's innovation, "It has been a tacit assumption in English tragedy that the dramatic hero must commit some deed from which he suffers. The deed may be a crime, as in Macbeth; it may issue from a fault in judgment, as in the case of Lear...George Eliot, somewhat like Shakespeare, traced the events of her somber novels to free individual acts of will... Tess is the main and central actor, who, from first to last, Hardy insists, is free from any wrong doing. In this reversal of the traditions of tragedy both in our drama and our novel, Hardy is an innovator."

In a Shakespearean tragedy, order is restored in the end; the king is dead, long live the king. Angels sing Hamlet to his rest, after Macbeth's death the righteous prince sits on the throne. The villain is punished and though tragic waste is there in the form of the death of good persons, yet the ultimate note is one of continuity and calmness, of 'all passion spent.' In Hardy's novels, on the other hand, we find that though tragic waste is prominently there, the sense of calmness and serenity is missing. However, Hardy attempts to provide a sense of continuity in the end somewhat against his will. In *The Return of the Native*, he makes Thomasin remarry after the deaths of Wildeve and Eustacia; in *Tess of the D'Urbervilles* he makes Angel and Liza-lu walk together after the death of Tess; in *The Mayor of Casterbridge*, he makes Elizabeth-Jane marry Farfrae. However, the end of a Hardy novel is disturbing because it does not end in serenity and lacks the completion of catharsis. The last paragraph of *Tess of the d'Urbervilles* refers to a malevolent President of the Immortals and the last line of *The Mayor of Casterbridge* is perfectly disturbing, *'happiness was but the occasional episode in a general drama of pain.'*

4. Democratization of Tragedy

Tragedy before Hardy was restricted to great personages as in the Shakespearean or Greek drama. Hardy democratized tragedy from town-life and rooted it in a definite province of England called Wessex. All his great tragic novels, except perhaps *Jude the Obscure*, are rooted in the Wessex soil geographically as well as temperamentally. His chief characters are not from the upper-class society or higher echelons of state, they are common men as far as their class is concerned. Their strength lies not in their family background or financial status; their real strength lies in their powerful rustic nature with which they act and react to the alien circumstances and experiences. His heroes or heroines are at the root deeply rustic; all of them possess nobility in nature, but not in society. In Shakespeare, the thrust of the characters is upward; Macbeth is a general and he becomes a king, Hamlet is a prince and he wants to become the king. In Hardy, the thrust or progress of the characters is downward. In *Tess of the D'Urbervilles*, the heroine is an independent girl, then she becomes a caretaker of fowls, then she becomes an unmarried mother or a fallen woman depending upon our viewpoint, then she becomes a dairymaid, then a common agricultural labourer, then an adulteress and ultimately a murderess. In *Jude the Obscure*, the hero wants to be a clergyman, but his ambitions are mercilessly thwarted and he ends up being an ordinary stone-mason. In *The Return of the Native*, Clym is in diamond-business at the beginning, then he hopes to become a teacher and then he is reduced to the miserable state of a furze-cutter. In *The Mayor of Casterbridge*, Henchard is a common hay-trusser, then he becomes a rich man and a Mayor, but ultimately in the end he again becomes a common hay-trusser. Hardy democratized the English tragedy from city life and noble heroes to portray rustic life and rustic characters. His characters may be from the low class but, as David Cecil puts it, 'Hardy's characters are all greatest in their most tragic moments.'

5. Destiny is Character

Hardy as a novelist believes in fatalism, which was a common pagan belief of the Wessex people. George Sampson writes, 'Hardy saw man living, loving, labouring and perishing against a background of remote, indifferent, implacable forces, themselves unconscious and uncontrolled...As far apart in spirit as in time from the great Greek writers, he had their view of man as born to endure that which was to befall him; and he expressed his faith in creations that often rise to the dignity of tragedy.'

In Hardy's novels, character is less important than destiny. The characters suffer not due to their actions or thoughts, but due to their destiny. David Cecil sums up Hardy's craftsmanship, 'A struggle between man on the one hand and, on the other, an omnipotent and indifferent Fate — that is Hardy's interpretation of the human situation...Man in Hardy's books is ranged against impersonal forces, the forces conditioning his fate.'

In Hardy's novels, we find that destiny works through chance events and coincidences; and human beings are too weak and powerless to win against their fate. Edwin Muir avers, 'Hardy takes a short cut to tragedy by reducing life to a formula.... His characters are passive.... He does not believe that character is fate; so that for him tragedy does not proceed from action, but resides with the power which determines all action.'

The belief in determinism may be a personal penchant, but it certainly is an artistic shortcoming, as the tragic force is crippled. If destiny cannot be changed by human will or action or thought, then what is the point in the struggle, and what is really tragic after all. Bradley, alongwith Hegel, believed that only that suffering or misfortune can be called tragic, which springs in great part from human agency. In Hardy's tragedy, there is a lot of sound and fury; but the splendour is missing. David Cecil writes; 'Shakespeare's tragic emotion is a blazing flame; Hardy's broods like a thundercloud.'

6. The Supernatural Element

The supernatural element is strong and striking in Shakespearean tragedies; it is the dominant note of the Greek tragedy. In Hardy, the supernatural element is conditioned by his undue reliance on chance events, but even in pure forms the elements of the supernatural lurk in his novels. David Cecil comments; 'It is striking that at the climax of his drama he often sounds a supernatural note. Henchard's neglect of the weather-doctor's warning is a contributing cause of his catastrophe; Eustacia goes to her death the very moment that her waxen effigy is wasting away before the fire of the avenging Susan. Even in *Tess of the d'Urbervilles* where Hardy is openly in rebellion against the old creeds, he strikes the supernatural chord. As Tess starts on her ill-fated marriage journey the evil omens gather round her as thickly as though she were the heroine of a saga.' A cock crows in the afternoon on her marriage-day; the coach is ominous, the foreboding sound of the superstitious d'Urberville coach is heard. Hardy used all these omens and superstitions in his novels, because in Wessex these were a real belief; the point of view was rustic and hence it was artistically correct to incorporate the supernatural element. Like the oracles of Delphi or the prophecies in Shakespeare, the ill omens of Hardy also prove correct and we find that Hardy uses this great tragic element judiciously and skilfully.

7. Pessimistic Outlook

The Greeks were disillusioned about the incongruity between human actions and their consequences. As Routh says, "The first and greatest of all poets Homer makes the King of the Gods declare that of all creatures which breathe and crawl, man is the most to be pitied;... Sophocles and Euripides both confess that death is preferable to life. Hardy himself seems to have been at one with them." Hardy's conception of life was essentially tragic. For him "happiness is an occasional episode in a general drama of pain." Man's existence between earth and sky is 'like a fly.' Hardy uses the fly image in *Tess* and he also quotes this determinist image from Shakespeare's *King Lear,*

> As flies are we to wanton gods;
> They kill us for their sport.

David Cecil propounds, "The tragic intensity of Hardy's work is increased by his conviction that there is a fundamental dissonance between man and his environment, by the ironical contrast he draws between poor striving humanity and the ruthless omnipotent destiny with which he vainly contends."

8. Hardy's Tragic Vision

Hardy, apart from his novels has also written about his tragic vision; his beliefs on the artistic requirements in a tragedy. First of all, he believes that 'realism is not Art.' By rejecting realism, he is rejecting all the naturalistic objections against his novels *e.g.*, the excessive reliance on fate and chance. Next, he believes that the best or the highest tragedy is that of a 'Worthy encompassed by the Inevitable.' Thus, he clarifies his philosophical background of his novels as Good man/woman *vs.* Destiny.

Hardy thought that 'human nature must never be abnormal.... The uncommonness must be in the events, not in the characters.' And this is true in the case of his novels. All of his major characters are probable and credible [except perhaps Sue], while the incidents are at times improbable. Hardy demands that 'A story must be exceptional enough to justify its telling. We taletellers are all Ancient Mariners and none of us is warranted in stopping Wedding Guests [in other words, the hurrying public] unless he has something more unusual to relate than the ordinary experience of every average man and woman.'

9. Construction-Pattern of His Tragedies

[i] Usually the setting is Wessex and the protagonist belongs to or resides in this rustic setting.

[ii] His major characters come into contact with some superior man, as Tess with Angel, Henchard with Farfrae, Jude with Sue, Eustacia with Clym.

[iii] His major female characters have pre-marital sex or romance [Sue, Tess, Eustacia, Lucetta]. Before the true love, false love enters their loves. This past love-affair is hidden by the characters and when it is revealed by some chance events, as is inevitable in Hardy's novels, the catastrophe comes.

[iv] His major male characters suffer disastrous separation from their wives [Henchard, Angel, Clym, Jude, Phillotson].

[v] Children talk philosophy and usually one or more children die in his novels, if there are any children in the novel. Father Little Time in *Jude*, Abraham in *Tess of the d'Urbervilles*, Tess's little child in *Tess*, hanging of the children in *Jude*, Elizabeth-Jane in *The Mayor of Casterbridge.*

[vi] Heredity is a complex issue and its influence on the present individual is traced; especially in *Tess of the d'Urbervilles* and *Jude the Obscure.*

[vii] Love is always a catastrophe in Hardy and his major characters find themselves in trouble due to frustrated or desperate or disclosed love-affair.

[viii] Chance events precipitate the crisis in Hardy's novels. Letters do not reach their destination [*Tess of the d'Urbervilles* and *The Return of the Native*]; secret letters are revealed [*The Mayor of Casterbridge*], people find unexpectedly their nemesis [in all his tragic novels].

[ix] The conflict of pagan *vs.* Christian is present in almost all his novels. In *Tess of the d'Urbervilles* this is a major issue, which is also true of the later tragedy *Jude the*

Obscure. In almost all his major novels, there is an adverse comment on the First Cause, God or Christian religion.

[x] His two tragic novels are divided into six Books or Chapters [*Jude* and *The Return of the Native*], *The Mayor of Casterbridge* alone has no such division, while *Tess of the d'Urbervilles* alone is divided into phases and with an unusual number of seven phases. This division of the novel in phases is a convenient plot-construction technique.

[xi] In all his novels, crisis comes in the very first chapter or early on. Henchard sells his wife in the very first chapter, Tess's ancestry is revealed quite early on and in the first phase, she is seduced.

[xii] In each of his novels, there are pairs of sexual/platonic love. [Thomasin/Eustacia {in *The Return of the Native*}, Alec/Angel {in *Tess*}, Lucetta/Elizabeth-Jane {in *The Mayor of Casterbridge*}, Sue/Arabella {in *Jude the Obscure*}]. Thomasin, Angel, Elizabeth-Jane and Sue come into the category of Platonic lovers, while Eustacia, Alec, Lucetta and Arabella are sexual.

[xiii] All his tragic novels are essentially the tragedies of a single person; the only exception is perhaps *Jude the Obscure*, which may be interpreted as the tragedy of two persons, Jude and Sue.

10. Defects

[I] *Limited in Geography* : Hardy's tragic vision is limited to a single geographical area : Wessex. The environment is not conducive to portray in full all the tragic issues bothering the modern world. Hardy's tragic world is extremely limited as war, poverty, industrialisation, exploitation and other major tragic issues are left out. The tragic vision of Hardy is basically a folk-vision which leaves the urban world untouched.

[II] *Limited in Range* : Hardy's range is extremely limited. He believes that a malignant destiny thwarts human efforts to achieve their goals. Hence, his art is essentially anti-realist and not a faithful portrayal of real life. All his novels are based on this thesis and they seem more arguments than novels proper.

All his novels show love to be fatal and marriages to be disasters; this is not always true. Hardy seems to be prejudiced in such portrayals.

[III] *Not realistic* : Hardy's characters are embodiments of ideas and not real. Even their conversation seems to be propaganda or arguments for or versus some cause. Even little children become mouthpieces of Hardy's philosophy. In Tess, Angel and Alec seem to be lifeless embodiments of intellect and flesh respectively. The dialogue is also stagey at times, as the situation is theatrical. Hardy puts his weighty philosophical musings into the mouths of his frail characters, who cannot carry the philosophical burden.

[IV] *A pessimistic vision* : In Hardy's tragedy, whoever acts is doomed to suffer. Tess takes the responsibility of Prince's death and she suffers excessively, Eustacia tries to escape Edgon Heath and she suffers. Lawrence points out, "This is the theme of novel after novel : remain quite within the convention, and you are good, safe, and happy in the long run, though you never have the vivid pang of sympathy on your side : or, on the other hand, be passionate, individual, wilful, you will find the security of the convention a walled prison, you will escape, and you will die, either of your own lack of strength to bear the isolation and the exposure, or, by direct revenge from the community, or from both."

[V] *Determinism* : Baker writes, 'Tragedy loses dignity and beauty in the exact measure that it is the play of alien forces controlling the actions of a mere pawn.... There is, moreover, no ethical significance left, such as characterises genuine tragedy, since personality is at a minimum.' Since suffering of the characters does not spring mainly from their actions, the causal relationship is broken, which is a serious blemish on Hardy's art. Edward Bright asserts, 'Too much machinery is employed in Tess to bring about the catastrophe; and in the latter part of the tale especially, disaster follows disaster in so close and yet disconnected a manner that all sense of verisimilitude is destroyed.'

11. Conclusion

Hardy as a tragic artist stands alone in the field of English novel. His is a strange combination of the primitive and the modern; folk and universal; determinism and melioration. He takes down tragedy from the bourgeois heights to proletarian depths and this was a revolutionary innovation. He discussed the taboos — about sex and God — in his novels fearlessly. He, like Ibsen, tried to raise problem-issues and moral questions. His citadel of reputation stands mainly on his four tragic pillars. He is the only great tragic novelist in English literature. In the words of Virginia Woolf, "if we are to place Hardy among his fellows, we must call him the greatest tragic writer among English novelists."

3

Hardy's Philosophy

1. Introduction

Hardy's novels are shaped by his philosophy, and this is why his philosophy becomes important when we evaluate his novels. Usually novelists change their viewpoints or ideologies in their career. They get affected by the current ideologies or societal changes. But Hardy's standpoint never changed. Right from his first novel, he had the vague idea of the relentless forces inflicting torture on the hapless man and throughout his career he tried to give a definite shape to this vague philosophical idea. Grimsditch asserts that the philosophic attitude "strongly colours the fabric of the greater novels, and it would be impossible to understand Hardy without examining it very fully as to understand Dickens or Jane Austen without taking into account the humour of the one or the irony of the other.... The invasion of the realm of metaphysics is the most outstanding characteristic of Thomas Hardy's art."

2. His Personal Opinion

Hardy humbly admits that he has no definite philosophical doctrine to preach, that his pessimism is not his consistent creed, that he should be treated as an evolutionary meliorist and his novels as 'explorations of reality.' In spite of Hardy's denials, critics keep on stressing the philosophical basis of Hardy's fiction. Hardy's so-called philosophy is partly shaped by various philosophers and thinkers like Schopenhauer, Darwin etc. and largely by the two Greek dramatists, Aeschylus and Sophocles. In Hardy's age, Darwin and his theory of evolution were popular and a scepticism about Bible's veracity was being doubted. Hardy's novels are set in a simple and primitive world, but the ideas actuating and pervading them are complex and modern. Philosophy is obvious enough in his novels, it is easily to be found in his poems and it is the basis of his epic-drama '*Dynasts.*' Baker writes, 'In "Hap," the poem written in 1866, the universe is contemplated as the sport of chance; in *The Dynasts*, forty years later, it is a complete system of determinism. The main trend of his thought was settled by his reading of the utilitarians and Darwinians : J. S. Mill, Spencer, Huxley, and others.... Much later on, it was from Clodd that he derived "the idea of the Unconscious Will becoming conscious with flux of time" which he wove into *The Dynasts*. His sense of a Will other and more compulsive than man's was deepened by his study of the Greek tragedians, as the novels attest; he knew these long before he became acquainted with Schopenhauer and Hartmann.'

3. Pessimistic Philosophy

"His philosophy," writes David Cecil, "from the time he began to write, was confirmedly gloomy." Baker points out, "Hardy's conception of life was essentially tragic : the conflict is one in which there is but the remotest chance of escape, so heavily are the scales weighted by man's impercipience, his inability to coerce his own insubordinate nature and the checks and snares plentifully sown in his path by some occult malice. *In The Mayor of Casterbridge*, Elizabeth-Jane thinks about Farfrae's viewpoint, 'He seemed to feel exactly as she felt about life and its surroundings — that they were a tragical rather than a comical thing'. And the last line of the novel more completely states the author's philosophy : 'happiness was but the occasional episode in a general drama of pain.' In *The Return of the Native* also, all major characters suffer invariably. Eustacia and Clym suffer most. Eustacia thinks, 'O, the cruelty of putting me into this ill-conceived world!' In Jude the Obscure, Phillotson speaks, 'Cruelty is the law pervading all nature and society' and Sue says, "All the ancient wrath of the Power above us has been vented upon us, His poor creatures, and we must submit. There is no choice. We must. It is no use fighting against God!" In *Tess of the d'Urbervilles* we find the reversal of the optimistic faith in a benign God,

'God's *not* in his heaven : all's wrong with the world.'

In his four major tragic novels, major characters die; Henchard *{The Mayor of Casterbridge}*, Eustacia & Wildeve *{The Return of the Native}*, Jude *{Jude the Obscure}*, and Tess & Alec *{Tess of the d'Urbervilles}*. Even before death, they suffer a lot and their suffering is greater than what their deeds deserved. Hardy everywhere makes his major characters suffer from chance incidents and there is a clear suggestion that suffering is their destiny.. Hardy's God is not a benevolent one, but a ferocious one like the pitiless beast of Yeats' The Second Coming. Hardy's characters are pitted against their environment, society, social norms, moral and ethical codes of the Victorian generation, and above all, against a ruthless omnipotent power, 'the ingenious machinery contrived by the gods for reducing human possibilities to a minimum' [The Mayor of Casterbridge].

4. The First Cause

Hardy did not believe in God. He didn't think that the omnipotent has a definite shape. According to him, the universe is evolutionary, as envisaged by Darwin. Still he believed that there is an omnipotent presence, which should be called as the Immanent Will or the First Cause. The First Cause simply means that this omnipresent, omnipotent thing comes first, is responsible for all creation, and it causes the evolution of mankind. Hudson remarks, "Hardy held that there is not active intelligence, no just and loving God, behind human destiny, but that Creation is swayed by an unconscious mechanical force, sightless, dumb, mindless, and equally indifferent to either the sufferings or the joys of mankind." The universe is impersonal; its growth is automatic and the law of growth is cruelty as evidenced by 'survival of the fittest' theory. The First Cause of Hardy is equivalent to the traditional God; with the difference that Hardy's is cruel.

The First Cause has caused everything and all human miseries have resulted from the imperfections of the First Cause. Hardy regards the First Cause in theory as blind and indifferent to human beings, but in his novels he makes the First Cause hostile to man. Hardy makes explicit references to this First Cause in his novels. In *The Return of the Native*, he writes, "Human beings, in their generous endeavour to construct a hypothesis that shall not degrade a First Cause, have always hesitated to conceive a dominant power of lower moral quality than their own." In *Jude the Obscure*, Sue thinks, 'the first cause worked automatically like a somnambulist, and not reflectively like a sage.' In *Tess of the d'Urbervilles* also, he writes, "This consciousness upon which he had intruded was the single opportunity of existence ever vouchsafed to Tess by an unsympathetic First Cause." In all his major novels, Hardy repeatedly refers to the First Cause and makes ironical comment on it. In this manner he underlines the lower moral status of the deciding forces and the higher moral worth of the suffering humanity. In each of his tragic novels Hardy holds the First Cause responsible for the suffering of his protagonists.

In Hardy's philosophy Immanent Will is the First Cause, the prime mover, the cause of all phenomena. Hardy called the supreme energy or cause of things as Immanent Will. The First Cause of Hardy is nothing else than the supreme energy working within the universe. We must keep in mind that the word '*Immanentism*' coined in 1907 means 'a theory according to which God or an abstract mind or spirit pervades the world,' while the word '*immament*' means 'inherent, or having existence or effect only within the mind or consciousness.' Thus, the Immanent Will relates both to the will of the First Cause as well as the inherent will of protagonists, which is conditioned by the First Cause.

5. Nature as an Instrument

Nature plays an important role in Hardy's novels as the background of human misery. Nature remains unaffected by, indifferent to and unconscious of human suffering. However, nature is an expression of the Immanent Will of the First Cause. In Hardy's opinion, external nature is also responsible for the tragic fate. David Cecil writes, "For one thing, nature controls the conduct of life in an agricultural community.... Further, nature was to him the emblem of those impersonal forces of Fate with whom he presents mankind as in conflict...For Hardy, as for the ancient writers of Greece and Rome, landscape is always a landscape, with figures." Though Hardy's nature-descriptions are extremely visual and authentic, these are primarily in relation to human life. David Cecil writes, 'Hardy recorded nature primarily in its relation to the life of man. Human life, therefore, is an essential feature in his picture of the natural world.' In *Tess of the d'Urbervilles* natural world is shown in relation to the human world. Tess is seduced sleeping in the lap of nature; rats and mice are killed during harvesting by machines; Tess is finally captured in the lap of nature; her romance with Angel and Alec's lustful designs both proceed against the natural background. 'Nature, first of all, played a larger part in his books than in those of any other English novelist. It is not just the background in his drama but a leading character in it. Sometimes it exercises an active influence of the course of events : more often it is a spiritual agent, colouring the mood and shaping the disposition of human beings.'

Hardy uses nature in the human sense also, for example, he thinks that pre-marital sex, though immoral, is a natural thing. Even in *Tess of the d'Urbervilles* we find the two opposing elements : the laws of nature and the laws of Victorian movement. In *Tess of the d'Urbervilles*, Hardy also varies the scenic background for artistic purpose, he nowhere show nature sympathetic towards Tess. Thus, we find that in Hardy, nature is an extension of the First Cause and hence cruel to the protagonists.

6. Irony of Circumstance

In Hardy's philosophy, irony of circumstance holds an important position. In every novel, this irony is present. This irony has two features; when a person desires one thing and the outcome is opposite and when a person marries, he usually makes a mismarriage. The novel is based on the irony of circumstance; the d'Urbervilles residing at The Chase are not the true d'Urbervilles. Had the parson told this to the father of Tess, her tragedy could have been averted. Tess expects help from the d'Urbervilles of The Chase, but ironically she gets troubles. The right man Angel comes first, but he does not pay much attention to her at the May dance and the wrong man enters her life. Angel asks forgiveness for his pre-marital affair, but is unable to forgive Tess for the same fault. Tess goes to Alec as she does not expect Angel to return and forgive her, but ironically he returns to forgive her. Tess and Angel are opposites in nature; Tess and Alec belong to the 'pagan' creed and had Tess married Alec, all would have been right but ironically this does not happen. In the seduction-scene, Tess sleeps when Alec returns, and her sleepy state causes her deflowering. At the crucial time, Queen of Diamond starts fighting Tess and Alec gets the opportunity of getting Tess on the horseback. In Hardy's thought, irony of circumstance springs from the Cosmic Irony. M. H. Abrams explains, "Cosmic Irony or the irony of fate exists, when God, or destiny, or the universal process, is represented as though deliberately manipulating events to frustrate and mock the protagonist. This is a favourite structural device of Thomas Hardy. In his Tess of the d'Urbervilles, the heroine, having lost her virtue because of her innocence, then loses her happiness because of her honesty, finds it again only by murder, and having been briefly happy, is hanged."

In *The Return of the Native* also, we find irony of circumstance in the marriage of Clym and Eustacia, 'Take all the varying hates felt by Eustacia Vye towards the heath, and translate them into loves, and you have the heart of Clym.' Irony lies in this mismatched marriage, like other marriages of the same kind in Hardy.

7. Chance and Fate

"A struggle between man on the one hand and, on the other, an omnipotent and indifferent Fate — that is Hardy's interpretation of the human situation...the conflict is not, as in most novels, between one man and another, or between man and an institution. Man in Hardy's books is ranged against impersonal forces, the forces conditioning his fate," writes David Cecil. In Hardy's philosophy, fate is responsible for the tragedy of life. Man is destined to suffer, and his suffering is caused by external as well as internal forces. Even the internal forces are guided by the external forces. The human will, the thinking process, the energy to act — all these are determined by the First Cause and this is why men are mere pawns on the panoramic chessboard of this universe. David Cecil explains, "Fate is an abstraction, and in order that it may play an active part in a human drama... Hardy embodies Fate in various forms. Sometimes it appears as a natural force. Henchard's plans for making himself rich are brought to nought by a bad harvest. Chiefly, however, the forces of Fate in Hardy's novels incarnate themselves in two guises — as chance and as love. Of these, chance is the most typical. In no other novels does chance exercise such a conspicuous influence on the course of events."

> Edward Bright asserts, 'Too much machinery is employed in Tess to bring about the catastrophe; and in the latter part of the tale especially, disaster follows disaster in so close and yet disconnected a manner that all sense of verisimilitude is destroyed.' There are too many coincidences and chance events in his novels.

[i] The first coincidence is that Tess sleeps while driving the cart, and, the morning mail-cart kills her horse. Had her father not got drunk she would not have driven the cart. Even if she had not fallen asleep, the tragedy could have been averted.

[ii] The second coincidence is that she falls asleep when Alec returns and seduces her. Had she kept awake, she could have resisted the attempt and retained her purity.

[iii] The most significant coincidence is that her confessional letter is thrust beneath the carpet.

[iv] By chance, Angel's parents are at church when Tess goes to seek them. And she does not choose to wait for them.

[v] By chance, she finds Alec preaching and then he re-enters her life.

[vi] Another coincidence is that at Flintcomb Ash, all her friends of Talbothays and her foes of Trantridge reappear.

[vii] Her letter to Angel in Brazil is delayed and he reaches home a few days too late.

The reliance on coincidences and chance-events as the external expression of the malignant Fate is Hardy's favourite technique, and Church writes, "coincidence plays too large a part in these tales. But so it does again in the Greek records of human fate. And so it does too in real life."

8. Love as Destructive Element

Love is the only source of happiness in this miserable world, but the First Cause has deprived human beings of getting love in this world. Love, conceived by Hardy is "the Lord of terrible aspect" — a blind, irresistible power, seizing on human beings whether they will or not; intoxicating in its inception, but, more often than not, bringing ruin in its train. Love is especially pre-marital love in Hardy and hence love becomes guilt after marriage. Love-affairs are kept hidden but in Hardy's fiction, past love-affairs are revealed regularly and due to that protagonists suffer. In *The Return of the Native*, Eustacia suffers for her pre-marital love to Wildeve, in *The Mayor of Casterbridge*, Lucetta's love-affair with Henchard is exposed and she dies thereof; in *Jude the Obscure*, almost everybody has an affair with somebody or the other; in *Tess of the d'Urbervilles*, the seduction when confessed causes her misery. The problem is more complex in *Tess of the d'Urbervilles*; here Alec terribly loves Tess and Tess loves Angel. This cross-connection of love-passion is responsible for their doom.

9. Resigned attitude is best

Hardy's rustic characters do not suffer; only his major characters suffer. This is so because the rustic characters are fatalistic and they do not try to improve their lot by fighting their destiny. The major characters passionately try to improve their lot and this attitude is responsible for their suffering. Hardy believed that if man lived patiently and did not try to force his own will upon events, destruction could be avoided. Tess undertakes responsibility for things beyond her control, and that is what destroys her. She holds herself responsible for Prince's death as well as for the welfare of her family and due to this aggressive attitude her life becomes tragic. Had she remained content with fatalistic resignation, she could have remained normally.

Hardy thought that passions and obsessions are obstacles in the path of happiness. Had Henchard not hated Farfrae so deeply, had Tess not hated Alec so much, had Sue and Jude been normal, had Eustacia not had the passion to escape the Heath or had Clym not had the passion to become a school-teacher in the Heath itself — their lives would have remained normal. They struggled to get out of their allotted destiny, and due to this they suffer.

10. Meliorist

Hardy calls himself an evolutionary meliorist, meaning evolution with further improvement. Charlotte Thompson writes, "Tess's imaginative process also shows traces of Hardy's evolutionary meliorism, his theory that man, consciously suffering, compassionating, exhibiting noble or humane behaviour, modifies the Unconscious by teaching it what it means to be conscious, so that in time the Universal mind acquires the requisite sympathy to reform its indifferent, mechanical ways." In *Tess of the d'Urbervilles*, we find in the final scene the evidence of this evolutionary meliorism. Liza-Lu is an improved version of Tess, inheriting all her good qualities and not possessing the streak of sexuality enveloping Tess. When Angel and she walk together, Hardy means it to be an example of his evolutionary philosophy, although it distracts and is implausible on the artistic grounds.

11. Defects of Hardy's Philosophy

[i] *Inconsistent philosophy* : Throughout his career, Hardy's philosophy kept on changing; what did not change was his pessimism. Sometimes he said that the First Cause is neither good nor bad; but in his novels we find that the First Cause almost always works malevolently against mankind. Baker writes, 'It was unfortunate that he kept shifting his ground... Hardy was always seeking a better theory to substantiate his tragic view of things... Hardy was a confused thinker.' In Tess, Hardy sets his story in the pagan setting but he uses the sun-god motif inconsistently. The Sun-god on one hand is shown as the creative source of energy helping growth and fertility; on the other hand it is scorching and destructive, on whose altar Tess is sacrificed.

[ii] *Unnecessary propaganda and preaching* : David Cecil remarks, "The most fatal error into which he was led by his lack of critical sense was preaching. At moments, obsessed by his views about the universe, he turns from an imaginative creator

into a propagandist. Just when we are spellbound by Hardy the novelist, Hardy the preacher bobs up, and instantly the spell is broken." In *Tess* this preaching is too obvious. Tess is an eighteen-year-old girl, talking philosophy with her little brother,

> "Did you say the stars were worlds, Tess?"
>
> 'Yes."
>
> ....
>
> 'Which do we live on — a splendid one or a blighted one?'
>
> 'A blighted one' [chapter 4].

David Cecil writes, "Here is no unsophisticated country girl speaking. Through her lips comes the voice of a middle-aged novelist, brooding in gloomy mood on the riddle of the painful earth. For 'Tess' is a late book. The preaching tendency grew on Hardy." Even in *Jude* we find Hardy puts philosophy in the mouth of a little child called Father Little Time, who says, 'I should like the flowers very very much, if I didn't keep on thinking they'd be all withered in a few days' [p. 293]. In the same novel, Father Little Time and the heroine Sue are talking just like Tess and her little brother; the little boy asks her,

> "It would be better to be out o' the world than in it, wouldn't it?"
>
> "It would almost, dear" [p. 327].

Hardy reiterates that Fate is responsible for the downfall of his characters and all his novels are based on this premise. There is always a touch of argument, a sense of writing a thesis present in his novels. The novels seem to be a philosophical propaganda in the garb of a pagan preaching. Dorothy Van Ghent writes, at the end of the book, with the "Aeschylean phrase" on the sport of the gods, we feel again that intrusion of a commentary which belongs to another order of discourse. The gibbet is enough. The vision is deep and clear and can only be marred by any exploitation of it as a datum in support of abstraction. We could even do without the note of "ameliorism" in the joined hands of Clare and Tess's younger sister at the end.' According to Baker, 'A story by Thomas Hardy continually betrays that he has a case to state, an indictment to argue; there is an obvious overplus of mischance leading to a solution.'

[iii] *Authorial Intrusion* : David Cecil objects to the intrusion of unnecessary philosophy in his fictional work, "Not only... is the catastrophe highly improbable, but we feel that Hardy has devised it too obviously in order to prove his point. He twists reality, partly to get the requisite tragic effect, but still more to draw a moral."

According to Baker, Hardy's philosophy does not allow breathing space to his characters, and it takes life out of the fictional work. His characters, especially young children, speak and think in terms of Hardy's philosophy and the whole novel is designed in the shape of an argument. The impression is that the novelist wants to conclude the novel on a predetermined note and he does it with the help of bizarre coincidences, originating from his philosophy of an indifferent First Cause.

12. Conclusion

Hardy never called himself a philosopher and hence he cannot be blamed for any inconsistency or defects in his philosophy. However, it is true that his works are thought-loaded and full of philosophical material. Baker sums up Hardy's philosophical penchant, "Tragic as are such novels as The Mayor of Casterbridge, Tess, and Jude, they all have in them something that exceeds the scope of tragedy : they are an arraignment and an accusation, in other words they embody an emotive exposition of Thomas Hardy's philosophy.... His philosophy precedes and determines his fiction."

4

Hardy's Pessimism

1. Introduction

The word 'pessimism' [1815] has the Latin root word 'pessimus' meaning 'worst.' The word 'pessimism' means (1) 'an inclination to emphasise adverse aspects, conditions, and possibilities or to expect the worst possible outcome.' (2A) : 'the doctrine that reality is essentially evil.' (2B) : 'the doctrine that evil overbalances happiness in life.' Thus, we find that pessimism highlights the gloomy rather than glittering, the shady rather than sunny, the graveyard rather than fashion show. None before Hardy deserves to be called a pessimistic novelist [only Swift in his *Gulliver's Travels* comes near, yet he was not prolific in writing novels]. Hardy is the father of the pessimistic novel and the predecessor of the modern novel. Pessimism is the core of Hardy's simplistic doctrine [the doctrine that evil overbalances happiness in life]. In Hardy's philosophical creed, men are mere puppets in the hands of a malicious, omnipotent First Cause. In *Tess of the d'Urbervilles*, 'the President of the Immortals had ended his sport with Tess.'

Pessimism is the foundation-stone of Hardy's novels. It runs through all his major works as the novelist's vision of human life on this 'blighted' planet. Hardy believed that happiness was an occasional episode in a general drama of pain. In spite of the fact that his novels do contain rustic humour, the dominant mood of a Hardy novel is elegiac. This is so because of Hardy's philosophy of life, his personal experiences and his reading impressions. Hardy was much influenced by the Darwinian theory of evolution. He rejects Christianity as a historically unreal dogma, and he accepts predeterminism as the guiding principle.

2. Pessimistic Philosophy

His philosophy, writes David Cecil, from the time he began to write, was confirmedly gloomy." Baker points out, "Hardy's conception of life was essentially tragic : the conflict is one in which there is but the remotest chance of escape, so heavily are the scales weighted by man's impercipience, his inability to coerce his own insubordinate nature and the checks and snares plentifully sown in his path by some occult malice." In *The Mayor of Casterbridge*, Elizabeth-Jane thinks about Farfrae's viewpoint, 'He seemed to feel exactly as she felt about life and its surroundings — that they were a tragical rather than a comical thing.' And the last line of the novel more completely states the author's philosophy : 'happiness was but the occasional episode in a general drama of pain.' In *The Return of the Native* also, all major characters suffer invariably. Eustacia and Clym suffer most. Eustacia thinks, 'O, the cruelty of putting me into this ill-conceived world!' In *Jude the Obscure*, Phillotson speaks, 'Cruelty is the law pervading all nature and society' and Sue says, "All the ancient wrath of the Power above us has been vented upon us, His poor creatures, and we must submit. There is no choice. We must. It is no use fighting against God!" In *Tess of the d'Urbervilles* we find the reversal of optimistic faith in a benign God,

'God's *not* in his heaven : all's *wrong* with the world.'

In his four major tragic novels, major characters die; Henchard {*The Mayor of Casterbridge*}, Eustacia & Wildeve {*The Return of the Native*}, Jude {*Jude the Obscure*}, and Tess & Alec {*Tess of the d'Urbervilles*}. Even before death, they suffer a lot and their suffering is greater than what their deeds deserved. Hardy everywhere makes his major characters suffer from chance incidents and there is a clear suggestion that suffering is their destiny. Hardy's God is not a benevolent one, but a ferocious one like the pitiless beast of Yeats' *The Second Coming*. Hardy's characters are pitted against their environment, society, social norms, moral and ethical codes of the Victorian generation, and above all, against a ruthless omnipotent power, 'the ingenious machinery contrived by the gods for reducing human possibilities to a minimum' [*The Mayor of Casterbridge*].

3. Reasons of pessimism

[i] *Gloomy personal temperament* : Since his childhood, Hardy was a sensitive child, rather given to melancholy, easily moved to tears, and fond of solitude. Baker writes, "All his life he had a weakness for gruesome incidents, grim legends, creepy stories, accounts of spells, omens, ghosts, murders, suicides and the like. He was always jotting down such things in his diary, and would visit the scene to find out all he could about some sinister event and enjoy its full flavour. He never seems to have missed a funeral." When he became young, due to circumstances he was forced to learn the art of architecture. The time-consuming architectural occupation frustrated his attempts to study Greek literature for some time. Later on, his first marriage proved to be unsatisfactory and unsuccessful due to the incompatibility of temperaments. Significantly enough, incompatibility of temperaments in marriage is the favourite theme of Hardy. Hardy's both marriages were childless and the lack of children also influenced his writing. This is responsible for the Malthusian note to be found in his novels. In *Jude the Obscure*, the reluctance to propagation comes in the forefront through Father Little Time,

> 'Then if children make so much trouble, why do people have 'em?....But we don't ask to be born.'

Father Little Time hangs himself and his two little brothers, and leaves a note, 'Done because we are too menny.' In *Tess of the d'Urbervilles* also, there is the Malthusian mention as Tess's brothers and sisters are 'too many.'

Hardy's tragic view of life was conditioned by his early experiences in life. In his childhood, Hardy saw the hardships of agricultural life in Rural Dorset. He saw two hangings before he was eighteen. His sensitive temperament found it difficult to forget these tragic impressions. Hardy's novels portray the seamy side of the picturesque rural life. The sufferings of Tess at Flintcomb Ash were not fictional, they were seen at close quarters by Hardy in his adolescence. Hardy grew up in the lap of nature and his first-hand experience of rustic life is responsible for the fatalistic belief in fate and Destiny, which was deeply rooted in his mind. David Cecil comments, "His tragedy is village tragedy, composed of the drama of broken love and wronged girls, the feuds and the hangings which filled his early memories."

[ii] *Disintegration of Rural society* : David Cecil asserts, "As a countryman, he belonged to the world that was passing. That rural England, which was hallowed for him by every tie of childish sentiment, was beginning to crumble before his eyes. Every year he noticed that old habits were discontinued; that stories and songs were being forgotten; that families established for years in a place were leaving it."

Hardy distrusted modern civilisation because he found its progress dehumanising and decivilizing. The natural innocence, simplicity and honest rustic life was getting destroyed by the ruthless juggernaut of industrialisation. Hardy belonged to the modern age, but his heart was captivated by the past. In his novels we find the note of discontent with the present and nostalgia for the past. His tragic art is nostalgic; his masters were ancient Greeks, the creed he most admired was pagan, and the protagonists he portrayed were rustics in a rustic setting. Hardy felt little sympathy for the replacement of men by machines. He belonged to the peasant class and he writes as a spokesman of that class against the modern encroachment on the peasant soil. Hardy's all major novels [except *Jude the Obscure*] have a rustic setting and Hardy mentions again and again the crumbling of rural traditions. He was attached to the rustic culture and found their disintegration painful.

[iii] *Nostalgia for the past* : Intellectually Hardy was a man of future, but emotionally he belonged to the past. David Cecil writes, "He was stirred primarily by the life he had known as a child, and of his most famous books only 'Tess' and 'Jude' deal with the contemporary world of his mature years; the rest are set in the world of his childhood."

Hardy presented the past picturesquely, with all the glamour of nostalgia. Hardy belonged to an ancient local family, which had an illustrious past, though reduced in social prestige with the advent of time. This is why the idea of heredity fascinates Hardy, which is an important theme in *Tess*. The heredity issue is raised in the very first chapter of *Tess of the d'Urbervilles* and the shadow of her ancestors does not leave Tess till the end of her life. The dilapidated mansion, the graveyard, the superstitions, the old portraits of ancestors — all are mentioned in *Tess of the d'Urbervilles*. Hardy did not like the modern age with its industrialisation, 'sick hurry and divided aims.' He longed for a pristine medieval age when men would be bound in a harmonious society. The disintegration of the past values, past systems, and past rustic habitats made Hardy's temperament more melancholy.

[iv] *Tragic Study* : Hardy's mind was influenced by the great tragic writers like Sophocles, Aeschylus, and Shakespeare. Hardy was also influenced by Darwin, Swinburne, and Fitzerald's translation of Omar Khayyam. In particular, Shakespeare's *King Lear* impressed him, as it also has a rustic setting and pagan background. In *King Lear* the Nature is indifferent, even relentless, to the protagonist. This Hardy found congenial to his taste. The Greek dramatists also influenced and shaped his pessimistic outlook. The Greek drama has a pagan setting and its tragedy has a fatalistic bias. Hardy was deeply influenced by this fatalistic pessimism of Greek tragedy.

[v] *Crisis of Religion & Darwinism* : David Cecil comments, "The automatic principle of the universe becomes a God — not a Christian God, but a sinister 'President of the Immortals,' sporting for his own pleasure with wretched humanity." Hardy had lost his belief in Christianity. Like Jude, he had hoped to enter the Church, but just like Jude, he lost his religious fervour and started believing in the universal life-force called 'Immanent Will.' Darwin's '*Origin of Species*' had shaken the very foundation of the religion by proving that life on this planet had developed gradually and did not start with Adam and Eve. Christian religion believed in the concept of a just, benevolent, paternal God; but Hardy believed in an indifferent, even malevolent First Cause. "*Hardy,*" says Baker, "oppressed by his tragic view of existence sees wherever he looks 'Crass Casualty' thwarting man's best endeavours, and what the scientist described as natural

selection eliminating with blind indifference both the fit and the unfit to survive."

[vi] *Age of pessimism* : The last decades of the 19th century were the decades of spiritual crisis and religious anguish. Philosophers like Schopenhauer were questioning the optimistic religious beliefs and poets like Arnold, novelists like Fitzerald were feeling life to be a sad business. Moody and Lovett assert that Hardy's pessimism "was in harmony with the mood of the late nineteenth century, a mood of discouragement and disillusionment resulting in part from the decline of religious faith, and the account of the world and of man's position in it as given by Science." Schopenhauer's concept of life as a blind 'will to live' had influenced the late Victorian thinkers and writers and Darwin's *Origin of Species* in a way confirmed the hypothesis of Schopenhauer. David Cecil points out, 'for the first time, pessimism — conscious, considered pessimism — found expression in English letters : in the works of Arnold and Fitzerald, of Thompson and Hardy. Hardy was especially open to the melancholy implications of the new outlook.'

Hardy's personal experiences had endowed him with a tragic viewpoint and this pessimistic viewpoint was increased by the age in which he lived. At that time the industrial revolution played havoc with the rural life. The old agricultural England was dying fast; villagers were migrating to cities; money was becoming more central to mankind than religion. In religion, thinkers were raising doubts about the validity or authenticity of the Bible. Christianity was no longer the omnicorrect religion. The Darwinian theory of evolution also questioned the Biblical myth of the origin of man. New thinkers believed in the Darwinian principle of 'Survival of the fittest' and they could not reconcile themselves with Christianity. The thinkers were drawn towards pessimism. Each one of them saw life in its utter nakedness. They disapproved of the 'money-race' and materialistic pursuits, which were major preoccupations of the Victorian society. They could not find solace in the blissful heaven promised by the Christianity, as they did not believe in it. Thus life became gloomy for them on this planet as well as in their post-death existence.

4. Man *vs.* Destiny

"A struggle between man on the one hand and, on the other, an omnipotent and indifferent Fate — that is Hardy's interpretation of the human situation...the conflict is not, as in most novels, between one man and another, or between man and an institution. Man in Hardy's books is ranged against impersonal forces, the forces conditioning his fate," writes David Cecil. Hardy's novels are emblems of cosmic irony, in which no struggle is individual; all struggle is universal. Mankind seems to struggle against the unsympathetic First Cause. In his ironic closure of the novel comes the startling sentence : " 'Justice' was done, and the President of the Immortals, in Aeschylean phrase, had ended his sport with Tess."

5. Fate, Chance & Coincidences

In Hardy's philosophy, fate is responsible for the tragedy of life. Man is destined to suffer, and his suffering is caused by external as well as internal forces. Even the internal forces are guided by the external forces. The human will, the thinking process, the energy to act — all these are determined by the First Cause and this is why men are mere pawns on the panoramic chessboard of this universe. David Cecil explains, "Fate is an abstraction, and in order that it may play an active part in a human drama.... Hardy embodies Fate in various forms. Sometimes it appears as a natural force. Henchard's plans for making himself rich are brought to nought by a bad harvest. Chiefly, however, the forces of Fate in Hardy's novels incarnate themselves in two guises — as chance and as love. Of these, chance is the most typical. In no other novels does chance exercise such a conspicuous influence on the course of events."

Edward Bright asserts, 'Too much machinery is employed in Tess to bring about the catastrophe; and in the latter part of the tale especially, disaster follows disaster in so close and yet disconnected a manner that all sense of verisimilitude is destroyed.'

6. Love as Terrible Lord

Love is the only source of happiness in this miserable world, but the First Cause has deprived human beings of getting love in this world. Love as conceived by Hardy is "the Lord of terrible aspect" — a blind, irresistible power, seizing on human beings whether they will or not; intoxicating in its inception, but, more often than not, bringing ruin in its train. Love is especially pre-marital love in Hardy and hence love becomes guilt after marriage. Love-affairs are kept hidden but in Hardy's fiction, past love-affairs are revealed and due to that protagonists suffer. In *The Return of the Native*, Eustacia suffers for her pre-marital love to Wildeve, in *The Mayor of Casterbridge*, Lucetta's love-affair with Henchard is exposed and she dies thereof; in *Jude the Obscure*, almost everybody has an affair with somebody or the other; in *Tess of the d'Urbervilles*, the seduction when confessed causes her misery. The problem is more complex in *Tess of the d'Urbervilles*; here Alec terribly loves Tess and Tess loves Angel. This cross-connection of love-passions is responsible for their doom.

7. Hardy's Views about Pessimism

According to F. Manning, "His pessimism, after all, is only a habit of thought, a weariness with life that comes upon all of us sometimes, if it does not remain with us always." But pessimism is at the core of Hardy's philosophy and his novels. Hardy does not consider himself a philosopher. He writes, "positive views on the whence and the wherefore of things have never been advanced by this pen as a consistent philosophy...the sentiments in the following pages have been stated truly to be mere impressions of the moment, and not convictions or arguments.

"That these impressions have been condemned as 'pessimistic' — as if that were a very nice wicked adjective — shows a curious muddle-mindedness. It must be obvious that there is a higher characteristic of philosophy than pessimism or than meliorism, or even than the optimism of these critics — which is truth." [Hardy, General Preface to the Wessex Edition of 1912].

5

Role of Fate and Chance

1. Introduction

Fate, destiny, chance and coincidence are frequently found terms in Hardyan criticism. Fate and destiny are almost synonymous words. Fate implies an inevitable and usually an adverse outcome. The word *fate* originates from Latin word *'fatum'* which means 'what has been spoken.' Destiny implies something foreordained or a predetermined course of events often held to be an irresistible power or agency. Incidentally, *'Fates'* were the three goddesses who determined the course of human life in the classical mythology. 'Chance' means something that happens unpredictably without discernible human intention or observable cause. It is a subordinate agency of fate or destiny. In all these words, the emphasis is on a supernatural or extra-human agency and not on the cause-and-consequence chain of human actions. Hardy's anti-realism goaded him to use chance events rather excessively to highlight his pessimistic philosophy.

2. Fate as Cosmic Irony

Cosmic irony is the favourite mode of philosophical expression in Hardy's novels. In Hardy's philosophy, irony of circumstance holds an important position. In every novel, this irony is present. This irony has two features; when a person desires one thing and the outcome is opposite and when a person marries, he usually makes a mismarriage. The novel is based on the irony of circumstance; the d'Urbervilles residing at The Chase are not the true d'Urbervilles. Had the parson told this to the father Tess, her tragedy could have been averted. Tess expects help from the d'Urbervilles of The Chase, but ironically she gets troubles. The right man Angel comes first, but he does not pay much attention to her at the May dance and the wrong man enters her life. Angel asks forgiveness for his pre-marital affair, but is unable to forgive Tess for the same reason. Tess goes to Alec as she does not expect Angel to return and forgive her, but ironically he returns to forgive her. Tess and Angel are opposites in nature; Tess and Alec belong to the 'pagan' creed and had Tess married Alec, all would have been right but ironically this does not happen. In the seduction-scene, Tess sleeps when Alec returns, and her act causes her deflowering. At the crucial time, Queen of Diamond starts fighting Tess and Alec gets the opportunity of getting Tess on the horseback. In Hardy's thought, irony of circumstance springs from the Cosmic Irony. Abrams explains, "Cosmic Irony or the irony of fate exists, when God, or destiny, or the universal process, is represented as though deliberately manipulating events to frustrate and mock the protagonist. This is a favourite structural device of Thomas Hardy. In his Tess of the d'Urbervilles, the heroine, having lost her virtue because of her innocence, then loses her happiness because of her honesty, finds it again only by murder, and having been briefly happy, is hanged."

In *The Return of the Native* also, we find irony of circumstance in the marriage of Clym and Eustacia, 'Take all the varying hates felt by Eustacia Vye towards the heath, and translate them into loves, and you have the heart of Clym.' Irony lies in this mismatched marriage, like other marriages of the same kind in Hardy.

3. Fate as Omens and Signs

Hardy uses several omens and signs in his novels to great effect. First of all, he deftly tells us that fatalism is the way of life of Tess's family by showing that Joan reads and consults the *'Compleat Fortune-Teller'* on a regular basis and even tries to decipher the future of Tess, 'I tried her fate.' And she finds out that some noble gentleman will marry Tess. This prediction or sign is fulfilled, though rather late; when Angel marries Tess. Later on, Farmer Dick recalls the superstition of 'butter not coming' as somebody in the house must be in love. The superstition is found to be true because Tess is in love with Angel. Later on, on the marriage-day the cock crows in the afternoon at Tess, foreboding ill events to her. The omen is found to be correct when Tess confesses her past guilt and she is deserted by her husband. Then the popular superstition about d'Urberville coach is also used ominously. Whenever its sound is heard, tragic events take place in the d'Urberville family.

The legend of the d'Urberville coach is heard by Tess on her marriage-day from Angel's mouth, 'that well-known superstition.' Whenever any of the d'Urberville family hears or sees the old coach, it means that either they will die or they have committed a crime. Angel tells Tess all this, and we know that she has just married him, in that way committing a crime in not telling Angel of her past. The sound of d'Urberville coach is again heard by Tess, when she is going to live with Alec as his mistress. Alec tells her, 'it is held to be of ill-omen to the one who hears it. It has to do with a murder, committed by one of the family.' Just like the ancestor from whom the legend originates, Tess will also commit two crimes : adultery and murder. In this way, omens & superstitions are tied together in the plot quite skilfully.

4. Fate *vs.* Man

"A struggle between man on the one hand and, on the other, an omnipotent and indifferent Fate — that is Hardy's interpretation of the human situation...the conflict is not, as in most novels, between one man and another, or between man and an institution. Man in Hardy's books s ranged against impersonal forces, the forces conditioning his fate," writes David Cecil. In Hardy's philosophy, fate is responsible for the tragedy of life. Man is destined to suffer, and his suffering is caused by external as well as internal forces. Even the internal forces are guided by the external forces. The human will, the thinking process, the energy to act — all these are determined by First Cause and this is why men are mere pawns on the panoramic chessboard of this universe. David Cecil explains, "Fate is an abstraction, and in order that it may play an active part in a human drama.... Hardy embodies Fate in various forms. Sometimes it appears as a natural force. Henchard's plans for making himself rich are brought to nought by a bad harvest. Chiefly, however, the forces of Fate in Hardy's novels incarnate themselves in two guises — as chance and as love. Of these, chance is the most typical. In no other novels does chance exercise such a conspicuous influence on the course of events."

In Hardy's novels fate plays a predominant part. His characters are puppets in the hands of a malignant fate which is out to thwart them in their efforts and rob them of any chance of happiness. Fate works not only as an external power from without but also from within. Fate is also responsible for the pre-marital sex with an undesirable person. In Hardy's views the call seldom brings the caller and the two perfect halves never come together. In all Hardy's novels, the first experience of love is always with the wrong person. In *The Mayor of Casterbridge*, Lucetta wrongly loves Henchard and suffers due to it. In *The Return of the Native*, Eustacia loves Wildeve and they die in their attempt to elope. In *Jude the Obscure*, Jude and Sue indulge in extra-marital relationship, which creates havoc in their lives. In *Tess*, Angel does not take notice Tess at their first meeting and when he takes notice of her, it is too late; by then she has been seduced by Alec. Thus we see that fate in Hardy always works against mankind.

5. Fate as Coincidence & Chance

Edward Bright asserts, 'Too much machinery is employed in Tess to bring about the catastrophe; and in the latter part of the tale especially, disaster follows disaster in so close and yet disconnected a manner that all sense of verisimilitude is destroyed.' There are too many coincidences and chance events in his novels.

The reliance on coincidences and chance-events as the external expression of the malignant Fate is Hardy's favourite technique, and Church writes, "coincidence plays too large a part in these tales. But so it does again in the Greek records of human fate. And so it does too in real life."

{I} The first coincidence is that Tess is asleep while she drives the cart, and due to her sleep, the morning mail-cart dashes against her cart and kills Prince. This coincidence is rather far-fetched; Tess is out there, because her father is over-drunk; had he been sober, Tess would not have driven the cart. Father's drunken state is caused by another coincidence; the parson has informed him that he belongs to the illustrious d'Urberville lineage. This series of coincidences brings about the death of the horse, and the consequent sufferings on Tess.

{II} The second major coincidence is that she once again falls asleep when Alec returns, making it quite easy for him to seduce her. This in turn has been made possible due to another coincidence. When Tess is coming with her usual rustic company, Queen of Diamonds and Queen of Spades, the former beloveds of Alec, start fighting with her and at the same time Alec comes and offers her a rescuing lift, which she has to accept in desperation to avoid the incessant fighting. Even during the ride, she falls asleep and does not pay attention to the fact that Alec is taking her in the wrong direction.

{III} The most significant chance event in Tess is that she keeps on postponing her confession to Angel. And finally when she musters up enough courage to do so, unfortunately her confessional letter is thrust beneath the carpet. She doesn't ask him about the letter nor does she search for it till the morning of the marriage-day. And then, it is too late to stop the marriage.

{IV} The next chance event occurs, when Tess goes to seek help from the Clare family; but the day being Sunday, they are at Church and she finds the doors closed. Had she gone there some other day or had she waited for them, her life would certainly have been different. Moreover, Angel's brothers take out her shoes which she has hidden in a bush to maintain her dignity.

{V} While she returns from her unsuccessful visit to Clare family, she hears Alec's voice. That she finds Alec preaching is a ready-made coincidence; that she teases Alec for being reformed is almost suicidal; that she is responsible for Alec's de-conversion through her verbatim condensation of Angel's philosophy is still more incredible. Alec, like a leech, sticks to her and succeeds in keeping her as a mistress once again.

{VI} All her friends and enemies of Talbothays and Trantridge assemble at Flintcomb Ash. By chance, the painter of signs with the pot of red paint returns. The owner of the farm at Flintcomb Ash turns out to be the same person whom Angel has slapped. Her friends Izz, Retty and Marian also reappear. Even Alec re-enters her life at Flintcomb Ash. This reappearance of several characters en masse appears to be contrived and an incredible coincidence.

{VII} By chance, Tess's father dies and leaves his family homeless. By chance their Kingsbere house is refused to them. By chance, Alec's proposition comes at a time when Tess is desperate for providing a home for her family. By chance, her letter to Angel gets delayed and by chance again, Angel returns too late due to sickness.

6. Defects

[i] *Too Many Coincidences* : David Cecil asserts, 'In no other novels does chance exercise such a conspicuous influence on the course of events. Hardy has been blamed for this; and no doubt he does sometimes overdo it. But to condemn his use of chance altogether is to misunderstand his view of life. We are witnessing a battle between man and Destiny. Destiny is an inscrutable force...its acts always show themselves in the guise of inexplicable, unexpected blows of chance.'

Hardy uses chance events to get the desired tragic effect. Due to his anti-realist outlook he did not seek to prefer plausibility and probability. His belief in fatalism and determinism was strong and this was responsible for his philosophy that Fate shapes human destinies. Walter Allen writes, 'Hardy's chief weakness in plot arises from his view of causality. He is intent to show that the stars in their courses fight against the aspiring...Here his problem was difficult indeed, and it is not surprising he never solved it. For the universe itself to become suddenly hostile to man could only be shown through the working of what maybe called the freak coincidence. It is silly to blame Hardy for the emphasis he places on coincidence; simply, he believed in coincidence.' David Cecil comments, *"Hardy seems to be twisting his plot to suit his purpose. The characters seem puppets all right; but puppets not in the hands of Fate, but of the author."*

[ii] *Improbable events* : There is a disregard of probability in his novels. There are many improbable events in Tess, which convey the sense of anti-realism.

the man with the red paint who writes the biblical warning, '*THY, DAMNATION, SLUMBERETH, NOT.*' The line, and the next line also, are too apt to Tess's situation and the overall effect is one of improbability.

[1] Tess remained for a few days with Alec even after the seduction. If Tess was pure and virtuous, she should have come away from him at once. The situation as it is, is improbable.

[2] Angel's sleepwalking is also improbable. To believe that a sleeping man can carry his wife for so long a time and in such precarious circumstances, is not at all realistic, although Hardy has tried to make it convincing by supplying prior detail.

[3] The story of the bull, who kneels when the Nativity Hymn is played on the flute is also improbable.

[4] Tess kills Alec with a thin knife which is not at all probable and plausible.

[5] After the Alec's murder, the blood seeps through the floor and the landlady sees a red spot in the shape of a 'gigantic ace of hearts', which is also improbable.

[6] Alec's conversion and de-conversion are also too sudden to be probable.

[iii] *Preaching & Propaganda :* Hardy reiterates that Fate is responsible for the downfall of his characters and all his novels are based on this premise. There is always a touch of argument, a sense of writing a thesis present in his novels. The novels seem to be a philosophical propaganda in the garb of a pagan preaching. Dorothy Van Ghent writes, 'At the end of the book,' with the "Aeschylean phrase" on the sport of the gods, we feel again that intrusion of a commentary which belongs to another

order of discourse. The gibbet is enough. The vision is deep and clear and can only be marred by any exploitation of it as a datum in support of abstraction. We could even do without the note of "meliorism" in the joined hands of Clare and Tess's younger sister at the end." According to Baker, 'A story by Thomas Hardy continually betrays that he has a case to state, an indictment to argue; there is an obvious overplus of mischance leading to a solution.'

7. Conclusion

Hardy's philosophy is basically fatalistic and deterministic; this is why chance events play such a significant role in producing the catastrophe. Chance events are a significant external expression of Fate or Destiny. David Cecil writes that in Hardy's novels, "Man is working to one end, Destiny to another. These ends may coincide or they may not. Either way, it is destiny who decides what shall happen. Man cannot modify the will of Destiny.... Hardy is liable to over-emphasise the part played by chance in producing catastrophe. That it should play such a part is, of course, an essential element in his view of life. Chance is the incarnation of the blind forces controlling human destiny."

6

Limitations of Hardy and Defects in *Tess*

1. Introduction

Hardy, in spite of being a great novelist, suffers from several limitations. His work is more imaginative than realistic. Peter Widowson enumerates on Hardy's faults, "Hardy's faults are said to be : his tendency to melodrama, the excessive use of chance and coincidence in his plots; his pessimism, his parading of ill-digested ideas; his at times pedantic, awkward, mannered style; and, over and above all these — indeed subsuming them — his tendency to 'improbability' and 'implausibility;' in other words, his failure to be 'realistic,' or, to put it yet another way, to represent 'essential reality' accurately ...Perhaps Hardy was an anti-realist." These are the characteristic faults or flaws of Hardy as a novelist. In his novels, plots smack of artificial construction, events seem melodramatic, characters look flat and unconvincing, style appears awkward and pedantic; and the viewpoint seems to be didactic and pessimistic.

2. Limited Range

The first defect in Hardy as a novelist is that his range is extremely limited. He chooses certain types of characters, certain situations and certain scenes. Beyond that he does not go and if he goes, he utterly fails in the attempt. Hardy's work, like Wordsworth's, was limited to the rural setting and society and he leaves urban society largely untouched. In comparison to other great novelists, his is a limited range. His scene is too narrow.

David Cecil remarks, *"The subtleties of intellectual life, the complexities of public life, the sophistication of social life, these do not kindle Hardy's imagination to work.... The life he portrays is life reduced to its basic elements. People in Hardy's books are born, work hard for their living, fall in love and die : they do not do anything else."* The struggle of mankind is on a grand scale; his characters do not struggle against society, they struggle against a malevolent First Cause. Hardy does not lay bare the complexities of social systems; nor does he elaborate upon the individual consciousness.

3. Propaganda and Preaching

David Cecil remarks, "The most fatal error into which he was led by his lack of critical sense was preaching. At moments, obsessed by his views about the universe, he turns from an imaginative creator into a propagandist. Just when we are spellbound by Hardy the novelist, Hardy the preacher bobs up, and instantly the spell is broken." In *Tess* this preaching is too obvious. Tess is an eighteen-year-old girl, talking philosophy with her little brother,

> "Did you say the stars were worlds, Tess?"
> 'Yes"
>
> ....
>
> 'Which do we live on — a splendid one or a blighted one?'
> 'A blighted one' [chapter 4].

David Cecil writes, 'Here is no unsophisticated country girl speaking. Through her lips comes the voice of a middle-aged novelist, brooding in gloomy mood on the riddle of the painful earth. For 'Tess' is a late book. The preaching tendency grew on Hardy." Even in *Jude* we find Hardy puts philosophy in the mouth of a little child called Father Little Time, who says, 'I should like the flowers very very much, if I didn't keep on thinking they'd be all withered in a few days' [p. 293]. In the same novel, Father Little Time and the heroine Sue are talking just like Tess and her little brother; the little boy asks her,

> "It would be better to be out o' the world than in it, wouldn't it?"
> "It would almost, dear" [p. 327].

Hardy reiterates that Fate is responsible for the downfall of his characters and all his novels are based on this premise. There is always a touch of argument, a sense of writing a thesis present in his novels. The novels seem to be a philosophical propaganda in the garb of a pagan preaching. Dorothy Van Ghent writes, 'At the end of the book, with the "Aeschylean phrase" on the sport of the gods, we feel again that intrusion of a commentary which belongs to another order of discourse. The gibbet is enough. The vision is deep and clear and can only be marred by any exploitation of it as a datum in support of abstraction. We could even do without the note of "meliorism" in the joined hands of Clare and Tess's younger sister at the end. According to Baker, 'A story by Thomas Hardy continually betrays that he has a case to state, an indictment to argue; there is an obvious overplus of mischance leading to a solution.'

4. Too Many Coincidences

Edward Bright asserts, 'Too much machinery is employed in Tess to bring about the catastrophe; and in the latter part of the tale especially, disaster follows disaster in so close and yet disconnected a manner that all sense of verisimilitude is destroyed.' There are too many coincidences and chance events in his novels.

[I] The first coincidence is that Tess sleeps while driving the cart and the morning mail-cart kills her horse.

[II] The second coincidence is that she falls asleep when Alec returns and seduces her.

[III] The most significant coincidence is that her confessional letter is thrust beneath the carpet.

[IV] By chance, Angel's parents are at church when Tess goes to seek them.

[V] By chance, she finds Alec preaching and he re-enters her life.

[VI] Another coincidence is that at Flintcomb Ash all her friends of Talbothays and foes of Trantridge reappear.

[VII] Her letter to Angel in Brazil is delayed and he reaches home a few days too late.

The reliance on coincidences and chance-events as the external expression of the malignant Fate is Hardy's favourite technique, and Church writes, 'coincidence plays too large a part in these tales. But so it does again in the Greek records of human fate. And so it does too in real life.'

David Cecil asserts, 'In no other novels does chance exercise such a conspicuous influence on the course of events. Hardy has been blamed for this; and no doubt he does sometimes overdo it. But to condemn his use of chance altogether is to misunderstand his view of life. We are witnessing a battle between man and Destiny. Destiny is an inscrutable force...its acts always show themselves in the guise of inexplicable, unexpected blows of chance.'

Hardy uses chance events to get the desired tragic effect. Due to his anti-realist outlook he did not seek to prefer plausibility and probability. His belief in fatalism and determinism was strong and this was responsible for his philosophy that Fate shapes human destinies. Walter Allen writes, 'Hardy's chief weakness in plot arises from his view of causality. He is intent to show that the stars in their courses fight against the aspiring...Here his problem was difficult indeed, and it is not surprising he never solved it. For the universe itself to become suddenly hostile to man could only be shown through the working of what may be called the freak coincidence. It is silly to blame Hardy for the emphasis he places on coincidence; simply, he believed in coincidence.'

5. Improbable Events

There is a disregard of probability in his novels. There are many improbable events in Tess, which convey the sense of anti-realism.

[1] When Tess returns after being seduced, she comes across the man with the red paint who writes the biblical warning, '*THY, DAMNATION, SLUMBERETH, NOT.*' The line, and the next line also, are too apt to Tess's situation and the overall effect is one of improbability.

[2] Tess remained for a few days with Alec even after the seduction. If Tess was pure and virtuous, she should have come away from him at once. The situation as it is, is improbable.

[3] Angel's sleepwalking is also improbable. To believe that a sleeping man can carry his wife for so long a time and in such precarious circumstances, is not at all realistic, although Hardy has tried to make it convincing by supplying prior detail.

[4] The story of the bull, who kneels when the Nativity Hymn is played on the flute is also improbable .

[5] Tess kills Alec with a thin knife which is not at all probable and plausible.

[6] After the Alec's murder, the blood seeps through the floor and the landlady sees a red spot in the shape of a 'gigantic ace of hearts,' which is also improbable.

[7] Alec's conversion and de-conversion are also too sudden to be probable.

6. Inconsistent Philosophy

Throughout his career, Hardy's philosophy kept on changing; what did not change was his pessimism. Sometimes he said that the First Cause is neither good nor bad; but in his novels we find that the First Cause almost always works malevolently against mankind. Baker writes, 'It was unfortunate that he kept shifting his ground... Hardy was always seeking a better theory to substantiate his tragic view of things... Hardy was a confused thinker.' In Tess, Hardy sets his story in the pagan setting but he uses the sun-god motif inconsistently. The Sun-god on one hand is shown as the creative source of energy helping growth and fertility; on the other hand it is scorching and destructive, on whose altar Tess is sacrificed.

7. Clumsy Dialogue

Walter Allen writes, 'His prose is often clumsy to the point of uncouthness' Hardy's dialogue, as one critic points out, is stilted and clumsy except in dialect. In Tess dialect is almost eliminated and hence Hardy's dialogue, becomes artificial. At times, the dialogue is too sophisticated to be convincing. The thoughts of Mrs. Durbeyfield in chapter 3 are simply beyond her range. At times, there is unnecessary circumlocution in dialogue as in Angel's conversation with Tess :

> *Well, a certain place is paved with good intentions, and having felt all that strongly, you will see what a terrible remorse it bred in me when, in the midst of my fine aims for other people, I myself fell* [chapter 34].

The dialogue is stagey at times, as the situation is theatrical. Hardy wants to put his weighty philosophical musings in the mouths of his frail characters and sometimes the poor speakers cannot carry the burden on their tongue. David Lodge points out the dual dialogue devices of Hardy, 'There is the Hardy who can recreate dialect speech with flawless authenticity...and there is the Hardy speaking in orotund sentences of laboured syntax and learned vocabulary, the Hardy who studied The Times, Addison, and Scott to improve his style.'

8. The Role of Minor Characters

In his early novels, Hardy draws the chorus of minor characters very effectively. However, in *Tess* and later on in *Jude*, he discards the chorus. Tess has very few minor characters. Hardy not only takes Tess to Flintcomb Ash, but also manages to convey her friend circle as well as enemies to the new place. Due to it, there is a sense of improbability. However, Hardy gains a great deal from the concentration. People keep on coming and returning. The man with red paint-box reappears, so does the farmer of the Flintcomb Ash, so do Izz, Queen of Diamonds, Queen of Spades and Alec. This sudden reappearance and reemergence of characters is a favourite motif of Hardy.

9. Male Characters Unreal

Alec and Angel, both major male characters in *Tess*, are unreal in the proper sense. Hardy insists on making them the two sides of the coin; one is sensual, another ethereal; one materialistic, another intellectual; one seduces Tess, another forsakes her. Alec is drawn in the frame of the unconventional villain with a cigar, pouting lips, full lips. He is clearly a villain, but he is not life-like. his conversion as fictitious as his de-conversion. Even Angel, drawn more sympathetically, is also lifeless for he is an idea-guided person. Both these men are developed around the ideological dichotomy. This is why these men talk and walk;

chowever, vitality is missing in their characters. They are not as alive as the heroine of the novel.

10. Ambiguity in Tess

Ambiguity is the keynote of Tess. The ambiguity starts with the seduction itself. Whether Tess, dazed by Alec's flashy maners, somewhat voluntarily surrenders to his advances [as hinted several times] or she is raped against her wishes [as also hinted once or twice]. Hardy does not clarify the situation and he keeps the question open-ended. The next ambiguous note comes when she chooses to remain with Alec for a few days even after her seduction. Why does she stay, Hardy does not choose to clarify it?

In the same manner, several important scenes are obliquely presented, not given full detailed emphasis :

[i] The seduction of Tess

[ii] Tess's account of her past on her wedding night

[iii] Her return to Alec

[iv] Her murder of Alec

Kaja Silverman comments about these incidents which fall into a hiatus between phases. "Tess is curiously 'absent' from most of the key events in the novel; from the death of Prince, to the strawberry scene, the night in The Chase, Angel's return and her capture at Stonehenge, she is asleep or in a trance." Significantly enough, Hardy does not provide details about these significant events and perhaps he keeps back certain things to establish his heroine as 'a pure woman.' However, the ambiguity makes the interpretations multifarious, besides making it impossible to reach at a consensus.

7

Thomas Hardy as a Regional Novelist

Hardy's literary works have adopted the fictional name "Wessex" for their setting. No other writer has celebrated a region, with such deftness and accuracy as this South-Western part of England, fictionalised as "Wessex" in Hardy's works. A close study of his works reveals the changing perspectives of this viable region, subjected to harsh and detrimental changes of industrialisation and modernity.

The Wessex is a tradition bound region, well steeped in superstition, folk-lore, folk magic and folk customs. These are not mere decorations. They are integral to the world Hardy depicts. It is the world of 'the later balladry and folk-tale from which old beliefs have receded, leaving a residue of the merely strange. Improbability and accident have replaced the miraculous' [Donald Davidson].

1. Setting

Hardy's Wessex has been geographically identified with south-western England. The scene changes from place to place in his various works. However, Casterbridge can be closely identified with Dorchester, the region to which Hardy belonged. The scenes and the characters of Hardy's works belong to this region. The pastoral and the legendary aspects of these regions have been explored in great detail by Hardy. According to Entice Andrew, the early novels of Hardy can 'be grouped as enclosed landscapes' and establish him firmly as a regional novelist.

Yet, Hardy in his characters and their presentation and their inter-relationship with the setting, rises much above the narrow bounds of regionalism. The settings and characters, though identifiable with the place and spirit of their time have that element of universality which renders them timelessness and universality.

The region within a few miles of Hardy's childhood home at Stimford forms the setting of Hardy's major works. The ideas of love, marriage, divorce, social mobility and so on and so forth of the people inhabiting these surroundings find their expression in the works of Hardy. Strange simple dreams, superstitions, beliefs, aspirations and apprehensions of these people living in poverty-stricken circumstances fill the pages of Hardy's works. Lovers are separated, girls are wronged, feuds and hangings are executed here. Stern laws, harsh conditions of living and an indifferent and malignant fate combine to form a force that threatens to crush the indomitable spirit of the Wessex people. It is, however, in the stoicity and inherent strength of these characters that their chief attraction resides.

The town of Casterbridge in *'The Mayor of Casterbridge'* can be easily identified as the real Dorchester of the mid-19th century. It is an old-fashioned place — muddled all together. Hardy portrays it as a town that announced old Rome in every street. It looked Roman, bespoke the art of Rome and concealed dead men of Rome. Yet Rome is far removed from the lives of its people.

The setting of *Far from the Madding Crowd* is the valley of the River Piddle, just upstream of Puddletown. The 'Great Heath' of Hardy's Wessex stretches from Dorchester to Poole spreading southwards to Purbeck Hills, northward to Winterbome and Stow. In *Tess of the d'Urbervilles*, *The Woodlanders* and *Jude the Obscure*, the setting is not the geographical location of Dorset. He chose Melbury Sampford as the original landscape in *The Woodlanders*.

Tess is characterised by the emphasis of movement and the setting of the novel changes with the changes in the phases of her history. The village of Marlott, described as lying amid the north-eastern undulations of the beautiful Vale of Blackmoor is hard to be located on the map; though Hardy himself referred to Marnhull, as the original, the town is hardly described. Hardy presents however a very clear picture of the Vale of Blackmoor. Trantridge too is hard to locate, but Talbothays is quite familiar. Froom Valley is the fertile lowland of the *Return of the Native* on the distant edge of the heath. It reaches up to the very walls of Casterbridge. Flintcomb Ash is the area at the head of the Piddle Valley.

Hardy uses these places as contrasting with each other. Tess passes a part of her life in every setting. The physical features, agriculture and occupations too are contrasted. In Blackmoor Tess works at harvest, in Trantridge, it is poultry and at Flintcomb Ash it is swedes, straw and threshing. Thus the settings here serve as arenas of action for Tess.

Even the buildings hove a different significance. Th Trantridge is a modern fancy farm. At Blackmoor Nature and Man coexist in harmony, at Trantridge Tess is a little more than the caged animals. At Flintcomb Ash the relationship between the employer and the employee is further estranged. Tess is made to suffer both at the hands of a hard taskmaster as well as a dehumanising machine. Sandbourne is a pleasure house, with Tess reduced to the status of a pet and at Stonehenge, she is depicted as a sacrificial animal laid on the altar of the Sun-god.

2. Mental Landscapes

In *Jude the Obscure*, the rural community continues flourishing, yet Hardy's method of depiction has changed from that of involvement and sympathy to bleak objectivity. The new landscapes are of the mind. The town of Christminster keeps changing and ending in Jude's mind. It changes as a centre for studies, as an architectural town and as the centre of the changing 19th century society and culture. As in *Tess*, so in *Jude*, our centre of interest lies more in the individual than the setting. We are far removed here from the South Dorset world of the early Wessex novels, both in location and as well as character.

3. Tradition

The people inhabiting the 'Wessex' are tradition bound country folks, forced by the harshness of their circumstances to lead a harsh life. Their clothes, their manners are of the 19th century England. Their ideas are gradually changing to the changing pattern of the day. They sing and dance, work and make love and at times do desperate things like murder and suicide, but all for love. Love is the dominant feature of their life.

Life in Wessex is hard, and the sense of a tragic fate is strong. It is in fact a poet's reaction to the harsh unintelligible workings of the universe. The people are strong and are set against less powerful persons of greater modern experience. The focus is on erotic love and the preference is for tragic turn of events. Their code of conduct and morality run contrary to the convention but ultimately succumb to laws of a greater power. These characters are driven by their own passions and idiosyncrasies, and yet are universal.

4. Superstitions & Omens

Theirs is a world of superstitions & omens. The thorn pricks Tess's chin, and she fears it to be a bad omen. The afternoon crow is held in apprehension by the Dairyman Crick and his wife. The vision of the d'Urberville Coach, and its relationship with death and murder, the cross like structure which relations of a malefactor had erected, where he was nailed and hung, the blood stained paper that flies in front of her before she reaches her in-laws' house, find a place in this tragic drama of missed chances and lost opportunities.

Tess for all her individuality is a milkmaid who is seduced and who murders her seducer, a story oft celebrated in the ballads. In *The Return of the Native* Susan Nonesuch pricks Eustacia Vye for a witch and later makes a waxen image of her just before her death by drowning. The effigy of Henchard is seen floating in the river by Henchard himself. The supernatural, though at times forms a part of Hardy's narrative, is never allowed to take the main position.

5. Changelessness

The Wessex people have a non-changing and fixed character. Hardy felt that the uncommonness must be in the events and not in characters. These changeless characters are juxtaposed with characters of a more changeful or modern type. Their conflict forms the focus of Hardy's novels. These changeless characters, more aptly called the rustics of the Hardyan world accept nature as unchangeable and passively accommodate themselves to nature in the ordered ritual of their life. Tragedy strikes when they confront the changeful in bitter conflict.

6. Fatalism and Folk Magic

Their fatalism is related to their folk character; 'it was to be' seems to be the dictum : a passive acceptance of the earthly doom is common here. The fatalism is closely linked with magic, which is a knowledgeable mode of dealing with the unknowledgeable. As the folk-fatalism imbues the foreground accidents with the suggestion of necessity, the folk magic imbues them with the suggestion of supernatural motivations. Their intricate interlinking gives an authenticity to Hardy's tale.

Thus Hardy's Wessex is a viable region lending its texture to the personality of characters, that inhabit it. It colours their thoughts, their aspirations and their longings. It is also a world that was fast diminishing owing to the onslaught of modernity and change. Hardy regretted the change, though it was inevitable. His vision became more and more gloomy as he realised that the world he loved did not possess the necessary equipments to survive. Money and technical excellence were the tools with which the new order was equipped, as we see in *The Mayor of Casterbridge*. Farfrae succeeds by his superior knowledge, and Henchard is defeated by his own inherent faults. Tess and Jude too have a destructive element in their inherent nature.

Though capable of being traced geographically, Hardy's Wessex is as much a physical landscape as a region of the mind. It is greatly coloured by Hardy's thoughts and ideology. Rooted in the elemental substance of human life, warmed by the presence of nature and coloured by folk tradition, Wessex presents before us a picture of the world as Hardy saw it. He saw man working, labouring, loving against the background of a malignant indifferent fate. Hardy, for all the pains he takes to present before us the geographical landscape of Wessex, never lets us forget even for a moment that his Wessex is a part of the life of the whole human race. The local characteristics and the scenes of Wessex are seen in relation to ultimate destiny and this makes them individual and universal at the same time. The timeless and changeless spirit of Wessex broods over them and Hardy has immortalised this region through his poems and novels.

8

Treatment of Nature in Hardy

The Romantics' view of 'Nature' was a strange amalgam of deistic theology, Newtonian physics and pantheistic naturalism. Their sensibility had considerably changed from the neo-classical sensibility which found excitement in the '*Puffs, powders, patches, Bibles, Billet doux*' etc. and held that 'High mountains are a feeling but the hum of cities torture.'

Hardy viewed Nature as indifferent and neutral to man and didn't feel a presence benign and benevolent in Nature. It served as a backdrop to his tales, and at times, as in *The Return of the Native*, it assumed the shape of a very strong force that could clog or promote action in the form of Egdon Heath. Here as also in *Tess of the d'Urbervilles*, the earth becomes the factor of causation and clogs action and defies motives. In the long dream of Talbothays the earth conspires with ancient sensuality to provoke instinct and at Flintcomb Ash it demoralises consciousness by its flintiness.

Long stretches of land have to be covered to meet a person and then the person one goes to meet may or may not be there at the other end. The Heath acts doubly in *The Return of the Native :* (1) It has to be crossed from one end to another to reach any place and (2) It presents itself as a place where the action has to take place. In *Tess* it acts in its own motivating causational substantiality, obstructing human purpose and aspirations. Every journey that Tess undertakes sets off a new phase in her life-history. In fact, Tess is always on the move, finally resting at Stonehenge — the Sun altar where once upon a time sacrifices were made. The journey through night with Abraham, on the cart, when Prince meets with an accident, triggers off her race with time, and finally with the day breaking upon the horizon at Stonehenge the race ends. Tess is arrested for Alec's murder and hanged at Wintoncester.

Hardy is able to use the setting and the atmosphere, here, in a symbolic way. "*The green Vale of Blackmoor fertile, small, enclosed by hills, lying under a blue haze is the vale of birth, the cradle of innocence.*" The wide misty setting of Talbothays dairy, "oozing fatness and warm ferments," where the "rush of juices could almost be heard below the hiss of fertilization"— the sensual dream, the lost Paradise. The starved uplands of Flintcomb Ash, with their ironic mimicry of the organs of generation, "*myriad of loose white flinks in bulbous cusped and phallic shapes,*" and the dun consuming ruin of the swede field — the mockery of impotence, the exile, and finally, Stonehenge and the Stone of sacrifice. In such a setting, coincidence and accidentalism are not out of place and seem to fit in the very scheme of things.

Wide awake to the external world, Hardy's novels present a moving account of the natural life of Wessex. Every delicate shade of colour, be it of Tess's eyes or of the sky, is described in detail. In *The Hand of Ethelberta*, he describes the effect of Ethelberta walking on the soil — 'Her patient heels punched little D's in the soil with unerring accuracy whenever it was bare, crippled the heather-twig where it was hot, and sucked the swampy places with a sound of quick kisses.' The weather and even the time of day and their effect on the mood is included in his narrative. The early hours of morning when Tess and Angel meet at the dairies with their misty dreaminess create the impression of the first man and woman coming together. The delicacy with which the rays of the sun touch upon Tess, the glowing of her skin and myriad of colours spread in the sky are beautifully described.

The suffering of the injured pheasants, the rain pelting down on the farmers working in the swede-fields at the Flintcomb Ash, Tess resting on the wall of a cottage from fatigue and many other such incidents bring out Hardy's humanistic concerns. Sue and Jude are moved to misery on seeing a trapped rabbit and set out to bring its immediate release. There is even a comment that if each man had to do his own slaughtering there would be many more vegetarians in the world, in the novel.

Cazamian comments on Hardy's superb power of natural descriptions and says — "From his earliest works he tried his hand at the delineation of landscape; and while he at first added nothing new to the theme, he showed freshness, an accuracy of touch and tone which bespeaks an intimate knowledge of the country. The idyllic scenes in Far From the Madding Crowd are worthy of being compared with the most truthful pictures that English prose has yet produced in that line. With The Return of the Native, The Woodlanders, Tess we come upon effects more powerful and of a rare quality, aimed at with a sure and certain skill. A great poet of nature there freely displays an exceptional gift for description, which owes a vast range to the perception both of fine shades and of vast, solemn harmonies."

Hardy called his novels "seemings" and "impressions." He has an analytical as well as an impassioned approach to nature. His approach is innovative and based on actual observation of the sad and happy aspects of nature. His descriptions of the woods and hills and dales of his native district, the uplands, the valleys, the vast moor lands in tempests and in fertile seasons have no parallel. Referring to the importance of nature in Hardy's fiction Sir David Cecil remarks, "Nature, first of all, played a larger part in his books than in those of any other English novelist. It is not just the background in his drama, but a leading character in it. Sometimes it exercises an active influence on the events : more often it is a spiritual agent, colouring the mood and shaping the disposition of human beings. The huge bleak darkness of Egdon Heath, dominates the lives of characters in The Return of the Native infusing into them its grandeur and its melancholy; the solitary wistfulness of the woods is the keynote of sentiment of The Woodlanders who lived among them. As the title suggests, the distinctive mark of characters in Hardy's second novel comes from the fact that they dwell 'under the Greenwood tree.' His most living characters, moreover, are always natives of countryside. Out of their original environments they are aliens."

Hardy's attitude towards nature is not Wordsworthian. In fact in Tess, he makes fun of the Wordsworthian philosophy of seeing a benign spirit in the aspects of Nature. His approach is Darwinian and is based on his theory of evolution and the selection and the survival of the fittest in nature. Much in nature is cruel and antagonistic to man. The weaker are all the more trampled upon. Man is not the supreme creation of God, for whom the beauties of nature were designed. He is simply one of the many species of animals inhabiting the earth. The Nature is indifferent if not hostile to man. The ephemerality and insignificance of man in the universe is brought out consistently in Hardy's novels. Tess, like a fly on a billiard table, is an apt illustration of human insignificance. Nature, however, can be bountiful as in the Valley of the great Dairies or exacting as in the uplands of the Flintcomb Ash. Man does not have the power to change the character of his waste land, the choice lies not in his power.

The network of imagery around Tess reveals her close kinship with nature. Metaphor of flora and fauna continually describe her. In fact, we first see her as a girl of sixteen, dressed in white and carrying a peeled willow wand in one hand and a bunch of white flowers in another. The image that strikes us is one of purity, virginity and of course, if we have a mythical bent of mind, we can associate her with fertility and productivity, for the occasion is of May-Day-Dance, a festival of local Cerelia [Ceres being the goddess of fertility and productivity].

Next we see her with roses stuck all over — "roses at her breast, roses in her hat, roses and strawberry in her basket to the brim." Her hair is earth coloured, her breath tastes of bread and honey, on which she mainly lived. The dew falls on her as naturally as on grass, her arm as 'cold and damp' to his {Angel's} mouth as new-gathered mushroom. She is variously compared with many animals and her history further elaborates the metaphor of a hunted animal. She is 'sunned like a cat,' there is something of the habitude of the wild animal. When she falls a prey to Alec's desires, "Nature seemed harmoniously to mingle with the spirit of wine," and in the thick darkness of the Chase, she was just a 'pale nebulousness.' In her moments of guilt and self reproach when she ventured into the woods to withdraw from the world on lovely hills and dales "her quiescent glide was of a piece with the elements she moved in. Her flexuous and stealthy figure became an integral part of the scene." It is her consciousness that made distinction and felt antagonism "but no law known to the environment in which she fancied herself such an anomaly." Earlier she is referred to by Hardy as a 'beautiful feminine tissue, sensitive as gossamer and practically blank as snow.' Later the imagery becomes more pungent and sinister as the events of her tragic story unfold. She is described through serpentine images with the interior of her mouth red like a snake's. She is seen like a fly on the billiard table as she descends into the Vale of Great Dairies. At Flintcomb Ash, a starve-acre place, she becomes a field-woman — pure and simple and at the sacrificial altar of Stonehenge her breathing becomes like that of 'a lesser animal.' Thus, the character of Tess is defined and justified by metaphors of flora and fauna, and the changing face of the earth both directs and reflects her emotional life.

Yet viewed outside the range of Tess's vision, Nature is indifferent and neutral. It simply exists in the novel as the physical background in which the story of Tess moves. The Fly image brings the idea of the helplessness and defencelessness of Tess as also the inscription from King Lear, 'As flies to wanton boys....' the drabness and discoloration of the Flintcomb Ash is described by 'the white face looking down at brown face and the brown face looking up at white face, without any thing standing between them but the two girls crawling over the surface of the former like flies.'

Before coming to the Talbothays farm Hardy while referring to the raised hopes in Tess's heart says, 'Her hope mingled with the sunshine in an ideal photosphere which surrounded her as she bounded along against the soft wind.' While referring to the adjective "Pure" and the implications therein for Tess Hardy had stated its association with 'Nature.' In the Preface to the Fifth edition [1895] Hardy says of readers who had objected to the description of Tess as a 'pure' woman : 'They ignore the meaning of the word in Nature.' Thus Tess's purity resides in her deep and ultimate kinship with Nature. Hardy intensifies the natural processes around Tess to make them a part of her story.

9

Wessex — More than a Setting in *Tess*

The novel opens on a May evening with John Durbeyfield walking homeward to Marlott, from Shaston, in the adjoining Vale of Blackmoor. The village of Marlott lay amid the north-eastern undulations of the Vale of Blackmoor — "an engirdled" and secluded region, as yet 'untraversed' by the tourist or landscape painter. In this fertile land springs never dry, the sun blazes down on large fields, the atmosphere is '*languorous.*' Arable lands are few and limited. It was originally called the Forest of While Hart, but the forests have departed now. Old customs and their shades still remain, and the festival of the May Day Dance is one such old custom. It is a gay survival from days when May time and happiness were synonymous. Here the girls of the village have gathered in white dresses. We find our heroine Tess amidst the country folks. Like the secluded and virgin land, she too is untinctured by any experience. But as the forests and its customs are on decline, the course her life is to follow is also one of relentless decline.

Trantridge, a modern house constructed on the outskirts of the Chase, speaks of money. Life here is artificial quite contrary to the rising grounds of the Chase behind it, where Druidical mistletoe was till found on aged oaks and enormous yew trees grew as if when they were pollarded for bows. These two places have a basic dichotomy inherent in their structure and they finally prove to be detrimental to Tess, a creature of nature and instinct. It is in the misty wilderness of The Chase that Alec, the intruder succeeds in his designs of seducing Tess. It is the power of money that leads to deforestation and construction of a 'spurious' house on this ancient land and it is the economic drive that has sent Tess here.

Life at Talbothays speaks of nature's bounty and fruitfulness. It is a world drawn on a larger scale and here Tess achieves a fullness of growth and matures into a woman. The Froom waters were clear as the Pure river of Life shown to the Evangelist. They lend their purity and freshness to Tess who blooms into a beautiful woman in this idyllic atmosphere. Here she meets Angel and he has a harp too. The scene is perfect to the last details. The two of them meet often as they are both early risers. In these early hours she looks like a 'visionary essence of Woman — a whole sex condensed into one typical form.'

At Flintcomb Ash, a drab dismal place, we find that Tess mercilessly '*nipped her eye brows off*' and wore her oldest field-gowns. Hardy refers to her figure as '*part of the landscape.*' The Flintcomb Ash was an 'starve-acre place.' Life here is starved and devoid of the means of sustenance. Tess is abandoned and her lonely condition is reflected in the starved condition of the land. The weeds that were growing abundantly at the milk idyll of the Talbothays emit offensive smell here at Flintcomb Ash.

The pleasure house of Sandbourne reduces Tess to the status of a richly decorated pet. Finely attired, Tess is blemished for the first time. But this stain upon her conscience, she washes through the blood of Alec. The huge naked stony structure erected at the Stonehenge — the sacrificial altar of Sun worship receives Tess completely exhausted and worn out. Tess finds herself completely at home here. She is ready for the policemen who come to fetch her.

Thus the setting in Tess keeps on changing but always bears an integral relationship to the physical as well as the psychological state of the heroine. It becomes an arena in which Tess acts out a part of her life. Hardy purposefully wants to create different atmospheres here for illuminating different aspects of Tess's life. The Blackmoor Valley has Man and Nature co-existing in a working harmony. Trantridge is idiosyncratic, the Froom Valley is a new exciting world, where 'Tess steps into a world redolent of sensuality and rich fruitfulness.' The lush landscape and Tess's experience of sensuality and love synchronise. The Flintcomb Ash with its drabness symbolises the Winter of Love, as experienced by Tess. The house where Angel and Tess take refuge after the killing is the image of Wellbridge without the terrors of her ancestral background. The Stonehenge is the sacrificial altar. Thus Tess's life runs parallel to the place where she finds herself; in fact her plight is so linked with the land she inhabits that critics have referred to her as the symbol of agricultural purity. Hardy has totally identified her with his settings.

'*The dilemma of Tess,*' feels Dorothy Van Ghent, 'is the dilemma of morally individulising consciousness in its earthy mixture. The most primitive antagonist of consciousness is, the earth itself. It acts so in Tess, clogging action and defying conscious motive; or in the long dream of Talbothays, conspiring with its ancient sensuality to provoke instinct; or on the farm at Flintcomb Ash, demoralising consciousness by its mere geological flintiness.'

The earth acts here as the main causal factor. Long stretches of land have to be crossed in traversing from one place to another. In the incident of Prince's death it acts as the cause of death, by being the same road through which the mail cart travels. The distance between Chaseborough and Trantridge leads to Tess's seduction and Alec is able to win her again due to the distance between Emminster and Flintcomb Ash. This in fact corresponds to the system of accidentalism and coincidence deeply interwoven in the narrative.

Thus, the setting [Wessex] is an integral part of the basic fabric of the novel and serves to highlight the novelist's aim and purpose in this tale of a milkmaid's tragedy as well as the tragedy of the rural community. The novel presents the plight of Tess against the background of the rural Wessex. David Cecil finds in Hardy a combination of the botanist's microscope and the astronomer's telescope. Character and setting are intricately linked in Hardy.

10

Hardy's Views on God and Religion

1. Introduction

Hardy had iconoclastic views on God & religion, which were far more advanced than those of the Victorian society. He believes that there is no God in the universe; instead there is a driving force called the First Cause or Immanent Will. However, in his opinion the First Cause is neither human nor benevolent; it is mechanical and malevolent. David Cecil comments on Hardy's advanced opinion, "Intellectually, Hardy was a man of the new age, a so-called advanced thinker, in open rebellion against traditional orthodox views about religion, sex and so on. — and he used his novels to preach these heretical opinions."

2. Hardy and Church Career

As a boy Hardy was firmly brought up as a Christian. His parents were devout Christians and he himself was well-versed in the Scriptures. Although Hardy rejected Christianity intellectually, he was fascinated by it throughout his life. He himself attended Church sporadically, and his characters also seldom attend Church. However, the amount of Christianity he absorbed in his youth is demonstrated by the large number of quotations from the Bible. Biblical allusions are too frequent in Hardy to be ignored by the readers. Intellectually Hardy rejected the Christian faith, but emotionally he clung to his childhood belief.

At one stage, Hardy thought of entering the church. It is noteworthy that Jude in *Jude the Obscure* also wants to join the church, but cannot; and Angel in *Tess of the d'Urbervilles*, destined for a clergyman, later on refuses to join the church. This conflict of entering the church, reflected in his later protagonists, was deeply influenced by Hardy's personal beliefs and autobiographical events. Hardy could not reconcile the idea of redemption, the idea of a benevolent God and several other beliefs prevalent in Christianity such as the indissoluble marriage. He developed certain intellectual objections to Christianity and finally he was disillusioned from it.

3. Disillusionment with Christianity

The last decades of the 19th century were the decades of spiritual crisis and religious anguish. Philosophers like Schopenhauer were questioning the optimistic religious beliefs and poets like Arnold, novelists like Fitzerald were feeling life to be a sad business. Moody and Lovett assert that Hardy's pessimism "was in harmony with the mood of the late nineteenth century, a mood of discouragement and disillusionment resulting in part from the decline of religious faith, and the account of the world and of man's position in it as given by Science." Schopenhauer's concept of life as a blind 'will to live' had influenced the late Victorian thinkers and writers and Darwin's *Origin of Species* in a way confirmed the hypothesis of Schopenhauer. David Cecil points out, "for the first time, pessimism — conscious, considered pessimism — found expression in English letters : in the works of Arnold and Fitzerald, of Thompson and Hardy. Hardy was especially open to the melancholy implications of the new outlook."

David Cecil comments, "The automatic principle of the universe becomes a God — not a Christian God, but a sinister 'President of the Immortals,' sporting for his own pleasure with wretched humanity." Hardy had lost his belief in Christianity. Like Jude, he had hoped to enter the Church, but just like Jude, he lost his religious fervour and started believing in the universal life-force called the 'Immanent Will'. Darwin's *'Origin of Species'* had shaken the very foundation of the religion by proving that life on this planet had developed gradually and did not start with Adam and Eve. Christian religion believed in the concept of a just, benevolent, paternal God; but Hardy believed in an indifferent, even malevolent First Cause. "Hardy," says Baker, "oppressed by his tragic view of existence, sees wherever he looks 'Crass Casualty' thwarting man's best endeavours, and what the scientist described as natural selection eliminating with blind indifference both the fit and the unfit to survive."

Baker asserts, "His God is not a Christian. The good in man is confronted by evil which seems to be omnipotent. Like that other determinist, Meredith's Sir Austin Feverel, overwhelmed by the general malevolence of things, Hardy sees the devil." Hardy's disillusionment with Christianity is reflected in Tess, with potent force. He reverses Browning's line to convey his stand on Christianity :

God's *not* in his heaven : all's *wrong* with the world.

In Angel's rejection of Christianity we find Hardy's own prejudice against it, culminating in the Aeschylean phrase, '*President of the Immortals.*' In chapter 12 we find, "Some people might have cried 'Alas, poor Theology!' at the hideous defacement — the last grotesque phase of a creed which had served mankind well in its time."

4. Ironical References to Religion

Hardy refers to Scriptures in an ironical manner. The ease with which Alec is converted and then retracts are symptomatic of the failure of Christianity to make any real impact on the modern, mercantile world. After Tess's seduction Hardy asks ironically, 'Where was Tess's guardian angel? Where was the Providence of her simple faith? Perhaps, like that other god of whom the ironical Tishbite spoke, he was talking, or he was pursuing, or he was in a journey, or he was sleeping and not to be awaked' [Chapter 11].

Hardy in his description says about 'her own long family of waiters on Providence' and comments on the Biblical knowledge of village girls, 'Like all village girls she was well grounded in the Holy Scriptures' [Chapter 14], but also adds ironically that these village-girls have 'far more of the pagan fantasy of their remote forefathers than of the systematized religion taught their race of later date' [Chapter 16]. The village folk treat the sacred Sunday as the chosen day for fashionable frivolity, "but on this day of vanity, this Sun's day, when flesh went forth to coquet with flesh while hypocritically affecting business with spiritual things" [Chapter 23].

Hardy also refers to the basic irony of human life : the dichotomy of stern moralistic expectations and the limited choice in a hostile environment. He makes it quite plain when he says, "She — and how many more — might have ironically said to God : with Saint Augustine, 'Thou has counselled a better course than Thou hast permitted'."

Hardy's anti-Christian mood is at its bittermost in Chapter 14, wherein Tess buries her dead child. 'The Midnight Baptism' was not published in the serial publication of the novel in *Graphic*. It was published separately in *The Fortnightly Review* in May 1891, two months before the serial version began. This was excluded from the serial publication, because the Victorian public could have found the scene anti-religious. Jane Marcus comments on the sensitiveness of this scene and treats it in the light of gender-discrimination :

> 'She takes the law into her own hands, as she took Christianity into her own hands to get her dying baby into heaven. But Tess hands are a woman's hands. They are not supposed to administer sacraments and they are not supposed to administer justice.'

5. View of the First Cause

Hardy did not believe in God. He didn't think that the omnipotent has a definite shape. According to him, the universe is evolutionary, as envisaged by Darwin. Still he believed that there is an omnipotent presence, the Immanent Will, the First Cause. The First Cause simply means that this omnipresent, omnipotent thing comes first, is responsible for all creation, and it causes evolution of mankind. Hudson remarks, "Hardy held that there is not active intelligence, no just and loving God, behind human destiny, but that Creation is swayed by an unconscious mechanical force, sightless, dumb, mindless, and equally indifferent to either the sufferings or the joys of mankind." The universe is impersonal; its growth is automatic and the law of growth is cruelty as evidenced by the 'survival of the fittest' theory. The First Cause of Hardy is equivalent to the traditional God; with the difference that Hardy's is cruel.

The First Cause has caused everything and all human miseries have resulted from the imperfections of the First Cause. Hardy regards First Cause in theory as blind and indifferent to human beings, but in his novels he makes First Cause hostile to man. Hardy makes explicit references to this First Cause in his novels. In *The Return of the N*ative, he writes, "Human beings, in their generous endeavour to construct a hypothesis that shall not degrade a First Cause, have always hesitated to conceive a dominant power of lower moral quality than their own." In Jude the Obscure, Sue thinks, 'the first cause worked automatically like a somnambulist, and not reflectively like a sage.' In Tess of the d'Urbervilles also, he writes, "This consciousness upon which he had intruded was the single opportunity of existence ever vouchsafed to Tess by an unsympathetic First Cause."

In Hardy's philosophy Immanent Will is the First Cause, the prime mover, the cause of all phenomena. Hardy called the supreme energy or cause of things as Immanent Will. The First Cause of Hardy is nothing else than the supreme energy working within the universe.

6. Biblical Allusions

Baker comments on the strong influence of Bible in Tess, "Hardy could not clear his mind of a theistic conception of the governance of the world, however, much he assented to the protests of the science that the universe was a system of unconscious and unpurposive mechanism...Tess of the d'Urbervilles is almost a reading of the Bible backwards, so full is it of Biblical similes and allusions, above all, curses." It has a Biblical word for every occasion, but especially the occasion of guilt. It brands Tess who 'looked upon herself as a figure of Guilt intruding into the haunts of Innocence' [Chapter 13] with a ready biblical image : 'He little thought that the Magdalene might be at his side.' Alec's encounter with Tess in the juicy garden resembles the meeting of Eve and the Tempter in the Paradise and the strawberry effectively replaces the Original forbidden fruit. In Tess's misadventure with Alec she has 'eaten of the tree of knowledge.' Alec, too, descries himself as 'the old Other One' and can cite scripture for his diabolical purposes. A biblical vocabulary provides convenient models. Tess's sufferings are compared to Job's; her worship of Angel's wisdom is referred to as the Queen of Sheba's wonderment at Solomon's wisdom {I'm like the poor Queen of Sheba who lived in the Bible}; Angel Clare is linked to Samson, reviewing the damage after his tragic wedding night. Parson Clare compares himself to Abraham and compares his son, his 'misnamed Angel' to a 'doomed Isaac.'

However, the most strong biblical allusion, recurrently found in *Tess* is that of Adam-Eve. Angel is seen as Adam, Tess as Eve and Alec as Satan. When Tess and Angel meet before dawn at Talbothays, there is the strong environment of pre-creation Paradise, where Adam and Eve used to walk alone in all innocence and bliss. In the novel also they are alone in all bliss in the lap of nature. The association with Eve carries with itself the association of being *'fallen'* as well. She *falls* twice in the novel, first she falls from her virginal status at Trantridge, and secondly she falls when she returns to Alec at Sandbourne and thus is guilty of adultery. Tess also suffers a fall from her Talbothays paradise and the cause of her fall is her eating of the forbidden fruit at the insistence of Alec at Trantridge. Seen in this light, Tess must be a willing victim to the seductive machinations of the Satanic Alec. Tess not only falls herself, but like Eve again, is also instrumental to the fall of her man. Angel's misery begins with the knowledge of Tess's fall [as Adam's misery began with the knowledge of Eve's fall] and, however, unsympathetically we may think of Angel, it is true that his happiness suffered an eclipsed after the ill-timed confession of Tess.

In the paradise of Talbothays — this Garden of Eden...like Eve, Tess will worship her lover; but unlike the Christian Paradise this one is full of paganism and sun-worship, and ecstasy lies in warm, sensual love, not in the cold, perverted 'Christian' principles. Clare is not only seen as Adam by Tess, but also as her Apollo. Clare, to Tess, is a sublimation of the direct sensuality of the Sun, and of nature all around. The disguises of Alec also assume biblical significance. Alec is first dressed-up as a dandy, then he is dressed in the garb of the Methodist, then again in his normal clothes, then disguised at the reaping scene 'in a gathered smock-frock.' The frequent disguising of Alec suggests the disguises of Satan, the tempter of Eve and mankind, who, in the Bible, continually assumes different shapes.

7. Faith in Pagan Religion

Christianity is the outward religious mode in Wessex; the real religion there is pagan. Although the village-girls certainly know their Bible, they are full of pagan spirit. There, Sunday is not the day of worship, but the day of coquetry. Their life is in harmony with the natural world they live in. This is why pre-marital sex for them is not a sin, as it is not a sin in the eye of nature. Even Angel says that 'it might have resulted far better for mankind if Greece had been the source of the religion of modern civilization, and not Palestine' [Chapter 25]. Izz, Retty and Marian are full of sexual longings and Hardy as the omniscient author comments sympathetically on the pathetic situation : "cruel Nature's law...was but portion of one organism called sex; which lacked justification 'in the eye of civilization [while lacking nothing in the eye of nature]'" [Chapter 23].

Church-going is sporadic in this pagan setting and the people are fatalistic and superstitious. Tess, like Eustacia, has been called pagan. In *The Return of the Native*, Eustacia has been described as having *'pagan eyes,'* and as *'the raw material of a divinity on Olympus.'* In *Jude the Obscure*, Sue brings the pagan deities of Apollo and Venus into the most Christian city of Christminster and she suffers for the deed.

In *Tess*, the remote ancestor of the heroine is appropriately called Sir Pagan d'Urberville and her kinship is emphasised by her sense of peace at the pagan place of Stonehenge. When she arrives at the heathen temple at Stonehenge she says, 'One of my mother's people was a shepherd hereabouts, now I think of it. And you used to say at Talbothays, that I was a heathen. So now I am at home' [Chapter 58]. Here Hardy tries very hard to establish the credentials of Tess as a pagan woman; this is why he traces her heredity to the imaginary Sir Pagan, and also associates her mother with some shepherd. This sudden revelation and association of shepherd-connection is obviously an attempt to establish her pagan background, but Hardy here stretches his art too much. Even without the reference of the shepherd Tess is a pagan all right, but Hardy spoils the effect by over-emphasising the obvious.

The pagan family of Tess is skilfully contrasted with the strictly Christian family of Angel. The religious individual is a favourite area of concern for Hardy in Tess. From the painter of signs and clergyman [in the Baptism episode] to Alec's conversion to the Clare family — everywhere we find Tess's paganism in contrast with the Christian world. The really religious parents of Angel, and the religious caricatures of Angel's brothers, and the rebellious religious spirit of Angel — the Christian background is very strong in the novel, against which Hardy traces Tess's pagan roots consistently and effectively.

8. Conclusion

Tess has a strongly religious background. The biblical analogies are scattered throughout the novel and through them Hardy manages to put an ironic commentary on situation as well as to criticise the Christian practice. The novel is saturated in the Bible. Baker comments, 'He loved the church, though he was severe on its shortcomings.... He was always borrowing ideas, figures of speech, expressive phrases, as well as immortal sayings from holy writ, and put them with inimitable force and felicity in the mouth of his rustic sages.' In *Tess*, Hardy attacks the objectionable Christian malpractices and the lack of humanity in dogma. David Cecil sums up the situation, 'Tess is an indictment of Providence — a parable whose moral is that it is not possible to justify the ways of God to men.'

11

Morality, Marriage and Sex in Hardy's Novels

"Love is one of the great facts that mould human life. But it is a catastrophe," says Virginia Woolf regarding the novels of Hardy. Love, marriage and sex are the three issues that run as an undercurrent in the novels of Hardy. What we remember most about the people of the Wessex novels is their passion. Marriage is the natural outcome of love as far as the convention goes and sex naturally figures in these relationships. Hardy had written freely about these issues in his novels, though not as freely as he would have liked to, but much more than the Victorian people could digest. This can be corroborated by the reviews of his later novels, especially *Tess of the d'Urbervilles* and *Jude the Obscure*.

Hardy believed that man-woman relationship had to be redefined in the changing world situation. What had previously been said about it was not final for it didn't explain the issue completely. Hardy's novels are an attempt to redefine the man-woman relationships in the social context. The question raised by Tess seems to be of great importance to Hardy — "Was once lost always lost true of chastity?" and "Was the recuperative power of nature denied to woman alone?" In nature man-woman union was something quite natural and not an anomaly, it is society and its conventions that have made these relationships complex and objectionable.

In his letter to Edmund Gosse Hardy had remarked on the criticism of Jude, that he had feared the book to "seem High Churchy." He had also felt the subtitle of Tess to be the impression left on a 'candid' mind. Thus he did not hold the conventional outlook and so didn't find them in any way innovative or outrageous.

Hardy however displays different codes of conduct for the Wessex people and the people who do not belong to the Wessex region. In Wessex, seduction and adultery are not sins. In fact, here seduction and infidelity are 'natural,' while in the corrupt outside world they seem more reflective nastier evil.

Hardy's novels have been greatly concerned with the man-woman relationship and its implications for him, aptly expressed in the following words, 'I feel very strongly that the position of man and woman in nature may be taken up and treated frankly.' In *Tess of the d'Urbervilles* and *Jude the Obscure* Hardy had after many years of evasively writing about sexual tensions and conflicts, written openly. They reveal his final and definitive statement and stand on these issues. Woman in marital and sexual relationship is presented with extreme frankness. Tess brings together for the first time the 'types' of woman that have frequently been counterpoised in the earlier work — the woman compromised and doomed by her own sexuality, either as victim or as femme fatale [Fanny Robin, Lucetta], and the young woman poised at the moment of marriageability [Paula Power, Elizabeth-Jane Newson].

Ian Gregor says, the temptations of Su[k]e, the endurance of Marty, the troubled consciousness of Grace come together and find a fresh definition in *Tess*. The novel is structured on the sexual and marital history of Tess.

Her schooling and her analytic and questioning mind has segregated Tess from her surroundings. Her first trouble, feels Hardy, would only have been a 'liberal education,' if she would have been like Izz, Retty or Marian; and perhaps to any other Wessex inhabitant in place of Angel, for in Nature's scheme of happenings it was only an incident and not a catastrophe. It is the conventional outlook that made it a tragedy. In fact with Tess Hardy had become the novelist depicting the New Woman, and also the writer who took up the sex issue frankly and openly. The sub-title 'A Pure Woman' involved the moral concerns; for purity in its conventional mode exists side by side with morality.

The sex roles and double standards regarding men and women had already come to be questioned. Hardy's defence of his heroine's conduct by pronouncing her as 'pure' created a great controversy. The phallic imagery of pricking, piercing and penetration used in delineating Tess's experiences from the death of Prince to her final penetrative act of retaliation and the interiority of her sexuality satisfies the narrator's fascination with Tess. He uses recurrent motifs of red-white, blood & flesh, sex and death to show her suffering and express the violence perpetuated on her.

Hardy not only uses the word 'pure' for Tess, he also calls her 'an almost standard woman,' now standard involves values, moral, ethical & social. In *Jude the Obscure* the sexual issue surfaces more prominently although Hardy called it primarily the tragedy of a young student who could not make it to the university. The grossness of Arabella's behaviour, the strangeness of Sue's marital relationships with Phillotson and her sexual relationship with Jude, along with their bleak, dismal lives, created a great uproar in the later nineteenth century when the book was published. It is a kind of Anna Karenina from the male point of view. Both these novels raised the marriage issue very prominently — Sue deciding to leave Phillotson as she couldn't physically tolerate his presence, Arabella tricking Jude into marriage through false pregnancy alarm, both leaving their marriage partners and living together as man and wife begetting children without marriage; Tess thinking herself to be truly married to Alec because of her sexual relationship with him — what was the significance of the marriage ceremony and where was the Christian dictum — "joined till God does us apart?"

Earlier novels too show promiscuous relationships, but these two novels really stirred the hornet's nest. The end of these two novels was also quite extraordinary. Tess murdering Alec and feeling almost absolved of her sin and coming to Angel with a guilt-free mind, Sue going back to Phillotson as a punishment for her digression, Jude going back to Arabella, all reflect a conventional morality taking over the rebellious souls. Yet the judgement Hardy allots to them is not same. His punishments are for those Wessex inhabitants who had tried to be different, had separated themselves from the common stock; the other erring Wessex people like Angel and Arabella are not punished by death sentence. Henchard, Tess, Jude have to face death for their sin of rebellion.

Marriage, in Hardy's fictional world, means unhappiness. The married pair is never blessed with a happy life. Perhaps this accounts for the reluctance of the majority of Hardy's heroines to marry. So many marriage licences are cancelled and so many are sought for at the spur of the moment. Their men try to catch them in between these denials. Moreover, extra-marital affairs are quite common. The novels throng with heart-breakers as well as girls who are evasive, coquettish and enchanting. Hardy's world presents men and women in varying combinations, the star-crossed and ill-matched pairs and the wrong lover. Here the hour of loving rarely arrives for the truly faithful ones and love becomes an agent of the 'doomsters' bringing destruction and ruin. Characters submit to social morality. The dreaming mind perceives an ancient ethics that sees punishment as coming from without and intuitively observes punishment coming from within, which is where it does, after all, so often come from.

Regarding the charge of immorality against *Jude the Obscure* Hardy had written in a letter to Edmund Gosse [1895-96] :

> "The only point in the novel on which I feel sure is that it makes for morality; and that delicacy or indelicacy in a writer is according to his object.... And in writing Jude my mind was fixed on the ending."

In 'Candour in English Fiction' Hardy had said, "Life being a physiological fact, its honest portrayal must be largely concerned with...the relation of sexes and the substitution for such catastrophes as favour the false colouring best expressed by the regulation finish that 'they married and were happy ever after,' of catastrophes based upon sexual relation as it is."

Hardy's novels are an attempt to present man-woman relation as they are not contrived to get a happy or sad ending. He had witnessed many such relationships which did not end in a happy marriage. The forsaken girls married again, the reckless lovers and heart-breakers ditched their beloved and so on. The Wessex world was fraught with such instances. What Hardy presents is an ironic parody of the Providence which separates rather than unites the separated lovers. This is a world where the characters are gradually isolated in a universe abandoned or forgotten by a god who is after all only a fiction. There is a discrepancy between personality and environment, sensibility and circumstance.

In *The Mayor of Casterbridge*, Henchard violates and disturbs the moral order and hence brings upon a retribution, that works from without as well as within. Tess and Jude and Sue too suffer because what accuses them is their conscience which takes too seriously the external and rigid dictates of a moral code which is conventional and socially acceptable. The isolation and self-inflicted punishment of these characters leads to their downfall. The cruelty of the 'ill-conceived world' injures and blights and crushes them for ever. Like Job, these derelict figures think themselves to be the victims of a demoniac torturer. Hardy's fictional world has a gigantic flow in its very essence — the environment is at variance with human happiness and the conditions cannot be changed for it is a morally indifferent world.

Yet Eustacia, Henchard, Jude, Tess all inwardly consent to this moral order that defeats them. Like Henchard who said, "I — Cain — go alone as I deserve — an outcast and a vagabond." Tess too says, 'I do not want to go any further...I am at home,' she is ready to face the gallows —' It is as it should be ... I am almost glad...This happiness could not have lasted...I have had enough.' She visualises a better life for her sister Liza-Lu — her spiritualised image — untarnished and untinctured, as the future mate for Angel, and thus gives up her claim and also her struggle, bowing down to the conventional social morality and accepting its dictum.

Jude too towards the end reconciles himself to his endless disappointments and accepts them. He reconciles to Arabella. Sue on the other hand blames the universe for the failure of her marriage. Thus in a dialogue with Phillotson she says,

"But it is not I altogether that am to blame?"

'Who is then? Am I?'

"No—I don't know! The universe, I suppose—things in general, because they are so horrid and cruel."

Sue is the type of New Woman — intellect and wit and even charm to some extent, extremely masculine and lacking the feminine component. Jude calls her a 'spirit,' 'a disembodied creature,' 'a tantalising phantom.' Hardy said that she was the type of woman who had always had a great attraction for him. Jude comments upon the havoc the two women have created in his life — 'Is it that women are to blame, or is it the artificial system of things under which normal sex-impulses are turned into devilish domestic gins and springes to hold back there who want to progress?' Faced with the idea of matrimony, Sue can only see a sequence of external gestures from which all inner significance has been drained. The ironic remarks of the widow Edlin further throw light on the change time has brought upon the institution of marriage — "Nobody thought o' being afeared o' matrimony in my time...Why when I an my poor man were married we thought no more o't than of a game o' dibs!" Their going back to their original partners is a parody of marriage as it exists in the Christian world.

12

Recurrent Motifs in *Tess*

Tess is a simple story told in a complex way. It has the architectural structure and Hardy consciously repeats several threads and ideas to build up the requisite atmosphere. The most important devices applied to this end are symbolism, animal imagery, anthropomorphism and motifs. 'Motif' is 'a usually recurring salient thematic element in a work of art, especially a dominant idea or central theme.' In *Tess*, there are several motifs repeated at regular intervals, besides the motifs of animal imagery, Adam-Eve parallels, Biblical motifs which will be dealt with elsewhere.

1. Red colour motif
2. Sun motif
3. Mist motif
4. Movement motif
5. Dressing up motif

1. Red Colour Motif

Red colour symbolizes sexual passion [as it is the colour of rose and lips] as well as violence and murder [as it is the colour of blood]. In *Tess* Hardy carefully uses the red colour motif, as this novel is about sexual passion as well as murder. The red colour has been associated with Tess from the very beginning. In May dance festivity, she is the only one of the group to wear 'a red ribbon;' others are in white. Thus, Hardy singles her out as different from other members of her group and connotes that others will keep their virginity, but she will not. The second memorable 'red colour motif' comes in the death-scene of Prince.

The horse is pierced through his heart and blood is spouting in a stream. "In her despair Tess sprang forward and put her hand upon the hole, with the only result that she became splashed from face to skirt with the crimson drops." This blood-bath signifies that her family has suffered a great financial setback due to the death of the horse. Symbolically, it also foreshadows the whole career of the heroine. Like Prince, she will also walk on the dark road of life while the Omnipotent Driver will be comfortably asleep as Tess sleeps in the ride sitting on the driving seat. Tony Tanner reads the death-scene of Prince as a prophecy of Tess's loss of virginity, "It adumbrates the loss of her virginity, for she, too will be brutally pierced on a darkened road far from home; and once the blood of her innocence has been released, she too, like the stoical Prince, will stay upright as long as she can until, all blood being out, she will sink down suddenly in a heap. Compressed in that one imponderable scene we can see her whole life" [Casebook, p. 186].

When Tess goes to meet Mrs. d'Urberville, her house is of 'rich red colour'. The name of the 'The Slopes' is also symbolic as hedonistic and the red colour perfectly communicates Alec's sexual designs on Tess. Red colour marks the house of sex and death. In Tess, her rapist's house is red. The entry of the Talbothays dairy-house, where she loves and marries Angel, is also red. The prison where Tess dies, is also 'a large red-brick building' [Chapter 59].

When Tess meets Alec for the first time, he decks her with roses [red-coloured flowers] and forces strawberries into her mouth [red-coloured fruits]. On the evening of the rape, Tess sees 'red coal of a cigar' in Alec's mouth. The constant association of red colour with Alec and Tess is symbolic; Hardy rarely associates red with Angel. Angel is more spiritual than sexual, hence red is not his colour. Tess is a pagan creature and Alec a sensual Bohemian; hence red is their proper colour.

After seduction Tess returns home and she finds a man with 'a tin pot of red paint' [Chapter 12] writing Biblical threats to erring mortals. The emphasis on red colour is significant, as the words are meant to be a warning or caution and red is the colour of warning besides being the colour of lustful passion. Soon after,

Hardy describes the reaping machine 'ruddy.' Later on also, Hardy associates red colour with 'red thresher' [Chapter 47], and 'red elevator'[Chapter 47]. Hardy takes machines as symbols of modernization invading the countryside, this is why he associates the colour of violence and anger with various harvesting machines.

Red colour is not only traced in external objects, but also in the body of Tess. Tess before seduction speaks to Alec' revealing the red and ivory of her mouth;' of course, her teeth are ivory-white and tongue is red, but here Hardy relates red colour to the sexual passion which is latent and inherent in Tess and white colour to her virginity. Later on, Angel also watches the interior of her mouth, 'She was yawning, and he saw the red interior of her mouth' [Chapter 27]. Here Hardy excludes the mention of ivory or white because Tess is no longer a virgin.

White colour is associated with purity and virginity. Hardy is aware of the colour symbolism and in May dance he uses it to denote the dance of the virgins. It is significant that in the seduction scene Tess is a 'white muslin figure.' Later on, Hardy insistently uses white colour to describe Tess, particularly his face, to denote her essential purity of character.

When Angel kisses the inside vein, her blood was driven to her finger-ends and when she madly rushes to hear Angel's music through apple-trees, her skin got 'madder stains' [Chapter 19]. the noun 'madder' means 'red' and by this single colour-association Hardy conveys to its readers the sexual impulse of Tess for Angel. Hardy endows Tess with a 'usually ripe red mouth' [Chapter 36].

In the pheasant-suffering scene we find pheasants 'dabbled with blood,' which is meant to be a parallel to the death-scene of Prince. When Tess goes to meet Angel's parents she finds 'a piece of blood-stained paper.' When Alec once again tries to renew his relationships with Tess, she hits him 'and in a moment the blood began dropping from his mouth.' Later on, she kills him and the landlady finds the red spot in a memorable description : 'it was red. The oblong white ceiling, with this scarlet blot in the midst, had the appearance of a gigantic ace of hearts' [Chapter 56].

There are innumerable 'red colour' associations in the background, particularly with sunlight or fire as 'red-coaled glow' [Chapter 34]. significantly, Alec calls Tess a 'bled calf' at the end of her torturous work on the thresher. And he means more than he intends. At Flintcomb Ash Tess is a woman without sexuality and, in that sense, bloodless. This is why in the Flintcomb Ash chapters, Hardy does not associate red colour with Tess. Colours become dull and ashy at Flintcomb Ash.

However, as soon as Angel returns, Tess once more becomes passionate and kills Alec. Tess and Angel rest into a vast bed with 'crimson damask hangings' in an empty house to be 'let furnished.' And in that red curtained bed she gets real sex [not described or mentioned at all] and peace. Thus, we find that red is the most important colour used in Tess to highlight sexual passion and violence and it has been used so repetitively that it becomes a significant recurring motif in the novel.

2. Sun Motif

References to the sun and the moon are extremely common in novels and they cannot be generally treated as motifs. But Hardy elevates the sun-figure in Tess to the significant status of a Pagan God and hence in this novel it is essential to trace the sun motif. Hardy reiterates the pagan or heathenish setting of Tess [Heathen or pagan religion does not acknowledge the God of the Bible and usually believes in several nature-gods]. Sun-worship is perhaps the most ancient form of worship on this earth. As a deity of light' Sun [called Apollo or Phoebus in Greece and Rome] helped to ripen crops, prevent sickness, maintain growth. In his kind aspect, Sun helps growth, gives energy and warmth. In *Tess*, Hardy uses the positive features of the sun in his recurrent motif.

Sun is an important feature in the structure and substance of the novel. The novel begins at sunset and it ends at sunrise. The sunset at the beginning symbolizes the fallen status of the d'Urberville family and the sunrise at the end symbolizes the consoling togetherness of Angel and Liza-Lu. In the beginning of the novel, sun makes its presence felt in the May-dance festivity, when 'Sun lit up their figures' [Chapter 2]. 'And as each and all of them were warmed without by the sun, so each had a private little sun for her soul to bask in; some dream, some affection, some hobby, at least some remote and distant hope which, though perhaps starving to nothing, still lived on, as hopes will' [Chapter 2].

As Tony Tanner writes, 'They are creatures of the sun, warmed and nourished by the sources of all heat and life.' In a cold climate, sun easily becomes the potent symbol of physical longing for warmth. The Sun as generative energy helps creation to procreate. Hardy gives a detailed discussion of the sun-motif in the novel itself.

The sun, on account of the mist, had a curious sentient, personal look, demanding the masculine pronoun for its adequate expression. His present aspect, coupled with the lack of all human forms in the scene, explained the old-time heliolatries in a moment. One could feel that a saner religion had never prevailed under the sky [Chapter 14].

Hardy here mentions 'heliolatries' meaning 'sun-worships,' which he will use so effectively at the end when Tess is going to be sacrificed at Stonehenge. Hardy describes the sun at length, 'The luminary was a golden-haired, beaming, mild-eyed, God-like creature, gazing down in the vigour and intentness of youth upon an earth that was brimming with interest for him' [Chapter 14].

In mythology, Apollo is a bachelor but a promiscuous lover. The implication is that pre-marital sex is admissible in pagan societies which worship Sun-god. The word 'pagan' also carries the meaning 'one who delights in sensual pleasures, a hedonistic person.' By making Tess a member of the pagan religion Hardy thus finds an excuse for her, which is altogether difficult to find in the Christian religion. It is significant that Hardy again and again pinpoints the pagan setting, just as Shakespeare does in *King Lear*.

The pagan *vs.* Christian attitude towards Sun is highlighted by Hardy in a subtle manner :

'...but on this day of vanity, this Sun's day, when flesh went forth to coquet with flesh while hypothetically affecting business with spiritual things' [Chapter 23].

The statement is deeply ironical, even satirical. Hardy here implies that all are pagans underneath, Christianity is a facade. Hardy significantly uses 'Sun's day' instead of 'Sunday' to highlight the importance of the luminary. The outdoor love-walk of Angel and Tess happened to be 'on Sundays, when it was quite dark'. Incidentally, Tess is also seduced at the early hours of Sunday. It is noteworthy that except one or two remarkable love-scenes, Angel-Tess courting takes place before sunrise or after sunset. Perhaps Hardy intended to underline the inherent Adam-Eve parallel and the pre-creation setting, which was possible only before sunrise. Besides, daylight is not proper to promote romantic atmosphere; night is rather more appropriate time for romance. This is why Hardy carefully imbues his romantic scenes with the recurrent motifs of mist and fog.

"Tess and Angel rise very early, before the Sun. they seem to themselves 'the first persons up of all the world.' The light is still 'half-compounded, aqueous,' as though the business of creating animated forms has not yet begun. They are compared to Adam and Eve."

In this sunless light Tess appears to Angel as unsexed, sexless, 'a visionary essence of woman.' As soon as sun appears, the reality comes. Tess is more physical than spiritual in daylight, 'her teeth, lips and eyes scintillated in the sunbeams, and she was again the dazzlingly fair dairymaid only.'

Hardy indirectly suggests that the sun has chosen Tess as a victim. On her marriage-evening the Sun is shown as casting an ominous spotlight on Tess. The sun 'formed a golden staff which stretched across to her skirt, where it made a spot like a paint-mark set upon her' [Chapter 34]. Here Hardy intends to remind the readers that the bride has already lost the virginity; she has already become an unwedded mother and hence she is stained.

The only great love-description in the sunlight is also ominous;

"The sun slanting in by the window upon his back, as he held her tightly to his breast; upon her inclining face, upon the blue veins of her temple, upon her naked arm, and her neck, and into the depths of her hair. Having been lying down in her clothes she was warm as a sunned cat" [Chapter 27].

Here the sun interferes too much and Hardy is more eager to tell us about the warm touch of the Sun on the lovers, in particular Tess. Angel is casually mentioned because he is rather cold emotionally hence sun-warmth is only upon his back; but on Tess, the Sun is everywhere. Angel also praises Tess, 'You are like an undulating billow warmed by the sun' [Chapter 23].

Tess is a pagan at heart, though a Christian in life. She suffers mostly when the sun is absent — Prince's death, her seduction, her capture — all the significant events including her rift with Angel take place just before sunrise, including her romance with Angel. Many more events like her separation, sleepwalking scene take place in the night. Tess has a complaint against the pagan god, 'Why the Sun do shine on the just and the unjust alike?' [Chapter 19]. By this question, Hardy makes Sun an indifferent, neutral god, who, regardless of virtue or vice, is distributing freely.

The setting sun gives rise to some remarkable similes,'The evening sun was now ugly to her, like a great inflamed would in the sky' [Chapter 21]. Of course, it is the transference of character-feeling to inanimate object, a simile which is more true about Tess. In another sunset scene 'At half-past six the sun settled down upon the levels, with the aspect of a great forge in the heavens' [Chapter 28]. In the May-dance, 'the rays of the sun had absorbed the young stranger's retreating figure' [Chapter 3].

In the last phase of her life, Tess sleeps on the altar of Stonehenge, the heathen temple, knowing fully well that people sacrificed innocent animals here to the Sun-god and realizing, 'And you used to say at Talbothays that I was a heathen. So now I am at home' [Chapter 58].

Tess is indeed a victim, sacrificed to the sun by the society as its best specimen [the Corn King theory]. The heathen temple is appropriate, as Tess has descended from Sir Pagan d'Urberville, and Hardy moreover believed that women 'retain in their souls far more of the pagan fantasy of their remote forefathers than of the systematized religion taught their race at a later date.'

3. Mist and Tear Motif

Mist or fog is as natural a phenomenon as sunlight. But Hardy has used it as a recurring motif. The misty surroundings have been associated with sexual longing and amatory anticipation. Mist makes a person short-sighted; one cannot see far in a misty setting. And this is why mist/smoke is an appropriate symbol for the forbidden sex which also makes a person morally short-sighted.

Whenever Tess meets Alec there is mist/smoke motif present. Although mist and smoke are being used here together; there is a difference. Mist suggests coldness while smoke suggests warmth. Whenever Alec confronts Tess there is smoke; the smoke of Alec's cigar becomes a symbol of his brazen sexuality burning in his heart. In their first garden-walking scene 'the skeins of smoke that pervaded the tent' and 'the narcotic haze' are clearly creating a shady atmosphere. In the seduction scene also fog and absence of light are important, 'On account of the fog The Chase was wrapped in thick darkness.' In the seduction scene itself we find 'Upon her eyelashes there lingered tears' [Chapter 11]. Mist is an image or symbol of passion and dizzy sexuality, but here mist is reacting on the heroine's body. Nature has produced mist and Nature has endowed men and women with the ability to have sex and thereby procreate. So if mist settles as tears on Tess's eyelashes it suggests that she will be miserable on account of her sexual experiences. Mist, again and again, will decorate her eyelashes. When she is with Angel, 'Minute diamonds of moisture from the mist hung, too upon Tess's eyelashes' [Chapter 20] and fog 'settling on the lashes of her eyes, where it rested like crystals' [Chapter 31].

When Tess is raped or seduced it is foggy, when she first approaches Angel by madly running to hear his music, there are mists of pollen in the atmosphere. Their courtship goes on in the misty light of the dawns when Sun and human beings are sleeping as yet. Thus, pre-creation togetherness of Adam and Eve is suggested here by segregating them from the rest of the human beings. 'The spectral, half-compounded, aqueous light which pervaded the open mead, impressed them with a feeling of isolation, as if they were Adam and Eve' [Chapter 20]. The face of Tess is enveloped in the 'mist stratum, seemed to have a sort of phosphorescence upon it.' Their romance develops in 'faint summer fogs.' In the proposal scene itself, 'she might have been in a trance, her eyes open, yet unseeing' [Chapter 24]. In her drive to the station with Angel, atmosphere is foggy and rainy with moistening road enveloped in smoke. In their walk 'they saw tiny blue fogs in the shadows of trees and hedges' [Chapter 31]. Even when she is going to be married, Hardy employs the mist motif, 'She knew that Angel was close to her; all the rest was a luminous mist' [Chapter 33]. The mist-motif is discarded, as soon as she is separated from Angel. Thereafter images are hard in Flintcomb Ash such as rain. Only when Tess is with Alec or Angel, mist-motif is applied to suggest the forces of sexuality reinforced by the atmospheric suggestive patterns of nature.

4. Movement Motif

In the novel, Tess is always kept moving and walking incessantly and reluctantly. The novel opens with a man staggering on rickety legs down a road and it is his daughter who will walk throughout the book. Phase the Second opens with her walking back to home after her seduction. At the start of Phase the Third, again Tess moves, 'she left her home for the second time.' In Phase the Fifth, she returns home after her nightmarish marriage. At the beginning of Phase the Sixth, she confronts Alec while she is returning from her 15-mile walk. At the beginning of Phase the Seventh, Angel returns from Brazil and thereafter they move like nomads in the natural habitat.

The motif of movement is associated with Tess, and the movement is always reluctant. "Tess's instinct is for placidity, she recoils from rapid movements. Yet at crucial times she finds herself in men's carriages or men's machines. She has to drive her father's cart to market and Prince is killed" [Tony Tanner]. Alec forces her into his speedy dog-cart and 'the least irregularity of motion startled her.' Angel, by contrast, takes her to the wedding in an ominous carriage. "And yet she is bound to be involved in travelling, and dangerous motion, because she has no home" [Tanner]. At the beginning of the novel, Tess's father asks the parson 'Where do we d'Urbervilles live?' and he replies 'You don't live anywhere.' Tess also does not live anywhere. Her home at Marlott always drives her to travel, forced by financial pressures. Throughout the novel we see 'her uprooted, forced to the roads, ejected from houses, knocking on doors which remain close to her' [Tanner].

Again and again, Tess returns to her home: after Prince's death, after her seduction, after Angel's rejection, even from Flintcomb Ash. But Marlott drives them out of their home after Jack's death, they travel with their bag and baggage to Kingsbere where also a home is denied to them. Tess is kept by Alec at Sandbourne, more a house than a home. After Alec's murder Angel and Tess spend their days and nights in a 'to let' house, a house which belongs to none of them. In the end, the capture happens to be at Stonehenge, an open heathen temple.

Home connotes warmth, love and security; and these are the very things Tess does not possess and always longs for. Tess, as a representative of the agricultural labourers, also has to move. Agricultural labourers in England had 'temporary homes' due to their changing work-places. It is not for nothing that Tess and her family move out of Marlott on a day of 'general movement' of the labourers to their new places. The movement motif implies the migration syndrome in the rural agricultural class, which has to 'move' in order to live, which has to take risks in order to survive. It is significant that after each major episode in her life, Tess returns to her home; but her home does not welcome her arrival. She is forced again and again to go away to work in alien and hostile places [Flintcomb Ash] or to live as a kept-mistress in an alien atmosphere [Sandbourne]. Much of her tragedy is caused by her movement and she is always running like a hunted animal to escape disaster. But at last she is tired and spent, 'I don't want to go any further.' She treats the Stonehenge temple as her home, 'And you used to say at Talbothays that I was a heathen . So now I am at home' [Chapter 58].

The movement motif in *Tess* symbolises three major issues raised by Hardy : migration of the agricultural labourers in rustic areas; the inability of the rustic world to retain their homes; the dangers inherent in the movement in alien and hostile environment. Penny Boumelha writes, 'It is not only Alec who is associated with the gigs and traps that, on occasion, literally run away with

Tess; it is during a journey in a wagon driven by Angel that he finally secures Tess's acceptance of his proposal. Equally, the two ride to their wedding in a sinister, funereal carriage and when Angel makes his proposition to Izz, she is riding in his gig. It is noticeable, too, that during their wagon-ride, Angel feeds Tess with berries that he has pulled from the trees with a whip, recalling the scene at The Slopes when Alec feeds her with strawberries.'

5. Dressing-Up Motif

Dressing-up is an important motif which runs through the whole novel. This motif is used in the negative sense by Hardy; whenever Tess is dressed up, there is disaster. In dressing-up is implied the idea of ornamentation and beautifying for the appreciation of the external world and male gaze. Another deep image is that of a sacrificial animal dressed-up for the ritual [compare Keats' Ode to the Grecian Urn]. The dressing-up motif is a minor but significant thread in the large pattern of Tess.

First of all, Tess is separated from her fellow-maids by her dressing-up. She wears an extra 'red ribbon,' while others are in total white. This is when Angel first sees her. Later on, her mother dresses her up when she goes to work at d'Urberville house. She falsifies the appearance of Tess by the brushing of hair, by the broader pink ribbon, and by the airy fullness of her frock, all which 'imparted to her developing figure an amplitude which belied her age, and might cause her to be estimated as a woman when she was not much more than a child' [Chapter 7]. The falsification has an adverse consequence for Tess, 'This dressing her up so prettily by her mother had apparently been to lamentable purpose' [Chapter 8]. This dressing-up impresses Alec and his sexual advances towards Tess are the consequences of her dressing-up. Later on, when Tess goes to her in-law's house, her friends Izz and Marian dress her up. They argued that 'she should dress up in her very prettiest guise to captivate the hearts of her parents-in-law; though she, knowing of the austere and Calvinistic tenets of old Mr. Clare, was indifferent, and even doubtful" [Chapter 44]. Again this dressing-up proves fatal to her because she meets Alec while returning from her unsuccessful rendezvous. When Angel returns from Brazil and meets her, she is dressed in Alec's extravagant presents. Thus, we find that the dressing-up motif has been skilfully managed and manipulated by Hardy.

13

Salient features of *Tess of the D'Urbervilles*

1. Irrespective of the criticism the novel has received from the day of its publication, the fact remains that it is an exceedingly readable novel. Many novels, though well-acclaimed in their times have simply become great but have not gained the popularity *Tess of the d'Urbervilles* has achieved.
2. The first and foremost element is the story element. The story of Tess has still retained our interest through its universality. Taking the theme from the world of balladry, wherein it was common to find young milkmaids being betrayed and murder or suicide being a part of the tale, Hardy has given us the story of a girl who suffers relentlessly and through her suffering rises to tragic heights.
3. The novel is vividly realised. Many scenes of great natural beauty as well as of romantic strain come live to us. Rural Wessex and its inescapably scenic moments of the May-Day Dance celebrations, the sunset at Stonehenge, the romantic scenes in the lush Vale of the Great Dairies and the drab and lacklustre scenery of the Flintcomb Ash have all been presented before us with unparalleled beauty.
4. The proto-cinematic technique that Hardy has employed in presenting the various scenes makes the novel extremely realistic.

5. The very conception of the heroine is done with great care and love. The lines from Shakespeare's *Two Gentlemen from Verona* :

> Poor-Wounded name! My bosom as a bed
> Shall lodge thee....

speak of the love and fascination of the author for the heroine. In an interview Hardy had given the following account :

> "Tess, I only once saw in the flesh. I was walking along one evening and a cart came along in which was seated my beautiful heroine, who, I must confess was urging her steed along with rather unnecessary vehemence of language. She coloured up very much when she saw me, but — as a novelist — I fell in love with her at once and adopted her as my heroine."

Tess comes to us vividly visualised and vibrating with real life and blood. Though passive most of the time, she fascinates us with her feminine charm and vivacity. We meet her at the age of sixteen, at the Marlott village in the extremely picturesque May-Day Dance celebrations dressed up in the virginal white dress carrying a peeled willow wand in one hand and a bunch of white flowers in the other hand. She has a red-ribbon too in her hair; this prized possession marks her out and the dance of missed chances and missed opportunities begins. Angel, our hero, comes, but he wouldn't dance with Tess. He notices her, but has no time to spare for this 'pretty maiden,' little knowing that time would neither spare her nor him for the clock has struck and the race has begun.

6. John Bailey claims that "Tess is the most striking embodiment in literature of the woman realised both as object and as consciousness, to herself and to others." She is the subject of the novel. The title reveals this. The title also speaks of Tess's pedigree, her descent from Sir Pagan d'Urberville, one of the twelve knights who came from Normandy with William the conqueror. The novel thus illustrates the life history of Tess, a descendent of Sir Pagan d'Urberville. Her fall reveals 'how mighty have fallen;' her moral strength and the power of endurance elevate her to great tragic heights.

7. Tess is both an individual as well as a universal constant. She is a symbol of agricultural purity.
8. The story pattern follows the metaphor of hunting, "Tess is a hunted animal running from one place to another." She is finally caught and sacrificed at Stonehenge.
9. The universality of theme and the realistic presentation make it an extremely engaging novel for all times to come.
10. The writer has succeeded in inciting the reader's sympathy for his central character. We may find fault with the author or the character herself but we can't help loving her and sympathising for her. This accounts for the appeal the novel has for its readers.
11. In Tess's struggle for survival we perceive the human frailty and in her strength to surmount all difficulties we see the heights to which man, though weak he may be, can rise and challenge the forces that are too strong for him. This proclaims and restores our faith in humanity.
12. Hardy's novels generally have "Love" as the main factor of causation. It is also the universal "emotion" to which all can relate.
13. "Fate," "Chance," "Coincidence" though greatly criticised by the critics, have been so integrally assimilated into the pattern of the novel, that while reading we don't feel them to be out of place. Hardy's fictional world is the world of balladry, not ancient balladry where the supernatural intervened but of later balladry where coincidence and chance have taken over the role of the supernatural. The bleak world that he presents in these novels admits them; for they serve as the agents of a malevolent Fate working in antagonism to human hopes, aspirations and happiness.
14. The realistic pastoral settings nostalgically take us back to the days when 'Love,' 'Faith,' 'Joy' were living things. This communal life, its joys, its sorrows arouse our sympathy and we share close affinity with it. The impressionistic, cinematographer technique transports us into the world of the rural Wessex of late 19th century.

We feel with Hardy the loss of such a beautiful world and realise "what man has made of man."

15. Not only this, the novel though well steeped in the later 19th century tradition takes up many of the concerns of the modern world. The dismal unfaith, the anxieties of sexual maladjustment, social misemployment, chronic self-destructiveness are all modern elements. The total vision of a bleak, godless or indifferent God is a modern trait. The modern reader finds himself quite at home.
16. Joseph Warren Beach finds the greatest element of appeal in *Tess of the d'Urbervilles* to be the pathos inherent in the story. It is this pathos — voicing itself in accents of great beauty — that marks the superiority of *Tess of the d'Urbervilles* to any other English novel of its period.
17. *Tess* is the most poignant of all Hardy's stories because here Hardy is writing from the depth of his being about casual wrong, the will to recover, the growth of love, faithfulness, frail happiness and death. It is the simplest of Hardy's novels and yet contains his best writing.
18. The novel is well steeped in the history, folk lore and traditions of Wessex. A world in which typical ballad heroes and heroines can flourish with a thoroughly rationalised 'mythology' to sustain them. The structure is compact with no loose episodic structure. Action and events dominate rather than psychology or comment. This gives the novel a resemblance with classic drama. Its logic is the logic of the traditional story wherein the improbable and unpredictable is not only admitted but is also welcome. It is the element of strangeness or miraculous that makes a story interesting.
19. The balance between the uncommon and the ordinary on one hand to make the story interesting and on the other adherence to realistically portrayed characters gives Hardy's novels a unique charm. Superstition and omens are there in the background, but never come to the surface and dominate action.
20. Wessex characters do not change. It is their changelessness that imparts universality to them. The

changeful characters bring evil into the lives of the changeless characters. The changeless characters have aesthetic richness and the success of epics, ballads etc., show the insatiable human instinct for changeless characters. Hardy rationalised them by presenting them in a social order that could accommodate them. His Wessex is a tradition bound region allowing free play to superstition, omens, love, revenge, tragedy etc. Here human aspirations, passions are allowed a free play against the backdrop of a dark malevolent sky. Nature is the norm and Hardy's rustics are nearest to nature. They are not decorative but are integral to the scheme of events. Angel and Alec are both changeful characters bringing ruin in the life of Tess.

21. Hardy's world has polarities : simple versus complex temperament, rural versus urban. Hardy maintained a double standard of sexual morality — one code for Wessex and one for the rest of the world. Hardy's theme is mankind, man crushed by the indifferent forces of Nature and Fate. Tess, the innocent maiden, seduced, abandoned and waiting for the return of her true love, is like the heroine of an ancient ballad. And, in the best ballad style, her fate partakes of the strange and the mystical : she is haunted by a phantom coach; a fortune telling book forecasts her future; an unlucky cock crows on the afternoon of her wedding day. These Gothic touches add to the book's charm.

22. Hardy takes the stance of an omniscient narrator : he knows and understands Tess's thoughts, motives, feelings, responses etc. He even intrudes directly or makes certain characters his mouthpiece. He uses the summary narrative form generally and at times uses pictorial or cinematographic technique in describing scenes of great beauty.

23. Hardy builds up an intricate pattern of symbols, omens, and superstitions to prepare us beforehand for the tragic events that follow, for example, the reference to this world being a blighted one is followed by the accident

and Prince's death. The pricking of the thorn foretells the consequence of Tess-Alec relationship. The afternoon crowing of the cock prepares us for the tragic consequences of Angel-Tess marriage and the phantom coach prepares us for the forthcoming murder and so on.

24. The novel's initial title, *Too Late Beloved* and *A Daughter of the d'Urbervilles,* and *Body and Soul of Sue* [one of Tess's pre-names] also sheds a new light on the writer's point of emphasis in the novel. The hereditary theme of the novel and the moral concerns become quite obvious from the title. Later, however, Hardy tactfully made the necessary changes in the text as well as the name of the novel, keeping the original pieces intact and published them as a full-fledged novel in 1912 Wessex edition in its full definitive form. The novel is full of Hardy's comments on religion, Bible, morality etc. Two scenes specially the baptism scene and the scene in the Chase were deleted and published separately as *Saturday Night in Arcady*' and *The Midnight Baptism,* sub-titled *A Study in Christianity.*

25. The novel's sub-title, *A Pure Woman* created a great uproar but Hardy was working out a course of action, for a girl who has been wronged at a very tender age, that aimed at reflecting a striking individuality and moral courage. To leave her seducer because she considers it right to do so is a decision which her behaviour and her future course of action would support. Hardy's artistic, moral and emotional identification with Tess gives her a personality that leaves an everlasting impression in the mind of the reader. She is both 'ideal' and 'real.' Tess's verisimilitude in art and human quality is maintained throughout with a subtlety and a warmth and naturalness which can only be the work of a great original tale-teller, born and not made.

26. Clementina Blark of the Illustrated London News finds the essence of the novel in the perception that a woman's moral worth is measured not by any one deed, but by the whole aim and tendency of her life and nature.

27. The novel exemplifies Hardy's pantheistic conception that impulse is the law of the universe and pictures of unrivalled natural beauty characterise the novel.
28. D.F. Hannigan in the Westminster Review [Dec. 1892] called *Tess of the d'Urbervilles* the greatest work of fiction produced in England since George Eliot died. It is Hardy's magnum opus, one of the great novels of all time. Tess is the most loveable heroine of Hardy.

In the presentation of characters there is a figurative pattern as also in his descriptive sequences. He works through contrast in effectively evoking the kind of feeling he wants to generate. The Talbothays versus the Flintcomb Ash is the most obvious contrast at the descriptive level. At the symbolic level too it forms a great contrast through its effect on the central character, as well as on the minor characters. Tess begins as a part of a 'votive sisterhood' at Marlott — a part of nature with a bunch of flowers and a peeled willow wand, but with a red-ribbon — selected by gods for this tragedy of passion and blood-shed. The white dress signifies purity and innocence and the black flag at the end puts an end to everything.

Tess is also characterised by animal imagery as well as the metaphor of hunt. The reaping machine and the mail-cart with its noiseless wheels are the agents of machinisation bent on destroying the kind of agricultural communal life that had been prevalent from times immemorial. Other symbols are the 'Cross in hand,' 'the Sun,' 'the red tyrant' and so on.

29. Another important feature of the novel is the authenticity of dialogue. Each character is given a suitable and authentic speech. Joan Durbeyfield, Dairyman Crick, the Milkmaids — Izz, Marian and Retty, Alec, Angel, Tess all speak differently. The speech also reflects upon their character. Sometimes the characters serve the part of chorus and sometimes they become the author's mouthpiece. Then, of course, their speech changes.
30. Hardy presents himself as the omniscient narrator and here and there inserts his philosophical, ironic comments on characters, situations and incidents. Throughout the novel one can hear his distinct voice.

31. The novel has many themes :
    (i) The betrayed woman and her revenge.
    (ii) The social contrast of rich and poor.
    (iii) The economic pressures, the cheap woman-labour and class consciousness.
    (iv) The social and moral contrasts.
    (v) Christian / anti-Christian; old Christianity / new Christianity.
    (vi) The nature theme.
    (vii) Victimisation of man by hostile or indifferent forces.
    (viii) Exploitation of the labour in the economically governed society.
32. Thus, though Tess is a novel that nostalgically looked upon a way of life fast disappearing yet it is for all times to come. There is a verisimilitude that transcends the facts of place. It is imaginative, sympathetic, humanitarian contemplation of humanity in adversity.
33. The novel not only depicts the tragedy of a heroic girl but the tragedy of a proud community baffled and defeated by processes beyond its understanding and control.
34. The superb opening, the death of Prince, the lovely elegiac scene of the harvesting, the sequence in dairy-farm, the scene of the sleepwalking, the episodes of agricultural life at Flintcomb Ash and the climax at Stonehenge are all original imaginative inventions.
35. Douglas Brown speaks of *Tess* as Hardy's most tragic fable of agricultural defeat.

14

Summary of *Tess*

PHASE THE FIRST : THE MAIDEN

The rickety legs of John Durbeyfield traversing the grounds of the village of Marlott perhaps reflect upon the degenerate condition of the ancient families of great renown coming to dust through the passage of time. It is not surprising then, that the discovery of his great lineage further deteriorates his condition.

The history of Tess, the daughter of the above mentioned John Durbeyfield [as indicated by the 'phase' of the chapters significantly reflecting upon the periods of the heroine's life] perhaps begins here, with the discovery of the great lineage. John Durbeyfield gets drunk on this pretext and Tess is forced to leave the lush grounds of Marlott in search of livelihood, a search which ultimately ends her on the sacrificial altar of Stonehenge.

It is Parson Tringham, with his interest in history and genealogy, who imparts the disastrous information of the Durbeyfields being a descendant of Sir Pagan d'Urberville, a French Knight who had come to England in 1066 with William the Conqueror. Though extinct now, there was 'hardly such another family in England.' All that remained of this illustrious family was the vaults at Kingsbere-sub-Greenhill, with their effigies under Burbeck-marble caponies.

Puffed up by this information of great ancestry John Durbeyfield decides to go home in a carriage. He sees a boy Fred and tells him of his ancestry and asks him to carry his basket home and send a carriage to take him home to the village of Marlott.

The village of Marlott lies amidst the north-eastern undulations of the beautiful Vale of Blackmoor — 'an engirdled and secluded region, for the most part untrodden as yet by tourists or landscape painter.' In this Virgin land lives our virgin heroine, at present engaged in the local Cerelia of the May-Day Dance, dressed in white, carrying a wand, but marked by a red-ribbon, '*a pronounced adornment*' from the rest of the village maidens.

She is a fine, handsome girl with mobile peony mouth and large innocent eyes. She is described by Hardy as 'a mere vessel of emotion untinctured by experience.' The meekness, passivity and rawness of Tess is well-expressed during the May-Day Dance, where she misses the chance to dance with Angel Clare, our hero due to her backwardness.

Thus, the drama of missed chances and opportunities begins with Tess, selected by gods as sport. Hardy's comment is quite illuminating here, 'Pedigree, ancestral skeletons, monuments records, the d'Urberville lineaments did not help Tess in her life's battle as yet, even to the extent of attracting to her a dancing-partner over the heads of commonest peasantry.'

May-Day Dancing, says the writer has been reduced to mere social custom but once it was synonymous with good time and cheerfulness. The village of Marlott is a fertile and sheltered tract of country, a feature which it shares with our heroine herself. It is a virgin land as yet 'untrodden' by tourists or landscape painter, but the wheel has started turning and very soon, its peace and calm will be disturbed by two outsiders — Alec and Angel. The land's virgin status has given a proper background to the heroine's virgin status.

The land has a historical interest too, which further links it with our heroine. The Vale of Blackmoor was earlier known as the Forest of White Hart and a curious legend is attached to it. During King Henry III's reign, a certain Thomas de la Lynd killed a beautiful white hart, which the king had spared. He was heavily fined for it. Tess in her white dress — [seen as white shape, when Angel turns back to look] and wearing a red ribbon slighted by Angel and persecuted by Alec symbolically repeats the same plight.

Forced by the drunkenness of her father, Tess undertakes to deliver the beehives to Casterbridge twenty miles away over rough roads on a rickety carriage driven by an old, slow horse. During the journey Tess and her brother fall asleep and meet with an accident. Tess feels responsible for the tragedy as well as for the economic collapse that this tragedy ensues for her family.

It is this sense of responsibility that drives her to further tragedy, when she undertakes the charge to claim kinship with a certain d'Urberville family living at Trantridge.

The significance of darkness, when misfortunes strike Tess is variously hinted by the critics. The whole system of missed chances and lost opportunities seems to work under the cover of darkness when the individual has fallen asleep. Tess's tragedy is as much linked with the unknown, unforeseen forces of blind Fate as with the economic drives and the evils of industrialisation. It is quite in line with the scheme of things, that the lantern goes off and Tess falls asleep at precisely the same moment when the mail cart — with its noiseless wheels was speeding like an arrow on the very path which Tess had to traverse. The pointed shaft of the cart lets out all the blood which animated the poor old horse.

In a futile, yet symbolic gesture Tess tries to stop the blood, which is spouting from the body of the horse, but she only gets splashed from face to skirt with the crimson drops. From now on the journey to the final splattering of blood at the gallows will be a much more hurried one for Tess. Panting and out of breath, she would only find rest at Stonehenge, the sacrificial altar of the Sun God.

Racked with guilt and her sense of responsibility for the sustenance of her family Tess agrees to go to Trantridge, which to her surprise is a newly constructed red-coloured mansion, where 'everything looked like money — like the last coin issued from the Mint.'

Trantridge was situated on the outskirts of the Chase — a truly venerable tract of forest-land — one of the remaining woodlands in England of primeval date, where in Druidical mistletoe was still found on aged oaks, and yet it was a well kept modern house, a complete to the landscape of the Chase. Here we encounter Alec — a man of swarthy complexion, with full lips, badly moulded, a well groomed black moustache with curled points, with touches of barbarism in his contours and a bold rolling eye.

Tess is as much surprised by the place as by its owner, whom she had imagined to be of an aged and dignified face. Hardy's comment on this chance meeting is again quite illuminating,

> 'In the ill-judged execution of the well-judged plan of things, the call seldom produces the comer, the man to love rarely coincides with the hour of loving. Nature does not often say "See!" to her poor creatures at a time when seeing can lead to happy doing, or reply "Here!" to a body's cry of "Where?"

So Poor creature Tess is coveted by the wrong man and not the right and desired Alec. The scene where Alec, makes her eat strawberries from his hand rightly foreshadows the terrain of the coming tragic events. The thorn that pricks her chin is symbolic of more blood to be spilled in their relationship. The red colour of the ribbon, the horse's blood, the strawberries, the red mansion seems to completely obliterate the white vacuity that Tess seems to project.

Tess is offered a job at Trantridge and like Proserpine, she is carried over by Alec [like Pluto] in his carriage from the happy world of Marlott to 'a great country of which she knew nothing.' Nicely decked up to her disadvantage by her over-ambitious mother.

The 'Kiss of mastery' that Alec implants on her face, and the futile attempts of Tess to wipe it off symbolically speaks of Tess's endeavour to wipe off this relationship from her life. It also speaks of her refined character. Alec's comment that she is 'mighty sensitive for a cottage girl' reveals his lack of sensitivity and manners; in fact that nobility of spirit which Tess, a mere child-woman displays.

Phase One ends with the inevitable. Alec succeeds in his sexual designs when Tess agrees to be driven home by Alec, while returning from the town of Chaseborough, where the working people of Trantridge went every Saturday night. Tess evades a physical combat with Car Darch but can't evade the evil designs of Alec. *'Out of the frying pan into fire'* is a fine description of this bacchanalian revel. Hardy compares Tess's friends to Pan and Syrinx and Priapus and Lotis. According to Greek mythology, Priapus was the god of male generative power; Pan the pastoral god of fertility. Syrinx and Lotis were nymphs pursued by these gods. These references prepare us for the event of Tess's seduction. Alec purposefully deviates into The Chase, where darkness and silence ruled over the years and Oak trees. Hardy ironically remarks that Tess's guardian angel 'was talking, or he was pursuing, or he was in a journey or he was sleeping and not to be awaked.'

Tess has been variously described as resembling an animal by Hardy. The symbolism of a hunted animal being quite evident. The end of Phase One also tries to give an answer to the cause of this harsh judgement of the Providence. 'Doubtless some of Tess d'Urberville's mailed ancestors rollicking home from a fray had dealt the same measure even more ruthlessly towards peasant-girls of their time.'

The spirit of Nature mingled with the spirit of wine, Tess's guardian angel went on a holiday, and the providence of simple faith was betrayed; Tess became wiser and sadder at the same time, and her personality underwent a drastic change from the white, virginal, figure that we had first encountered at the Marlott village. She has 'fallen,' she has been seduced or raped in her sleep by the villain named Alec.

Critical Comments and Salient Features

1. The May-Day Dance festivities with the village maidens dressed up in white frocks, carrying white flowers in one hand and a willow want in the other hand take us back in time to the days when 'cheerfulness and May-time were synonymous.'
2. The lonely figure of Tess feeling dejected for not being chosen by Angel — a white shape standing all alone near the hedge.

3. The picture of Joan Durbeyfield rocking her child, and washing the clothes and at the same time singing lullaby.
4. The death of Prince : the iron shaft of the mail cart piercing Prince; Tess drawing out the shaft gets splattered with blood.
5. Alec d'Urberville's stuffing strawberries in Tess's mouth, her basket and rose blossoms to be put into her bosom.
6. Tess beautifully dressed by her mother, drives in a carriage with Alec, who during the whole journey harasses the heroine by his amorous advances.
7. Tess tending the fowls in the d'Urberville farm, whistling to them.
8. The dancing couples looking like 'satyrs clasping nymphs — a multiplicity of Syrinxes' Lotis attempting to elude Priapus and always failing' — at the Chaseborough fair.
9. Alec rescuing Tess from the fight with Queen of Diamonds and Queen of Spades and carrying her away to The Chase, where the spirit of 'Nature seemed harmoniously to mingle with the spirit of wine.'
10. Tess exhausted falls asleep amidst dead leaves and felt like '*a pale nebulousness at his feet...Everything else was blackness,*' with tears still lingering upon her eyelashes.

Hardy's Comments and Their Significance

[a] *On Tess* : Hardy wants to emphasise in this section the childish and inexperienced character of Tess. Next Hardy focuses on her innocence, inexperience and childish quality. "...for all her bouncing, handsome womanliness, you could sometimes see her twelfth year in her cheeks or hr ninth sparkling from her eyes; and even her fifth would flit over the curves of her mouth..." Her physical development may belie her age but mentally she is still a child. Such a criterion is extremely essential for the thesis that he wants incessantly to prove that Tess is a pure woman. Purity for him has a natural connotation, though he struggles hard to establish it as a conventional and even a moral principle.

[b] *On the world at large* : Regarding the Durbeyfield household Hardy comments, 'Some people would like to know whence the poet whose philosophy is in these days deemed as

profound and trustworthy as his sing is breezy and pure gets his authority for speaking of Nature's holy plan.'

Tess and her brother talk about this world —

'Did you say the stars were worlds, Tess?'

'Yes'.

'All like ours?'

'I don't know... They sometimes seems to be like the apples on our stubbard-tree. Most of them splendid and sound — a few blighted.'

'Which do we live on — ?'

'A blighted one.'

Such a dialogue between a 'mere vessel of emotion untinctured by experience' and a small boy is highly improbable. It seems to be aimed at working out a thesis for this world as being a 'blighted one'. Soon we see Prince being pierced and Tess being forced to go to claim kinship with the so-called d'Urbervilles, who are not genuine d'Urbervilles.

The mispairing of Tess and Alec is just another feature of this drama of missed chances. The question Hardy asks, 'Why it was that upon this feminine tissue, sensitive as gossamer and practically blank as snow as yet, there should have been traced such a coarse pattern as it was doomed to receive; why so often the coarse appropriates the finer thus, the wrong man the woman, the wrong woman the man, many thousand years of analytical philosophy have failed to explain to our sense of order' still remains unanswered. But it is a normal feature of the world that Hardy celebrates in his fiction. The answer that he hesitatingly provides doesn't seem to satisfy : '...the possibility of a retribution lurking in the present catastrophe' with Tess's ancestors dealing the same blow on some peasant girl, and the visitation of the sins of fathers upon children doesn't work out perfectly even in this universe of Hardy. For we may ask what did Alec's forefathers do to earn a dagger in Alec's heart?

It is the later thesis of 'It was to be,' that seems to be nearer to the scheme of things in this world, where the 'guardian angel' simply wanders away and the providence of simple faith is betrayed again and again.

[c] *On Wessex* : The novel is not only a faithful account of the betrayal and undoing of a pure and innocent girl, it is also a faithful account of a way of life, a virgin land being gradually destroyed. The old ways, old customs were fast disappearing. Though Hardy bewails the loss of this world, he also realises the shortcomings of such a world. New inventions, new technologies and scientific knowledge assured a progress which was hard to negate.

[d] Another important feature is the decaying of old illustrious families. Now extinct or on the verge of extinction, their plight he viewed with concern. The tragedy of Tess begins with the discovery of her ancient lineage; nothing good comes out of this discovery, in fact all evil is at loose.

[e] *Colour symbolism* : White and red criss-cross Tess's life from the beginning. Note their relation with purity and passion respectively. Sun and darkness too play a great role. Tess wears a red ribbon — in the May-Day Dance sequence and this presents a curious mixture of purity and passion, innocence and sexuality in Tess red is also the colour of blood.

[f] *Superstitions/Omens* : The fortune-teller's ironic revelation about 'some noble gentleman marrying her,' the thorn of Alec's rose-blossoms pricking Tess's bosom, the blood of Prince spluttering all over Tess's body and her futile attempts to stop the blood oozing out of Prince's body, the mail cart with its noiseless wheels piercing poor Prince's body, the temptation scene of Eve being re-enacted in Tess's eating of the strawberries from Alec's hands are omens and symbols that foreshadow the coming events.

PHASE THE SECOND : MAIDEN NO MORE

The Phase One ends with the inevitability and fatalism of 'It was to be.' The novel is described by Hardy in Preface to the fifth and later editions 'as being one wherein the great campaign of the heroine begins after an event in her experience which has usually been treated as fatal to her part of protagonist, or at least as the virtual ending of her enterprise and hopes.' The experience referred to, culminates the first phase of the heroine's life history. Phase two is devoted to the consequence of Tess's experience.

She gives birth to a baby who ultimately dies. This phase is remarkable for the growth of the heroine from a mere child to a full-fledged woman. It also shows the strength of her character and she rises in ethical and moral stature right before our eyes.

Phase Two begins with Tess returning from Trantridge. Alec follows her; but she rejects his offers of help and tells him, 'I have said I will not take anything more from you, and I will not — I cannot. I should be your creature to go on doing that, and I won't!'

Alec makes fun of her and finds the behaviour uncharacteristic of her class and her position. But Hardy makes it quite clear that Tess's fall and her pregnancy are no fault as far as Nature is concerned. It is only Tess who looks 'upon herself as a figure of Guilt intruding into the haunts of Innocence....She had been made to break an accepted social law, but no law known to the environment in which she fancied herself such an anomaly.'

While returning from Trantridge Tess meets a Painter of signs, who is writing religious texts of warning for the sinners like *THY, DAMNATION, SLUMBERETH, NOT* and *THOU, SHALT, NOT, COMMIT*.....a very crude form of symbolism is being used here by Hardy. Tess, however, is not deterred by such texts and exclaims — 'Pooh — I don't believe God said such things!' Perhaps Tess shares Hardy's reaction to such comments. Tess's tragic experience with Alec made her look upon herself as a figure of Guilt, but most of her misery 'had been generated by her conventional aspect.' Hardy describes her as an almost 'standard woman' except 'for the slight incautiousness of character inherited from her race.'

Tess gives birth to a child and after a brief period of rest starts working at a field. We see her with her child, a child's child. One of her co-workers comments, ' 't was a thousand pities it should have happened to she, of all others....' but it was to be and so it happened. The comments of the earlier chapter regarding this world as a blighted one prepare us for this fatalism. In the hands of a blind and malignant fate, human beings are mere puppets. Darkness assumes a symbolic meaning in Hardy.

It is this cosmic blindness which seems to favour first Prince's accident and next Tess's seduction.

However the baby, an 'offense against society' falls sick. Tess realises the implications of death without Baptism; her poor child will be consigned to the nethermost corners of hell; she decides to baptize him herself. She gathers her brothers and sisters together and performs the service, christening him 'Sorrow' from a phrase in the *Book of Genesis*. In this scene she emerges as a pathetic but strong heroic figure. 'The children gazed up at her...She did not look like Sissy to them now, but a being large, towering and awful — a divine personage.' Sorrow, the undesired ends his campaign in this world and after his death he is buried in a shabby corner of 'God's allotment' amidst unbaptized infants, notorious drunkards, suicides and other such conjecturally damned people.

The Phase Two ends with a pertinent question, 'Was once lost always lost really true of chastity?' The recuperative power which pervaded organic nature was surely not denied to maidenhood alone. Hardy's assertion is further corroborated by the earlier reference to Tess's experience being 'simply a liberal education.' The past was past; whatever it had been, it was no more at hand. Whatever its consequences, time would close over them. The 'turbulent experiences' did not demoralise her, and Tess with the 'unexpended youth, surging up anew' in her heart decides to leave her house for the second time, this time towards Talbothays.

Critical Comments and Salient Features

1. This phase, in the scheme of events is what we may call a dormant period in the life of Tess. The major events being the birth and death of 'Sorrow — the Undesired.'
2. The chapter begins with Tess's backward journey to Marlott from Trantridge with a heavy basket and a large bundle, the burden is even greater on heart.
3. Tess completely rejects any further relationship with Alec and refuses his help. She acknowledges her weakness in being 'dazed' by Alec for a while. She had not understood him 'till it was too late.' Alec tells her that

he is 'ready to pay to the uttermost farthing,' and as we see in the long run, he does pay with his life for the injury he had done to her.

4. Tess meets a man painting religious texts : *THY, DAMNATION, SLUMBERETH, NOT* and *THOU, SHALT, NOT, COMMIT*......—— over crude and overt symbolism is being introduced by Hardy. Tess's reaction, 'Pooh — I don't believe God said such things' is worth noting, for her little experience of life and her sixth standard study, she appears to be quite modern in her outlook. She also doesn't confirm to the Wessex còde of behaviour where pre-marital sex and adultery are no taboos.
5. Hardy explains her case as one of temporary infatuation: 'She had dreaded him, winced before him, succumbed to adroit advantages he took of her helplessness; then, temporarily blinded by his ardent manners, had been stirred to confused surrender awhile, had suddenly despised him and disliked him, and had run away. That was all'. Her agonised cry to her mother further reveals her pathetic plight, 'Why didn't you tell me there was danger in men-folk?' Hardy makes such statements to prove Tess's innocence. Again the field-women working with Tess refer to Tess's case as : ''twas a thousand pities that it should have happened to she...'tis always the comeliest!' Hardy now calls her 'an almost standard woman.'
6. Tess's plight has no effect on nature. It is a normal occurrence and no anomaly. Most of her plight is generated by her 'conventional aspect.'
7. We see the reaping machine and rabbits, hares, mice, snakes etc. put to death by its quick and merciless action.
8. Tess is seen here as a child-mother, a mixture of love and hate characterises her relationship with the child.
9. The most prominent scene of Phase Two is the towering personality of Tess, viewed by her brothers and sisters as she baptises her dying child.
10. Hardy describes some more of Tess's physical traits — her 'flower-like mouth, tender eyes, neither black, nor blue

nor grey nor violet, rather all those shades together, and a hundered others' and her face — 'a thing of immaculate beauty with a touch of dignity which was almost regal.'

11. We also come to know Hardy's attitude towards religion. It is as ambiguous as is his attitude towards sex and morality.
12. Tess to him now is 'a woman whom the turbulent experiences of the last year or two had quite failed to demoralize.' She now changes from a 'simple' to 'complex' woman, with 'a pulse of hopeful life still within her.'
13. The Phase Two ends with a pertinent question, 'Was once lost always lost really true of chastity?' The recuperative and regenerative power which pervaded organic nature was surely not denied to maidenhood alone.
14. The chapter's end is on the note of new life surging within Tess, and without spring bringing new life into nature and its creatures, 'The stir of germination was almost audible.' Denying her past, her ancestry Tess looks forward to her future work at the Talbothays farm as a milkmaid in search of pastures new.

PHASE THE THIRD : THE RALLY

The Phase Three ironically again brings us to a 'thyme-scented, bird-hatching' morning in May and while the earlier May-morning ended with Tess undertaking the fatal journey to Trantridge, this May morning finds her moving to Talbothays, the Dairy farm in the Valley of the Great Dairies. 'The world was drawn to a larger pattern here' and 'the Froom waters were clear as the pure River of Life shown to the Evangelist...' Here Tess's 'hopes mingled with the sunshine in an ideal photosphere which surrounded her as she bounded along' with 'a pleasant voice in every breeze' and joy in everything. Hardy would like us to believe that this phase of Tess's life would be different. In this Valley of milk and butter, Tess meets our hero Angel and he has a harp too! Again Hardy's comment,

'Let the truth be told — Women do as a rule live through such humiliations, and regain their spirits, and again look about them with an interested eye. While there's life there's hope is a conviction not so entirely unknown to the "betrayed" as some amiable theorist would have us believe.'

is a sly reflection upon the course of events as such. The Dairyman Crick's world presents a complete contrast to the field at Flintcomb Ash. Here the members live as a family in complete harmony with each other. Life at Trantridge too revealed a wide chasm between the employer and the employee.

Life at Talbothays is ideal for Tess and Angel to fall in love. They are both early risers and in this Froom Vale at a season when the rush of juice could almost be heard and amidst the oozing fatness and warm ferments 'it was impossible that the most fanciful love should not grow passionate.' Tess and Angel come closer and closer. The Phase Three ends with Angel declaring his love.

This chapter brings us in close contact with the life of Wessex people, well steeped in superstitions and folklore. The life at Dairyman Crick's place is full of idyllic charm and beauty. Tess responds to the rhythm of seasons and reaches a fullness of growth. Life at Trantridge had reaped the harvest of guilt and misery. The mechanical reaper that Tess encounters during the days of misery was a monster of the industrial Revolution threatening and engulfing her identity but the beauty and richness of her innermost being is revealed here in the lush atmosphere of the Dairies. In the 'luminous gloom' Angel envisions Tess as a goddess and calls her by fanciful names like Artemis.

Critical Comments & Salient Features

1. Another spring has come over, the earth rejuvenates and so does Tess, it is with her best face that she ascends the uplands of Egdon.
2. The Froom Valley is a complete contrast to the Vale of Little Dairies, Blackmoor Vale.
3. The world was drawn to a larger pattern here. Instead of beauty, cheerfulness is its chief characteristic. Instead of the 'intensely blue atmosphere,' here we have 'clear bracing, ethereal' air. Like the waters of the pure River

of Life, the Froom waters were pure and clear, there the water flower was lily; the crow-foot here.

4. Tess's hopes 'mingle with the sunshine, in an ideal photosphere which surrounded her...' There was a pleasant voice in every breeze and joy in every bird's note.
5. Tess once pink, then pale, now is in an elevated mood. The thyme scented spring has rejuvenated and revitalised her.
6. Hardy gives another generalisation — 'Let the truth be told — women do as a rule live through such humiliations, and regain their spirits, and again look about them with an interested eye. While there's life, there's hope is a conviction not so entirely unknown to the betrayed'.
7. The companionship and family atmosphere of the Talbothays presents a contrast to the life at Flintcomb Ash this life is full of superstitions and omens.

   In this photosphere of Tess's hopes and sun's bounty, we meet Angel and he has a harp too. Again the garden and temptation scene is repeated with the roles changed. The characters here are not all that simple, they have a past behind them, but they somehow manage to keep it hidden. Tess is more experienced now and Angel is a man of the world. Their relationship presents a contrast to Tess-Alec relationship which is characterised by materialistic and sexual concerns. Tess is 'a visionary essence' to Angel and Angel is more of 'an intelligence' than a lover to Tess. 'Sex' does not come in their relationship. She is Artemis, Demeter to Angel.

9. Superstitions like [1] the butter not coming up when someone is in love and [2] the milk turning sour are found in this superstitious place.
10. Hardy gives Tess a modern aspect too. When she refers to her inherent fears and death wish which Angel calls 'the ache of modernism.' Tess though of Wessex, exhibits characteristics which make her an inhabitant of the modern contemporary world.

11. Tess and Angel meeting in early hours of the day remind one of the beginning of the world. Adam and Eve in their garden of Eden before the Fall; and ironic reflection [as we know each has had an unwelcome experience].
12. The story of Jack Dollop, a man who betrayed his beloved and the treatment he received at the hands of the girl's mother serves to remind Tess of her past.
13. We become aware of the feelings of the three milkmaids, Izz, Retty and Marian for Angel. Love is everywhere in this lush Valley of Great Dairies. They serve to present a contrast to Tess. Tess feels that they would be better wives for Angel and tries to draw Angel's attention to them.
14. 'Amid the oozing fatness and warm ferments of the Froom Vale, at a season when the rush of juices could almost be heard below the hiss of fertilization, it was impossible that the most fanciful love should not grow passionate..', says Hardy and soon we see Angel clasping Tess in an embrace declaring his love for her. With the declaration of love by Angel the Rally comes to an end.
15. The chapter is conspicuous for the beautiful dairy scenes. Hardy has faithfully depicted the life at dairies. The gradual stirring of passions in Tess and Angel, in the favourable surroundings, with the sprit of romance permeating the whole valley. Next, we have the scene where Angel carries the dairymaids in his arms over the foaming river. While serialising Hardy had to change the scene and make Angel carry them in a cart. Due to the objection of the publisher. Here Hardy implies that Nature conspires to bring the lovers together.

PHASE THE FOURTH : THE CONSEQUENCE

In this universe of Hardy 'but to think is to be full of sorrow'. Love can hardly bring happiness. In fact, love is one of the most potent causative factor of tragedy in Hardy. It is the factor through which the malevolent and dark forces work out their nemesis. The chapter as the title shows, reveals the consequences of this idyllic love of Tess and Angel. Marriage is the natural sequel of love but

That never would become that wife
That had once done amiss.

The ballad of the mystic robe of Queen Ginevere which her mother used to sing to Tess comes back to Tess with full force, as she looks upon the wedding dress that Angel gets for her.

No amount of dilly-dallying could deter Angel from his resolve of marrying Tess and he even asks his parent for their permission which they reluctantly grant him, as he plans to lead the life of a farmer. Tess plainly tells him that she is not worthy of him but doesn't have the courage to speak of her past experiences. Her love for Angel is too much and as he keeps pestering her, she agrees to write to her mother for advice.

Tess's past hovers upon her, she 'had been caught during her days of immaturity like a bird in a springe.' She wants to tell everything to Angel and asks her mother who advises her against it. Tess asks her again but gets no reply. Meanwhile very little female help is needed at the farm in winters as the cows are rapidly going dry and Angel proposes to marry by Christmas. While shopping for Christmas they come across a Trantridge man who recognises Tess and passes a sly remark; Angel strikes him a blow and the man amicably apologises. Tess is visibly shaken and again asks Angel to postpone the wedding. She wrote a letter relating her past and slipped it under his door.

Angel's behaviour doesn't change and Tess comes to believe that his love for her has made him forgive her. Yet her doubts are not fully dispelled and on the eve of her wedding she decides to find out, and to her dismay she discovers the letter under the carpet. But now she couldn't let him read it as the house was in full bustle of preparation.

The ceremony is marked by two major events, the reference to the legend of the d'Urberville coach and the crowing of an afternoon crow.

It is not simply by chance that Angel takes Tess to the ancient mansion of the d'Urbervilles for his wedding night. The huge mansion, with its portraits of the awesome ladies of the d'Urberville family, enhances the gloom that seems to be gradually becoming stronger and stronger. The crazy behaviour of Izz,

Retty and Marian adds to it. Tess decides to tell her past there and then. Angel confesses of a similar mistake in sexual relationship with a woman. Encouraged by this, she tells her tale of woe and undoing. The Phase Four ends with Tess still telling her story.

Critical Comments & Salient Features

1. Again and again, Tess resolves to tell Angel everything and every time her courage fails.
2. Angel orders her wedding dress and Tess is reminded of one of her mother's ballads

   That never would become that wife

   That had once done amiss.

   Hardy makes a reference to Queen Guinevere's robe which changed colour due to her infidelity; the implication to Tess is obvious.
3. Hardy often takes recourse to chance and coincidence. The letter Tess writes slips under the carpet and is not to be discovered till the wedding day. The vehicle they drive in happens to be an old one, the postillion was a man of sixty with a running wound on his right leg. The carriage, Tess felt she had seen before — the legend of the d'Urberville coach is related, another superstition — the members of the family see it before murder or some other crime.
4. Tess's thoughts now run on quite different lines, is she not more truly Mrs. Alexander d'Urberville? Her culpable reticence can't be justified by the intensity of her love for Angel.
5. Friar Lawrence's words '*These violent delights have violent ends*' again looks forward to the imminent tragedy.
6. It is ironic that Angel chooses the d'Urberville mansion for their honeymoon.
7. The treachery in the faces of Tess's ancestors, the evil, sinister wink like a toad's that the diamonds of Tess's necklace give Tess's confession an ambiguous meaning. The tragedy is further intensified by Retty's attempted suicide. Angel's confession gives it an ironic twist. As

the novel is about 'purity' and 'morality,' what about Angel's sin? In this man-made world there are two codes of conduct and morality one for man and another for woman. The Phase Four ends with Tess's confession.

PHASE THE FIFTH : THE WOMAN PAYS

That Never would become that wife
That had once done amiss.

The lines from Mrs. Joan Durbeyfield's ballad hovering Tess's mind before her marriage now strike her with full force. The plight in which we find Tess after confession, has been gradually brought to our notice. The seeing of the d'Urberville coach and the legend attached to it, the afternoon crow, the legend of the mystic robe, the sinister winking of the diamonds have already prepared us for the events that follow. Angel's reaction, though Tess can't quite figure it out, is also expected. His words to Tess — 'Forgiveness does not apply to the case. You were one person; now you are another' show the hollowness of his learning and scholarship. Tess in her simplicity doesn't take a moment in forgiving him. The hopelessness of their situation makes it difficult for them to live together. They decide to separate. Tess suggests divorce/suicide as a means of ridding Angel of her presence but Angel wouldn't allow it. Finally Tess goes back to her parents and Angel decides in desperation to go to Brazil.

Tess goes home and tells her mother everything. Mrs. Joan Durbeyfield is astonished at her simplicity and calls her a simpleton and a fool. Mr. Durbeyfield was mortified at the insult the whole affair brought to his great ancestry. His remark to his wife about Tess's marriage — 'D'ye think he really have married her? Or is it like the first —' finally makes Tess leave her home. Clare's note informing her about going to North of England, gives her the pretext of doing so, and she leaves Marlott, telling her friends that she is going to join her husband.

Three weeks after marriage, Angel goes to visit his parents at Emminster and tells them of his plans to go to Brazil. They ask him about his wife and he tells them of their temporary separation, but he does not tell them the truth that he has deserted his wife. They are naturally inquisitive about his wife and Mrs. Clare asks if she is pure and virtuous, Angel replies in the affirmative.

Angel next goes to the town to deposit some money for Tess as well as to get money for his future plans. He meets Mercy Chant who is shocked by his decision to go to Brazil. Next he goes to the house at Wellbridge where he had spent three days with Tess after marriage to settle the rent. The rooms bring back the memory of happy days and he pitifully cries :

> 'Oh, Tess! If you had only told me sooner, I would have forgiven you!'

He meets Izz, who had come to visit them. Izz, one of the dairymaids at Talbothays and a close friend of Tess, tells Angel about the love-sick condition of Marian and Retty. Angel finds Izz also in the same love-sick condition. He asks her if she would have married him, had he asked her. She replies in the affirmative. Angel then asks her to accompany him to Brazil without marriage, which she readily accepts. However, when Angel asks her whether she loves him more than Tess, she confesses that Tess loved him more than any one in the world. This brings Angel to his senses and he asks her to forgive him and forget what he proposed.

Meanwhile, life has not been easy for Tess. She has not succeeded in finding a permanent job. Her money too has vanished as out of the thirty pounds Angel sent her, she sends twenty to her parents.

Marian informs her of a job at an upland farm. Tess decides to go there. While marching towards Chalk-Newton, she is overtaken by a man, who knew her at Trantridge and whom Angel had knocked down at the inn for addressing Tess coarsely. She quickly runs away from him and takes shelter in a plantation amidst the dry leaves of some bushes. She didn't get a good sleep and heard strange noises in her sleep. She felt the injustice of it all. In the morning, she discovered some dead pheasants lying about her with their bodies dabbled with blood. Their miserable condition leads her to exclaim,

> 'Poor darlings — to suppose myself as the most miserable being on earth in the sight o' such misery as yours!'

She finds her condition much better, her body not being mangled and her hands and feet intact. She, however, without further risking herself clipped her eyebrows and wore a faded old gown, tied a handkerchief round her face. Defacing herself from the comeliest milkmaid to 'a mommet of a maid, Tess becomes 'a part of the landscape.' Neither bad weather nor elemental enmity can deter 'the pulsating life which had learnt of the dust and ashes of things, of the cruelty of lust and the fragility of love.'

From light labour Tess proceeded to work on a rough land — the roughness of which was such that she would never have voluntarily applied for. But she was forced by her circumstances to take up the job at Flintcomb Ash, the place of Marian's sojourn, and Hardy explains, 'There seemed to be no help for it; hither she was doomed to come.' She meets Marian here and requests her not to refer to her marriage. Marian's comment on her condition is very apt, 'You've no faults, deary; that I'm sure of, and he's none. So it must be something outside ye both.'

Life at Flintcomb Ash is very harsh. It is only the memory of the happy days and the presence of the friends at the Talbothays that gives their dreary life some charm. In fact that 'green, sunny, romantic' world presents a complete contrast to the present situation. Hardy's comment again is quite illuminating :

> 'So the two forces were at work here as everywhere, the inherent will to enjoy and the circumstantial will against enjoyment.'

Tess trudges on relentlessly in morning frost and in afternoon rains. The dampness and frost brought strange birds with 'tragical eyes.' The working conditions became still worse. Izz joins them and two other women from the Trantridge days — Queen of Diamonds and Queen of Spades — too join Tess and Marian at the Flintcomb Ash. Next to join was the man from Trantridge who had insulted Tess. He turns to be her employer named Farmer Goby.

Marian tells Tess about Angel's offer to Izz, and Tess instead of reproaching him feels that she should write to him more often. She even started thinking of visiting Angel's parents to seek help.

One Sunday she decides to go there, however, when she reached Emminster, she found no one at home. Moreover, she overhears Angel's brothers talking about her as being the cause of their estrangement from Angel. Moreover the boots she had left near the hedge to changed into fine thin ones of leather, are picked up for some poor person by Mercy Chant. All this drives out the last bit of courage to meet her in-laws and Tess starts her journey back without meeting them :

'Her journey back was rather a meander than a march.' As she comes near the barn where a preacher was lecturing, Tess finds to her dismay that the voice belonged to some one she knew. Yes, it was her seducer who faced her in the form of Angel the convert.

Critical Comments and Salient Features

1. All tragic omens come true. The chapter begins with the end of Tess's narrative. Though nothing around them changed physically — yet the 'essence of things had changed.' Angel's attitude is one, which conforms to the Victorian morality and not to the character that the writer has sketched up till now. He appears quite unnatural in not perceiving the sameness of their faults. His words, 'forgiveness does not apply to the case!' seem unnaturally idealistic. He calls Tess's fault as grotesque prestidigitation, that can't be forgiven. Now 'prestidigitator' is a juggler or a conjuror, his horrible laughter also signifies something sinister, he even tells her, 'the woman I have been loving is not you...another in your shape.' He speaks of her past mood of self-preservation. The reason why he had not confessed of a similar crime was also the same for Tess but his hypocrisy doesn't let him acknowledge it. He only grants that Tess was 'more sinned against than sinning' but he doesn't show the charity of forgiving her.
2. Hardy seems to suggest another reason for Tess's tragedy — the discovery of her ancestry, which Angel now associates with her 'want of firmness.' He says, 'Decrepit families imply decrepit wills, decrepit conduct.' From 'a new-sprung child of Nature', she now becomes for him 'the belated seedling of an effete aristocracy.'

3. Angel's idea of a wife rested upon securing 'rustic innocence' while he himself couldn't offer that to his wife. They spend three days under one roof, but as strangers.
4. the idea of killing Alec to secure life with Angel is suggested when Angel asks, 'How can we live together while that man lives?...if he were dead it might be different.'
5. The most vividly presented scene of this phase is Angel's sleep-walking scene when he carries her in his arms and puts her in a coffin saying 'Dead! Dead! Dead!' Critics have found this scene suggestive of the superhuman force of Destiny compelling Tess towards her doom, with Angel as its instrument.
6. They separate after three days and Tess goes to her parents and Angel too goes back to his parents.
7. He decides to go to Brazil to begin his life afresh.
8. Angel meets Izz and asks her to go with him to Brazil without marriage. His fling with Izz can't be excused, for now he is a married man.
9. Tess's mother believes her to be a fool to tell her husband everything and the father even starts doubting whether her marriage materialised or not. Tess finds it hard to stay in such circumstances and leaves her home at the first opportunity.
10. Tess's mother had spoken of her face as being her 'trump card,' now Tess considers it to be her undoing. The incident with the man from Trantridge makes her believe it. She then nipped her eyebrows off and tied a handkerchief round her face to guard herself against 'aggressive admiration.'
11. Flintcomb Ash has the flintiness of steel and is a 'stave-acre' land. The lack of colour and spirit in the land reveals Tess's life — colourless and hopeless. The harshness of weather combines with the severity of the job that Tess undertakes. She is bodily shaken from morning till night, stopping only for meals. This appears to be her endurance

test. Angel's desertion has already left her spiritually, if not dead, then paralysed. Even the work of swede-hacking is very tiresome.

12. Izz also joins them and Tess comes to know of Angel's flirtation. The farmer is the same man with whom Angel had picked up a fight. The farmer asks Tess to beg his pardon and upon her refusal puts Tess to greater hardships.
13. Tess's journey to Emminster to seek help from her in-laws ends in futility. She sees her brothers-in-law and forms an idea of her father and mother-in-laws accordingly. The most eventful incident of this journey was her coming face to face with her seduce, but now he has become a preacher, a convert, through the teachings of Mr. Clare, Angel's father.
14. The chapter is conspicuous for the re-assembling of all the characters from Tess's past — Izz, Retty and Marian as well as Queen of Diamonds and Queen of Spades and Farmer Goby and the painter of signs.

PHASE THE SIXTH : THE CONVERT

Alec, as a preacher was to Tess 'a ghastly bizarrerie, a grim incongruity.' Hardy's comments are more apt — 'animalism had become fanaticism.' Tess can never believe it of him. The moment his eye alights on her, his religion and his resolve are both forgotten. The moment he sees Tess, Alec starts following her and tells her of his duty towards her, as the woman he had grievously wronged. Tess rebukes him and says he is a person who has taken his full 'of the pleasures on earth' and now he wants to secure his 'pleasure in heaven too.' Alec makes her to swear by putting her hand on the 'Cross in Hand' that she would never tempt him. Tess, though aghast at such a conjecture, promises him. But the promise doesn't help them. Very soon Alec follows her to Flintcomb Ash. He tells her that he was solely to be blamed for her trouble and now he wants to make amends by marrying her. Tess tells him that she is already married. Alec's repeated meetings greatly disturb Tess. He calls her temptress, the 'dear damned witch of Babylon' who has completely bewitched him.

Farmer Goby gets a threshing machine and Tess has to work on its platform close to the man who fed it. She had to untie the sheaf of corn and pass it on to him. The work continued from early morning till late at night, stopping only for meals. The whole exercise left her physically shaken. Apart from this the recurrent pestering of Alec d'Urberville tormented her beyond endurance. He reproaches her for driving away the religious thoughts from his mind. Tess hits him with her leather gloves and blood starts oozing from his mouth. Alec controls his anger and leaves her with the threat, '...I was your master once! I will be your master again. If you are any man's wife, you are mine.'

Tess falls in a kind of stupefied reverie; her relentless physical labour and spiritual torments take a heavy toll. And consequently her limbs had acquired a motion independent of her consciousness. She worked and moved as if in dream. in fact this dreamy quality has been inherited from her parents and it had initially been her undoing at Trantridge.

Now, the only course left to her is to apply for help to her husband. The letter she writes speaks of her torments. She refers to her defenceless position and the temptations and snares of the world, and she also writes that if she falls again, her 'last state will be worse' than her first.

Meanwhile life had not been easy for Angel too in the strange land. Illness, bad weather troubled him greatly. His companion dies of fever. Moreover, his feelings for Tess had also gradually changed, 'from being her critic he grew to be her advocate.'

In the meantime Tess is surprised by the arrival of Liza-Lu who tells her of their mother's illness. Tess immediately decides to go home. She finds her mother very all. She takes all the responsibilities in her hand, sees to the allotments of the spring tillage, takes up digging and other duties of the house.

One night she finds a strangely attired figure digging close to her and is surprised to see Alec. The temptation scene is repeated, Alec again comes to tempt her like Satan in his disguise. Precisely at this moment Tess's father dies and with him the lease of the cottage also comes to an end, leaving Tess and her family houseless and homeless.

On Old Lady's Day [25th March] the family is finally uprooted and they decide to move to Kingsbere. Alec again comes and offers his house at Trantridge to let them live but Tess again rejects the offer. In her misery she reproaches Angel and writes, 'Oh why have you treated me so monstrously, Angel! I do not deserve it...I can never, never forgive you...It is all injustice I have received at your hands!'

Critical Comments & Salient Features

1. We meet Alec now in a new role and disguise; that of a preacher. Our first meeting with him was as a typical villain of the melodrama; Hardy describes him as, 'there was the same handsome unpleasantness of mien, but now he wore neatly trimmed, old fashioned whiskers...his dress was half clerical, a modification which had changed his expression sufficiently to abstract the dandyism from his features.'
2. Tess notices something incongruous in him. The words of the Scriptures look out of place when spoken by him; instead of reform she notice a kind of 'transfiguration' in this new role of Alec. The reformer's zeal vanishes as soon as he sees Tess and his passions are again aroused. Here Hardy implies the shallowness of Christianity, which allows anyone to become a preacher whether he himself deserves it or not; and also that every man can be a preacher unless he has temptations in front of him.
3. In Tess's treatment of Alec the roles are reversed now. Critics find Tess devoid of charity, in her conduct of Alec had she been more tolerant with him and not said the harsh words of mistrust he wouldn't have relinquished his faith so quickly. Here she proves to be inviting trouble, when she accuses Alec of hypocrisy and de-converts him from his professed faith by repeating verbatim Angel's ideas.

4. We meet Tess also in a new role — as a temptress. Alec asks her not to looks at him 'like that,' with those eyes that kindle the fire of passion in him. Geoffrey Thurley in *The Psychology of Hardy's novels* claims that Tess's weakness is in fact her overwhelming sensuality. To maintain her purity, it is necessary to blacken Alec's character.
5. Tess is not a victim but a victimiser. She, says Laura Claridge, fails Alec in charity — charity that would have saved her as well as him from destruction. She had earlier asked Angel to forgive, as she has forgiven him but when it comes to her to forgive Alec, she has only sneers and ironic outbursts for him. She tells him about their baby and 'another better man' whom she loves.
6. Alec now emerges as a victim. He not only loses his recently found faith but also his peace of mind. Earlier too he had proposed marriage and now he produces the marriage licence. He tries to alleviate her sufferings and also those of her family. He even offers to gladly help her husband. When Farmer Goby ill-treats Tess, he gets mad as he has no legal right to protect her.
7. It is perhaps visualising of Alec in the role of a sexual threat that he resumes the role of a predator.
8. The world of omens and superstitions is again encountered. The gruesome tale behind the 'Cross in Hand' on which Alec makes Tess swear not to tempt him brings us back to the world of murder and hangings; the two things they both will encounter in future.
9. Alec keeps following her and pestering her to accept help from him, as her husband, it seems to him, has forsaken her. On the other hand, Tess's desperation is revealed in the letter she writes to Angel : '...I must cry to you in my trouble — I have no one else! I am so exposed to temptations...if I break down by falling into some fearful snare, my last state will be worse than my first...come to me and save me from what threatens me!'
10. Meanwhile Angel too suffers both physically and financially. He finds a friend who rebukes him for his old-

fashioned ideas and tells him to think not about what Tess was but what she would be and it was wrong of him to leave her. This friend died due to fever and now his words favourably affected Angel in his feelings for Tess and he only now became her advocate from her critic.

11. Another of Tess's journey begins, from Flintcomb Ash to Marlott in the 'chilly equinotical darkness.' Her past comes alive before her. She takes up the household responsibilities and procures the garden allotment for spring tillage.
12. Hardy comments on the uprootment of Tess's family from their home and makes it a universal rustic phenomenon. Several families shift on the Old Lady Day. The 'rhythm of change' and 'flux and reflux' catches up and the landless labourers have to wander like nomads. The Durbeyfields are also landless labourers and once the great d'Urbervilles are today rendered homeless. Here Hardy gives us the fate of those people who own no land, they have to migrate from one place to another seeking jobs. This movement of the rural population was viewed nostalgically, for it changed their lives completely at times. Lovers were separated and tragedy struck those who were forced to move from the village to the cities.
13. Her mother proposes to shift to Kingsbere, the land of their forefathers. At Kingsbere, as chance would have it, the lodgings they had booked were rented out to some one else. They take shelter in the building known as the d'Urberville Aisle, beneath which the vaults which contained the thousands of their ancestors lay.
14. Tess reaches the door of her ancestral sepulchre and moves to the altar tomb where stood an effigy, which moved as she drew near. She found it to be Alec d'Urberville. He tells her to become his mistress in order to relieve the sufferings of her family.

PHASE THE SEVENTH : FULFILMENT

This chapter, as the name suggests, brings a sense of fulfilment to all. Alec succeeds in getting Tess back; Angel comes back to Tess and the dark forces gradually gathering force finally overpower everything.

The chapter begins by narrating the events at Emminster Vicarage. Angel comes back much reduced and weak. He gets Tess's letter of reproach and Marian's letter of alarm and decides to search for Tess. His letter of inquiry receives no positive response from Mrs. Durbeyfield. He goes to the Flintcomb Ash, but 'No Mrs. Clare had ever been heard of by the cottagers there.' The inquiry at Marlott reveals that they had gone to Kingsbere. Angel goes there and meets Mrs. Durbeyfield, who after great persuasion tells him that Tess is at Sandbourne.

Angel goes to Sandbourne, a pleasure city. Angel asks the postman about a Miss Durbeyfield, and he tells him a d'Urberville at the Herons. The landlady opened the door to Angel at the Herons and when Tess appears, he finds her fashionably dressed. Her words shock him. She tells him that he has come too late and now nothing can be done. She had waited for him so long and that Alec had persuaded her that Angel would not return and that 'He has won me back to him.' The author's comment on Tess's condition is quite striking, 'Tess had spiritually ceased to recognise the body before him as hers — allowing it to drift like a corpse upon the current.'

Later Hardy objectively depicts the scene from Mrs. Brooks' viewpoint, Tess's landlady. She had witnessed the meeting of Angel and Tess and being of a curious bent of mind goes up to Tess's room to spy. She looked through the keyhole and saw the breakfast table and Tess sitting on a chair with her face bowed. A murmur of extreme despair comes from her lips like a soul bound to some Ixionian Wheel. Mrs. Brooks then heard Tess speaking to Alec in mournful tones about the husband who had come to her, but now is gone for ever. She blames Alec for all this. She believes her husband to be dying for her sin, but she is helpless to do anything.

Mrs. Brooks, afraid of being discovered, retreats and goes back to her room. Suddenly she saw a scarlet blot in the midst of the white surface of the ceiling, become gradually bigger and bigger. In panic she goes out in the street and brings a man she knew to search the chamber of her tenants. The man looks and sees Alec lying dead.

Meanwhile Tess runs after Angel and overtakes him, after a while. She tells him that she had killed Alec and now Angel can forgive her. Tess now looks content and happy. Angel is with her, her Antinous, her Apollo, 'all that was perfection, personally and mentally.'

They take refuge in a locked up house and enters through an open window. They stay for three days in this state of perfect happiness. On the third day, fearing that the woman, who looked after the house, might come and discover them, they leave the house. Moving northwards they reach the prehistoric shrines of Stonehenge — the heathen temple. Tess completely feels at home here. She anticipates her doomed death and asks Angel to marry Liza-Lu when she is not there. She falls asleep, with 'her breath quick and small, like that of a lesser creature than a woman.' Tess wakes up all ready for the final parting and the final act of sacrifice. Policemen come to catch Tess and at the first ray of the sun she is caught. Hunted, harried from one place to another by the so-called dark forces, she has reached her goal — the gallows. As the curtain falls on Tess's history faithfully told, we see the black fly gradually moving up the staff and extending itself upon the breeze. Hardy comments on her death in a memorable paragraph. " 'Justice' was done, and the President of Immortals, in Aeschylean phrase, had ended his sport with Tess."

The figures of Angel and Liza-Lu — a spiritualised image of Tess, pure and virtuous, walking hand in hand, with no serpent lurking in the vicinity remind us of Adam and Eve as they move out into the world.

Critical Comments & Salient Features

1. The wheel is about to come full circle. The forces that had been driving Tess, hecticly up till now ultimately triumph. We see Angel coming back, completely changed and also defeated. He begins his search for Tess and goes to every place where she had drudged like a common labourer, without even taking his name to help her. This greatly touches his heart.

2. Angel's trip to Marlott, the native place of Tess Durbeyfield, as she is called there, reveals that they had not even been able to pay for the tombstone at Mr. Durbeyfield's grave; Angel pays for it before going to Kingsbere. Here he meets Mrs. Joan Durbeyfield who after much coercion tells him that Tess lives at Sandbourne.
3. Sandbourne is a pleasure town and we see Tess here beautifully dressed in rich attire, obviously living as Alec's mistress. She tells Angel to go back as he is too late.
4. Tess attempts the first conscious act of her life. She kills Alec by a bread knife. The incident is not shown but described through the eyes of the landlady who sees a spot of blood gradually filtering through the ceiling and enlarging into a 'gigantic ace of heart.' Free of guilt, she now rushes after Angel sure of gaining his love, now that she has 'done it.'
5. The brief period that Angel and Tess spend together in the deserted house is the 'summum bonum' of Tess's life.
6. Angel wonders at this strange look of contentment upon Tess's face, weeping with happiness she clung to him. Angel wondered what obscure strain in d'Urberville blood led to this aberration. Again Hardy seems to condone his heroine's behaviour by relating her conduct to her ancestry. We see him shifting the blame of Tess's conduct on one thing or the other. Initially he had laid the blame of her weakness on her race.
7. Now in this hopeless state of affairs Angel makes his first promise to Tess, 'I will not desert you! I will protect you.' How futile it is now?
8. The deserted house with its heavy furniture is a replica of their honeymoon house. The way they get in, through the lower window like thieves shows how they have been able to steal away their little happiness from the hands of fate.
9. Tess is caught when sun is just visible in the sky. The sun has played a great role in her life. In the scene at

Marlott May-Day Dance, the sun was setting when Angel goes away. Even at the beginning of the novel, the sun was setting. At the end of the novel, the sun is rising when Tess is hanged. At the death of Prince, the sun rises and the blood reflects prism rays. At the end of the novel the sun rises, anticipating the happy future of Liza-Lu and Angel. At the beginning, the setting sun signified the degeneration of aristocratic d'Urbervilles.

15

Hardy's Plot-Construction in *Tess*

1. Introduction

While the chronological construction is the foundation of a story, plot is its logical construction and causal base. E.M. Forster says, 'A plot is also a narrative of events, the emphasis falling on causality.' Hardy's plot-construction in *Tess of the d'Urbervilles* is superb; every single detail highlights the major theme. Interestingly, there is no sub-plot in *Tess* and the plot of the novel is carefully divided into seven phases :

[I] The Maiden
[II] Maiden No More
[III] The Rally
[IV] The Consequence
[V] The Woman Pays
[VI] The Convert
[VII] Fulfilment

It should be noted that all the seven phases are related to the different phases in the heroine's life. In the first phase, she is a virgin at home; in the second she is an unmarried mother; in the third phase she is in love at Talbothays; in the fourth phase she marries Angel; in the fifth phase she is separated from her husband; in the sixth phase she once again becomes mistress to her seducer Alec; and in the seventh phase she kills Alec, lives an idyllic life with Angel for a few days, and is then hanged till death for murdering Alec.

2. Seven Phases

Each phase narrates the visit or return of Tess from one place to another. In the first phase, she goes from Marlott to Trantridge and is there seduced. In the second phase she returns to her home at Marlott. In the third phase she goes to Talbothays; in the fourth phase she goes to d'Urberville farmhouse for her abortive honeymoon. In the fifth phase she returns to Marlott, goes to work at Port-Bredy, then goes to work at Flintcomb Ash, then goes to meet her in-laws at Emminster. In the sixth phase she while returning from Emminster meets Alec, she works at Flintcomb Ash, returns to Marlott, then with her family goes to Kingsbere, the old seat of d'Urbervilles. In the seventh phase she resides at Sandbourne, then she moves through woods with Angel, finally to be captured at Stonehenge and hanged at Wintoncester.

Phase 1 : Marlott—Trantridge—Marlott—Trantridge

Phase 2 : From Trantridge to Marlott

Phase 3 : Goes to Talbothays

Phase 4 : From Talbothays to d'Urberville farmhouse

Phase 5 : Return to Marlott, visit to Port-Bredy—Flintcomb Ash—Travel to Emminster

Phase 6 : Flintcomb Ash—Marlott—Kingsbere

Phase 7 : Sandbourne—Stonehenge

The central focus on the heroine is apparent from the phase titles. In every phase, Tess's successive journey to or from her home is shown. The constant movement of Tess 'always on the move' shows the dislocation of the rural working-woman, the emigration of rural populace in search of work and survival, the symbol of the hunter and the hunted is also there. The main function of this narrative structure is to emphasise that Tess is a creature who has her roots in her home and family, and when she is severed from her roots, her life becomes tragic. Again and again, after each tragic experience she returns to her home, but the home is unable to provide her sustenance and comfort.

In all his major novels, Hardy divides his story into six phases {*The Mayor of Casterbridge* has no divisions as such}; only in *Tess of the d'Urbervilles* does he adopt the idea of seven phases.

Significantly enough, in serial form *Tess* had only six phases; in revision for the book form Hardy divides the story into seven phases. 'Phase' was a popular word in history as well as natural history and as Hardy is 'faithfully presenting' the true life-story of Tess hc chooses it. In *The Return of the Native*, Hardy divides the novel into six 'books;' in *Jude the Obscure*, he divides the novel into six 'parts;' while in *Tess of the d'Urbervilles* he divides the novel into seven 'phases.' In *The Return of the Native*, the division is on the basis of general events; in *Jude the Obscure*, the division is based on the travels of Jude to different places; in *Tess of the d'Urbervilles* the division is on the basis of the heroine's experiences and emotions.

3. Architectural Plot-Construction

Hardy uses dichotomy to emphasise the incident and experience. He opposes one character to another in symmetrical antithesis. Angel Clare and Alec d'Urberville are compared and contrasted with each other. In the first two phases, and in the sixth phase Alec is present and Angel is more or less physically absent. In the third and fourth and seventh phases Angel is present and Alec is more or less absent. They do not come into her life at the same time. The story requires each of them to be completely absent from the scene for approximately half of the book. Hardy evolves the technique of comparison-and-contrast to avoid the complete forgetfulness of a character. By recalling the actions of one character as the other is placed in a similar situation, Hardy keeps both the men present in the reader's mind. When Angel drives Tess to the station [Chapter 31], we recall Alec driving Tess to Trantridge. When Alec offers her berries, we recall Alec offering her strawberries. When Alec offers to marry Tess and take her away to Africa [Chapter 46], we recall Angel's proposal to take her to Brazil. Alec was converted to Christianity by Angel's father and he was de-converted to paganism by Angel's own ideas. Alec's hot lust is everywhere contrasted with the cold intellectuality of Angel. Tess is put into the stone-coffin by Angel in his sleep-walking [Chapter 37] and Alec also rises from the coffin [Chapter 52].

Female characters are also contrasted with each other, and with Tess. In the first two phases, she is compared to Queen of Diamonds and Queen of Spades, the former beloveds of Alec who were seduced and deserted by him. In their fate, her own fate can be foreseen; she too will be seduced by Alec. However, the difference is that Tess in a way deserts Alec, while others were deserted by Alec. In her stay at Talbothays, she is compared and contrasted with three other dairymaids : Izz, Retty and Marian; all of whom are in love with Angel. She also loves Angel and hence is one of them; but she is the chosen one and herein lies her supremacy to them. At Flintcomb Ash, all the beloveds of Alec and the three dairymaids loving Angel come together to heighten the intensity of Tess's emotional anguish. Even in her absence, her passion is compared to Izz's passion, when Izz claims that she cannot love Angel more than Tess. At the end of the novel, Tess compares herself to Liza-Lu. The architectural technique of comparison-parallel-contrast has been frequently used by Hardy in *Tess*.

Baker comments, "There is a strict subordination of all the miscellaneous elements to the one dominant idea; everything and everybody co-operate to express that : casual hints, premonitions, converging indications repeated or recalled, produce a compulsive formality, a pattern in which chance is seen working systematically to an appointed end. However, intricate the events, the mosaic is the reverse of perplexing. Hardy was a trained architect, and carefully prepared the lay-out of his structures before he started building. More than that, he had an analytical mind, which was always seeking to impose an orderly pattern on the irregular features of human life."

4. Point of View

'Point of View' means 'telling a story from some consistent standpoint'. In *Tess*, Hardy follows the viewpoint of a local historian 'faithfully' presenting a well-known story. On the cover-page itself we find,

Tess of the d'Urbervilles
A Pure woman
Faithfully Presented
By
Thomas Hardy

In Chapter 2, we find the illusion of historical authenticity is maintained, 'The name of the eclipsing girl whatever it was, has not been handed down.' In chapter 34 we come across the mention of factual authenticity, 'features are so well known to all travellers.' In Chapter 14, 'which will never be forgotten by those who knew her' establishes its historicity. In Chapter 35, Hardy tells us specifically that the wedding-night walk was seen by a cottager, who remembered the incident a long time later. All these descriptions give the accumulated impression that Tess's story is a true one and the author's point of view is of a local historian. In his Explanatory Note to the First Edition, Hardy writes that he has attempted 'to give artistic form to a true sequence of things' and he quotes St. Jerome: 'If an offence come out of the truth, better is that the offence come than that the truth be concealed.'

But, curiously enough, Hardy's presence is not restricted to the role of a local historian. He becomes the omniscient narrator and supports his heroine by putting himself and his comments in the narrative. In chapter 36 we find, 'Some might risk the odd paradox that with more animalism he would be the nobler man. We do not say it.' In chapter 29, 'His manner was — what man's is not?' — 'the commentary between dashes is that of the omniscient narrator. Even the seduction of Tess is accompanied by the perspective philosophical commentary supplied by Hardy in her defence. Part of Hardy's omniscience is seen in the Biblical and literary analogies which are frequently to be found in *Tess*. Hardy is at times seen advocating for his heroine, trying to prove her purity and hence intruding into the story to justify or explain or comment on her actions. Much of the story is told in summary narrative form. Only during the idyil of the Talbothays dairy, while the love between Angel and Tess is developing, is there an extended pictorial presentation.

5. Serial Structure

Hardy's novel was originally published in serial form in *Graphic* Magazine in 24 weekly instalments. Although Hardy made several changes to the plot afterwards, we find the stamp of serial structure on the novel. In every two chapters we find an important incident, an eye-catching event — or at times more than one event. The serial structure was also responsible for the lack of sub-plot. Hardy had to take into account the popular interest of the audience, and he catered to the public by putting several melodramatic events and improbable incidents into the novel. In *Graphic* two episodes 'Saturday Night in Arcady' and 'The Baptism Scene' were deleted for the fear of public hostility; which were later put into the novel.

6. Plot-Analysis

David Cecil wrote, "He liked a story to be story. It should have a beginning and an end. It should be full of action. And, above all, it should be sufficiently unusual to arouse the interest of its hearers." The plot of *Tess* begins at the beginning and ends with her death. There is enough conflict and momentum, suspense and surprise and finally the catastrophe comes; partly from Tess's own deeds but largely from the Destiny's hands.

The plot of Tess is simple. It is a love-story; a love-triangle : Alec loves Tess, Tess loves Angel, Angel too can love Tess, but cannot love her as a fallen woman. David Cecil comments, "His tragedy is village tragedy, composed of the drama of broken love and wronged girls...There is always something of the folk-song about Hardy's plots. They are full of true lovers and forlorn maidens and dashing Don Juans...Even Tess, considered so modern and advanced in its day, has a story which, when peeled of its realistic trappings, reveals itself as a regular folk-tale tragedy. Tess, the beautiful innocent maiden, is betrayed by a wicked seducer and ends her life on the gallows tree."

The basic framework is that of a woman's struggle against fate. The plot has to run on two levels : personal as well as cosmic. At the personal level, Hardy tries to defend Tess's actions by insisting on her sense of responsibility for her family. At almost every stage of her life it is her concern for hr family which influences her actions, right upto her final decision to return to Alec. At every important moment of her life she is either unconscious or asleep or passive; in this way Hardy tries to make her blameless. When Prince is killed, she is asleep. While she eats strawberries from Alec's hands, she is in a half-dazed state. At her seduction, she is asleep. Even when she is finally captured at Stonehenge, she is asleep. In this simple love-story Hardy has put several reasons simultaneously working against his heroine : Heredity, economic forces, Victorian double-standards, timing of events, chance and fate.

7. Defects

The plot of *Tess of the d'Urbervilles* suffers from several defects. There are too many coincidences and improbable events; chance & fate are made too prominent. Hardy's penchant for preaching is also another shortcoming of his plot-construction.

[i] *Too many coincidences :* Edward Bright asserts, 'Too much machinery is employed in Tess to bring about the catastrophe; and in the latter part of the tale especially, disaster follows disaster in so close and yet disconnected a manner that all sense of verisimilitude is destroyed.' There are too many coincidences and chance events in his novels.

[I] The first coincidence is that Tess sleeps while driving the cart and the morning mail-cart kills her horse.

[II] The second coincidence is that she falls asleep when Alec returns and seduces her.

[III] The most significant coincidence is that her confessional letter is thrust beneath the carpet.

[IV] By chance, Angel's parents are at church when Tess goes to seek them.

[V] By chance, she finds Alec preaching and he re-enters her life.

[VI] Another coincidence is that at Flintcomb Ash all her friends of Talbothays and foes of Trantridge reappear.

[VII] Her letter to Angel in Brazil is delayed and he reaches home a few days too late.

The reliance on coincidences and chance-events as the external expression of the malignant Fate is Hardy's favourite technique, and Church writes, 'coincidence plays too large a part in these tales. But so it does again in the Greek records of human fate. And so it does too in real life.'

David Cecil asserts, 'In no other novels does chance exercise such a conspicuous influence on the course of events. Hardy has been blamed for this; and no doubt he does sometimes overdo it. But to condemn his use of chance altogether is to misunderstand his view of life. We are witnessing a battle between man and Destiny. Destiny is an inscrutable force...its acts always show themselves in the guise of inexplicable, unexpected blows of chance.'

Hardy uses chance events to get the desired tragic effect. Due to his anti-realist outlook he did not seek to prefer plausibility and probability. His belief in fatalism and determinism was strong and this was responsible for his philosophy that Fate shapes human destinies. Walter Allen writes, 'Hardy's chief weakness in plot arises from his view of causality. He is intent to show that the stars in their courses fight against the aspiring...Here his problem was difficult indeed, and it is not surprising he never solved it. For the universe itself to become suddenly hostile to man could only be shown through the working of what may be called the freak coincidence. It is silly to blame Hardy for the emphasis he places on coincidence; simply, he believed in coincidence.'

[ii] *Improbable Events* : There is a disregard of probability in his novels. There are many improbable events in Tess, which convey the sense of anti-realism.

[1] When Tess returns after being seduced, she comes across the man with the red paint who writes the biblical warning, '*THY, DAMNATION, SLUMBERETH, NOT.*' The line, and the next line also, are too apt to Tess's situation and the overall effect is one of improbability.

[2] Tess remained for a few days with Alec even after the seduction. If Tess was pure and virtuous, she should have come away from him at once. The situation as it is, is improbable.

[3] Angel's sleepwalking is also improbable. To believe that a sleeping man can carry his wife for so long a time and in such precarious circumstances, is not at all realistic, although Hardy has tried to make it convincing by supplying prior detail.

[4] The story of the bull, who kneels when the Nativity Hymn is played on the flute is also improbable.

[5] Tess kills Alec with a thin knife which is not at all probable and plausible.

[6] After the Alec's murder, the blood seeps through the floor and the landlady sees a red spot in the shape of a 'gigantic ace of hearts', which is also improbable.

[7] Alec's conversion and de-conversion are also too sudden to be probable.

[iii] *Propaganda and Preaching* : David Cecil remarks, "The most fatal error into which he was led by his lack of critical sense was preaching. At moments, obsessed by his views about the universe, he turns from an imaginative creator into a propagandist. Just when we are spellbound by Hardy the novelist, Hardy the preacher bobs up, and instantly the spell is broken." In Tess this preaching is too obvious. Tess is an eighteen-year-old girl, talking philosophy with her little brother,

> "Did you say the stars were worlds, Tess?"
> 'Yes"
> ....
> 'Which do we live on — a splendid one or a blighted one?'
> 'A blighted one' [chapter 4].

David Cecil writes, 'Here is no unsophisticated country girl speaking. Through her lips comes the voice of a middle-aged novelist, brooding in gloomy mood on the riddle of the painful earth. For 'Tess' is a late book. The preaching tendency grew on Hardy.' Even in Jude we find Hardy puts philosophy in the mouth of a little child called Father Little Time, who says, 'I should like the flowers very very much, if I didn't keep on thinking they'd be all withered in a few days' [p. 293]. In the same novel, Father Little Time and the heroine Sue are talking just like Tess and her little brother; the little boy asks her,

> "It would be better to be out o' the world than in it, wouldn't it?"
> "It would almost, dear" [p. 327].

Hardy reiterates that Fate is responsible for the downfall of his characters and all his novels are based on this premise. There is always a touch of argument, a sense of writing a thesis present in his novels. The novels seem to be a philosophical propaganda in the garb of a pagan preaching. Dorothy Van Ghent writes, 'At the end of the book' with the "Aeschylean phrase" on the sport of the gods, we feel again that intrusion of a commentary which belongs to another order of discourse. The gibbet is enough. The vision is deep and clear and can only be marred by any exploitation of it as a datum in support of abstraction. We could even do without the note of "meliorism" in the joined hands of Clare and Tess's younger sister at the end'. According to Baker, 'A story by Thomas Hardy continually betrays that he has a case to state, an indictment to argue; there is an obvious overplus of mischance leading to a solution.'

[iv] *Limited Range* : Another defect in Hardy as a novelist is that his range is extremely limited. He chooses certain types of characters, certain situations and certain scenes. Beyond that he does not go and if he goes, he utterly fails in the attempt. Hardy's work, like Wordsworth's, was limited to the rural setting and society and he leaves urban society largely untouched. In comparison to other great novelists, his is a limited range. His scene is too narrow. David Cecil remarks, "The subtleties of intellectual life, the complexities of public life, the sophistication of social life, these do not kindle Hardy's imagination to work... The life he portrays is life reduced to its basic elements. People in Hardy's books are born, work hard for their living, fall in love and die : they do not do anything else." The struggle of mankind is on a grand scale; his characters do not struggle against society, they struggle against a malevolent First Cause. Hardy does not lay bare the complexities of social systems; nor does he elaborate upon the individual consciousness.

[v] *Over-emphasis on Plot* : Hardy's training as an architect helped him in designing logical and symmetrical plots. George Meredith advised young Hardy to pay attention to plot after his first amateurish novel *The Poor Man and the* Lady and Hardy afterwards paid perhaps over-attention to plot-construction. E. M. Forster highlights Hardy's over-emphasis on plot-construction, "the characters have been required to contribute too much to the plot; except in their rustic humours, their vitality has been impoverished, they have gone dry and thin. This, as far as, I can make out, is the flaw running through Hardy's novels : he has emphasized causality more strongly than his medium permits." E. M. Forster makes it clear that Hardy always thinks of the plot and he twists the characters to fit in the plot. This is why his characters are not so lively, especially his male characters. 'They are finally bound hand and foot, there is ceaseless emphasis on fate.' In Tess we find Alec's character melodramatic and Angel's character unconvincing. In particular, Hardy's characterisation suffers from Hardy's emphasis on plot construction.

8. Conclusion

In spite of the impression that a malevolent fate seems to dog every footstep of Tess, the fact remains that Hardy has also provided human cause and agency to effect her suffering. Had Tess accepted Joan's proposal to send a young man on the mail-cart, Prince would not have died. Had Tess not remained in Trantridge even after the clear-cut sexual advances of Alec, she would not have lost her chastity. Had she not slept on both these occasions, even then her tragedy could have been averted. Had Tess told about her seduction to Angel before the marriage [and she had ample opportunity to do so], she would not have made the calamitous marriage. Had Tess been humble enough to insistently seek charitable help from Clare, she could have avoided the adulterous living-together with Alec. At each and every stage of her life, it is the wrong decisions of Tess or somebody else taken about her that cause her tragedy. As C. Day Lewis says, "It may be that an external Fate is working through them : but, on the face of it, little happens to Tess which could not be put down solely to human agency — to the harshness of custom and moral law, and man's perverse inhumanity." Thus, we find that the plot-construction of Tess is a perfect artistic construction, fulfilling the dual cause of Fate and human agency.

16

Hardy's Characterisation

Hardy's range of characters is not very great for he writes about a world limited to some extent to the late nineteenth century England and its southernmost region, which he named Wessex. The region bounded by the Thames on the north, the English channel on the south, on the east by a line running from Hayling Island to Windsor Forest and on the west by the Cornish Coast. Yet these people who throng the pages of the Wessex novels are meant to be typically and essentially those of any and every place where

> Thought's the slave of life
> and life's time's fool.

They are persons in whose minds and hearts that which is local has really become universal.

The characters of Dickens are from a wider range, yet Hardy's characters and Hardy's Wessex have acquired a timeless quality. Hardy's concern is for 'man' and not 'men,' in general. He sees man pitted against forces that are too strong, it is the struggle that his characters wedge against these forces that makes them heroic and elevates them to great tragic heights. What Hardy achieved through his characters can be better understood if we compare his art with other writers.

What strikes us most about Hardy's characters is their passion and their fatal love. We do not remember how they loved or what they said under duress of emotion : Their's is not a slowly smouldering love which depends on subtle perceptions and intellectual apprehension of each other's motives, feelings or ideas.

Love is one great emotion of their life, but it is also a catastrophe suddenly overpowering and consuming them. They do not burst into sudden passionate talk but enter into long philosophical dialogues. Hardy, says Virginia Woolf, lacks 'the perfection of Jane Austen, or the wit of Meredith, the range of Thackeray, or Tolstoy's amazing intellectual power.' In the great classical writers there is 'a finality of effect which places certain of their scenes, apart from the story, beyond the reach of change.'

Hardy's vision moves from the human heart and its passion to the dark world around it and rests on the turbulent forces of nature. Each of his men and women faces this storm in isolation. It is in these isolated moments, under utter distress, that these men and women reveal the strength of their character. In these moments, utterly alone, unobserved by even their fellow-beings, they steadfastly move forward to their goal. Hardy doesn't even reveal their motives and intentions through a thorough psycho-analysis. We do not know them as we know Elizabeth Bennett or Becky Sharp but we know them in their relation to time, death and fate. We see them in quick agitation against the earth, the storm and the season. They are people like us driven by their own passions and idiosyncrasies. It is in their resemblance to people like us that the chief strength of Hardy, the novelist lies. They may meet with certain improbable and unforeseen events but their character has nothing improbable or unforeseen in it. Hardy believed in the uncommonness of the story but his characters had to be authentic and real.

Geographically Hardy's people remain in the same stretch of the English countryside for the whole of their life. They are revealed to us through their confrontation with some of the most engaging problems of mankind, where they emerge magnified and regal. Thus Tess in her baptismal service, Marty South rejecting the attributes of her sex for loftier qualities of abstract humanism, laying flowers on Winterbourne's grave and so on. Their speech has a Biblical dignity and a force of love or hate defines them; a force that drives men to rebellion against life and gives women the strength to suffer infinitely.

Hardy's world is fraught with polarities of various kinds. There are the simple steadfast rustics who are pitted against the more experienced and sophisticated men from the wider world. His characters, both men and women, had infinite attraction for him. For women he showed a more tender attitude and presented them as weaker and fleshier, clinging to their men who are stronger. Vain might be their beauty and terrible their fate, but while the glow of life is in them their step is free, their laughter sure, and theirs is the power to sink into the breast of Nature and become a part of her silence and solemnity or to rise and put on them the movement of the clouds and the wildness of the flowering woodland. The men suffer through conflict with fate and extract our sympathy.

It is their passion that sets them apart. The faithful love of Oak for Bathsheba; the fleeting tumultous love passion of Wildeve, Troy, Fitzpiers, the filial love of Clym, the paternal love of Henchard stand out in our memory.

Hardy basically divides his characters into two groups [1] those who do useful work and [2] those who do no work. To the first category belong the positive characters *e.g.,* Marty South, Giles, Tess, Jude and to the second belong Eustacia, Lucetta or Mrs. Charmond, who are negative as well as disruptive. The capacity to work is usually linked with the ability to love in the world of Hardy. It also involves the ability to care and to sustain.

Another polarity is between the rustic and the sophisticated, modernised intellectual. The rustic have an elemental quality and their strength of character and steadfastness, tenderness and selflessness stands as a contrast to the fickle-minded reckless, heart-breakers. Gabriel Oak, Giles Winterbourne, John Loveday, Diggory Venn etc., present a contrast to Sergeant Troy, Wildeve, Fitzpiers, Alec d'Urberville etc., in every novel three or four figures predominate and stand up like lightning conductors to attract the force of elements. Oak, Troy and Bathsheba; Eustacia, Wildeve and Venn; Henchard, Lucetta and Farfrae; Jude, Sue and Phillotson. They live as individuals as well as types. Bathsheba is Bathsheba but she is a woman and a sister to Eustacia and Lucetta and Sue. Gabriel Oak is Gabriel Oak but he is a man and brother to Henchard, Venn and Jude. The vain and fickle-minded Cytherea, Fancy Day, Elfride, the early Bathsheba and the early Ethelberta seem to belong to the same sisterhood, while

Paula, Vivette, Elizabeth, Grace belong to one similar group. Tess and Arabella have affinities with Lucetta and Eustacia in their fleshy attributes and Tess and Marty belong to the realm of the pure woman — enduring and resourceful.

Lionel Johnson feels that Hardy mainly concentrates on powerful characters which are pitted against less powerful ones, though of more modern experience and no focus is on erotic love. These are persons who answer the call of personal fulfilment instead of submitting to *'the comparative imprisonment of conventions and society.'* The result if fatal for the society ultimately emerges victorious, not however, by any quality of its own but because they are inwardly connected with deeper bonds to the social structure from which they find it difficult to break off.

We can also have a different grouping among the women of Hardy's fictional world — as kind, gentle, forgiving, patient and devoted — Tess, Marty, Elizabeth-Jane; the wilful and capricious, yet kind-hearted like Bathsheba, Grace, Fancy, Anne. Passionate enchantress — Eustacia, Mrs. Charmond, Lucetta, Lady Constantine.

Angel Clare and Knight are idealists who fail to understand that ideologies may not be practical. In them learning and moralising has not been assimilated into practical wisdom. Their misery is caused by this disparity in their character. They cannot reconcile the ideal and real, in a composite whole.

Hardy's sympathy is always with the individual against the community. He makes his characters, more or less blameless and in fulfilling their aim they are destroyed by the community. They, however, have a certain weakness that leads to their downfall. It is true in Troy, Clym, Tess and Jude. They cannot completely break away from the community to which they belong and the forces that defeat them are within their own selves. Troy would have been faithful if his little unfortunate love had been a lady; Tess allowed herself to be condemned and judged by Angel, the most unfortunate incident in Jude's life was his failure to get admission to Oxford. They all succumb to what can be called public opinion in its most superficial aspect and in its deepest is the human compact by which we live.

Hardy's positive characters have an elemental quality. They are individuals with a distinct personality. They are generally fixed or 'non-developing.' They have the changelessness of the figures of traditional narratives from epic, saga, and romance to broadside balladry and its prose parallel. This gives them their universal character. Tragedy strikes when these changeless characters come in confrontation with the changeful characters. The two types form the focus of the struggle in the story. The rustics are the changeless characters and they are not mere curiosities but they form the integral structure of the novels and help in the development of the plot. They are much more than the Greek chorus. They form the norm from which the others may differ or to which they may conform. Eustacia, Clym, Jude, Alec, Angel are all changeful characters. Arabella, though changeless is too gross and Sue, though changeful is too refined. Alec and Angel are the changeful characters in Tess of the d'Urbervilles. In Alec the changeful character has taken a vulgar form. Angel is a refined form of alien yet both wreak miseries upon Tess.

D.H. Lawrence finds in Hardy that there is something fatal in the aristocrats — Elfride, Lady Constantine, Marty South, Tess, Troy, Wildeve, de'Stancy, Fitzpiers and Jude. Everyone of them is passionate yet they are doomed from the very beginning. The moral conclusion that he arrives at is :

1. The physical individual is in the end an inferior thing which must fall before the community *e.g.,* Marston, Henchard.
2. The physical and the spiritual individual is a fine thing which must fall because of its own isolation, because it is a sport, not in the true line of life : Jude, Tess, Lady Constantine.
3. The physical individualist and spiritual bourgeois or communist is a thing, finally of ugly, undeveloped, non-distinguished or perverted physical instinct and must fall physically. Sue, Angel, Clym, Knight. It remains, however, fitted into the community.

Another polarity in the world of Hardy is between the traditional and the modern, the rustic being symbolised by the traditional and the outsider as the modern intellectual. In *Return of the Native*, Hardy has stressed the revitalising power of the rustic life; and how it is able to overcome the challenges of modernity. In *The Mayor of Casterbridge*, the modern world, with its technical know-how ultimately triumphs over. In *Tess of the d'Urbervilles* too we notice the power of the machines to affect great changes in the life of the Wessex people. Gradually Hardy had come to realise the weakness of the old order. It was great, yet it did not possess within itself the strength to survive. This perhaps accounts to his giving up of novel writing after *Jude the Obscure*. He had said his last word on a number of issues and nothing more remained to be said on the statement of evil and mischance and self-destructiveness as well as on the social and cosmic absurd. He had completely lost faith in the traditional rural order as can be seen from the defeat of his great Wessex men and women. They are as much defeated by the changing modern world with its new knowledge and new ways, as by the inevitable forces that threaten their very existence. Hardy's men and women represent a dying world that has lost its strength to survive. Yet they emerge as the 'saviours of all creation' in spite of being defeated.

Hardy somehow contrives their defeats and frustrations as means of reducing to its final and minimal condition their saving heroism, dignity and integrity. The indestructible essence of human worth is what surfaces these tales of havoc and ruin. Out of blight and despair these tragic souls emerge victorious in spirit if not in form. Clym, Henchard, Jude, though defeated reveal the nobility of human spirit. Gabriel Oak, Giles Winterborne, Marty South, Diggory Venn, John Loveday etc., all proclaim our faith in human dignity.

Hardy's fictional world is poised between the traditional Wessex and the tumultuous later nineteenth century. There is in it a conflict between the two. Most of the characters can be broadly divided into these two worlds. Tradition clashes with modernity and the result is fatal. In the earlier novels traditional triumphed and modernity symbolised in the smart, educated men and women of the world was ultimately defeated. In the later novels the pattern was reversed.

Another polarity in the world of Hardy is between the community and the individual. Hardy always shows the individual as being defeated by the community. The individual is a freak, not the norm and so has to be defeated. He may or may not be bad but has an independent will, and independent code for conducting his life and its challenges. He is singled out by his independent will and in the interest of the community he is ultimately defeated and destroyed.

The basic polarity, is however, between the rustic and the modern. The revitalising power of the rural life is intrinsically greater than modernity. *The Return of the Native* affirms the assertion and triumph of the old order against the new one. The Mayor, however presents a changed attitude. Farfrae, though an agriculturist, is of the new world with his new and calculative knowledge. Henchard stands for traditional qualities and stands above others in his psychic virtues. His generosity and magnanimity, affection and humility imparts greatness and the rich stream of traditional culture sustains him even in adversity. Henchard surpasses all heroes of Hardy in his defeated strength, as Tess surpasses all heroines of Hardy.

In fact, Hardy's characters are dominated by plots. They are ordered to acquiesce in its requirements. The sense of tragic fate is strong, only Tess seems to surmount fate to an extent. Hardy like Tolstoy is condemned for making his characters submit to society or a morality which is socially induced. Hardy's subject is man in the tragic context of nature, where the novelist faith the poet takes over and fills the gaps. He succeeds in making us believe that these tragic figures are our fellow-beings driven by their own passions and idiosyncrasies as well as a malignant fate. They are each of them with a symbolic or universal element that gives them a timeless quality.

Tess, Henchard, Sue & Jude differ from earlier characters, in the sense that they seem to dominate the works; here character becomes Fate and not *vice-versa.* Jude and Sue vie with each other for the central position. Tess, however, dominates the novel as both Alec and Angel can be ultimately reduced to two different ideologies. Lionel Johnson says in *'The Characteristics of Hardy's art'* that Hardy loves to stress upon the strength and stability of his characters they have a pagan severity and their endurance is remarkable. They are simple, resolute and have great psychic strength. They have powerful natures and are men of country, with little or no sophistication and disciplined by life itself.

17

Rustic/Choric Characters

1. Introduction

Baker classifies Hardy's characters in three grades : [i] protagonists or major characters, [ii] minor characters involved in the action and [iii] lastly, the rustic bystanders who provide comic relief. Hardy's novels are set in rural Wessex and hence the rustics form an apt background for action. In all Hardy's novels we find the group of rustics commenting upon the action or providing comic relief by its gay zest for life. However, in the last two novels '*Tess*' and '*Jude,*' Hardy uses the rustic group sparingly for this purpose and this is why these two novels are not so rich in raucous humour and realistic delineation of the Wessex countryside.

2. Choric Function

In Greek drama, the chorus was a group of dancers who stood aside, not involved in the main action but offering commentary on the events. The chorus represented traditional, moral, religious, and social attitudes of society. Modern scholars use the term choral character to identify a character within a play or novel itself who stands largely apart from the action and often comments on the situation, for example, the Fool in King Lear. 'Choral character,' says Abrams, 'represents a communal point of view or the perspective of a cultural group, instances are Thomas Hardy's peasants, and the old Negro women in William Faulkner.'

In Hardy's novels the group of rustics formed the chorus. It commented on the situation and thereby provided a perspective to the readers. In almost all his novels we have the group of rustics : the choir led by Tranter Dewey in *Under the Greenwood Tree*; the Casterbridge gossipers in *The Mayor of Casterbridge*; Bathsheba's labourers in *Far from the Madding Crowd*; the gravediggers in *A Pair of Blue Eyes*. In *Tess*, there are three dairy-maids Izz, Retty and Marian at Talbothays besides the hedonistic Choric group at Trantridge including Queen of Diamonds and Queen of Spades. David Cecil comments, 'They cannot be compared with the central figures in the drama just because they are placed in the story to provide a chorus. They always appear in a group, never separately. They are not full-length portraits. Moreover, they are drawn in a different convention. Here Hardy is in the straight tradition from Shakespeare.'

3. Realistic Background

The superstitious and fatalistic quality of chorus characters provide a realistic background to the bizarre events in the novel. A. C. Ward comments, the men and women of Hardy's Wessex, though living in the nineteenth century, are subject to "curious fetichistic fears" and touched by a "lumber of superstitious folk-lore, dialect, and orally transmitted ballads."

Susan thinks Eustacia to be a witch and burns her waxen image and Eustacia dies soon after; the superstitious connection is made probable by the background provided by the rustic characters. In *Tess*, Mr. And Mrs. Crick are thunderstruck when the cock crows at noon, and the resulting tragic outcome of the marriage gains reality from this superstitious pattern. When the group of passengers comments on the foolish appearance of Tess overflowing with roses or when the painter writes damning words from the scripture; the attitudes of society in relation to Tess are being established.

David Cecil observes, 'They are eternal as the earth by which they live. And their very prosaicness anchors the story to reality. It gives the reader a standard of normality by which he can gauge the tremendous heights and depths to which the main characters rise and fall.'

They are realistic in another sense as well. Hardy like Wordsworth, believed that the conduct of the upper classes is screened by conventions, and thus the real character is not easily seen; whereas in the lower classes, conduct is a direct expression of the inner life and hence character can be directly portrayed and analysed.

Through these characters Hardy is able to introduce naturally the country stories and superstitions [as in dairyman Crick's stories] which contribute so much to the novel's individual character. He enlivens the novel by realistically portraying the rustics and strangely we never feel that his intellectuals are rather artificially done. Hardy is adept in presenting a picture of the decaying order of a rustic society, which is fastly migrating to cities [mentioned specifically in *Tess*] and thereby losing its identity.

Their reality is owned by Hardy himself, when he said that he took his minor characters from real life itself :

> "Old Mr. Clare was a Dorsetshire Parson whose name is still enshrined in the hearts of thousands. Girls resembling the three dairymaids in *Tess* used to get me to write their love-letters for them when I was a little boy. I suppose that unconsciously I absorbed a good deal of their mode of life and speech, and I have been able to reproduce it in the dairy at Talbothays." It must also be noted that Talbothays was one of his father's properties in the Vale of the dairies, and his brother and sisters at length lived there. Hardy personally visited Stonehenge and Flintcomb Ash. All this proved fruitful in adding the touch of reality to the characters and settings of *Tess*.

4. Philosophy of Fatalism

Hardy believed in fatalism and determinism; and this is essentially a primitive and rustic belief. The pagan and heathen setting of Wessex and the peasant and rustic characters living therein are the most appropriate mouthpieces for this fatalistic or determinist philosophy. We find that his rustic characters strongly believe in fate and destiny. Joan consults the Compleat Fortune-Teller and believes in its predictions. When Tess is seduced, the author comments, "As Tess's own people down in those retreats are never tired of saying among each other in their fatalistic way : 'It was to be.' There lay the pity of it." [Chapter 11]. Her mother also reacts fatalistically to her seduction : "Well, we must make the best of it, I suppose. "Tis nater, after all, and what do please God."

In *Tess*, even the old Clare is given to determinism : "His creed of determinism was such that it almost amounted to a vice, and quite amounted, on its negative side, to a renunciative philosophy which had cousinship with that of Schopenhauer and Leopardi" [Chapter 25]. His rustics are 'Waiters on Providence.' Alec says, 'It was my fate' [Chapter 8]. In chapter 6 the author comments, 'But the Fates seemed to decide otherwise.' There is somehow a comment or incident or coincidence connected with chance, fate or destiny and that is why makes a Hardy novel typical and singular.

5. Affinity with Nature

His rustic characters are earthy; they belong to their soil and environment. In *The Mayor of Casterbridge*, these rustics listen to Farfrae's nostalgic song and immensely enjoy the proceeding. In the famous inn-scene, where Lucetta's love-letters are being read; there also we find the chorus of rustics present, commenting on the deceitful lover as doing a natural thing. Later on, these rustics assemble in a group with 'two images on a donkey', carrying the images of Henchard and Lucetta and the disclosure proves fatal to Lucetta. In *The Return of the Native*, the rustic characters dominate the Book First, singing and dancing recklessly, oblivious of all the pain and suffering of their lives. They talk of 'ghosts' and superstitions, and they also serve the functional device of exposition. These turf-cutters assemble in procession for the performance of a dramatic allegory in which Eustacia also participates. Again, they come in procession to congratulate and sing in honour of Wildeve's marriage with Thomasin. The rustic characters create a convivial, jolly, thoughtless mood; as in the dance where Eustacia dances with Wildeve after her marriage with Clym. In *Jude the Obscure*, Arabella's friends serve the choric purpose. They teach her the amatory lessons of baiting and trapping innocent Jude. Then Philotson's friend serves the choric function when he criticises his friend for permitting his wife to commit adultery.

Baker comments, "In a sense they represent Hardy himself. They are quiet but deeply interested observers who see more of what is going on than the gentlefolks are aware, and they are continually dropping shrewd comments... They are not by any means an unthinking herd, no mere stage-furniture, but like Shakespeare's peasants have a droll logic of their own. And they impersonate the spirit of place; they are soaked in tradition, the traditions of a primitive class, rooted in the soil, which it is their function to typify. They are as eternal as the woods and fields and heaths." In the opinion of Compton-Ricket, *'Hardy's rustics are truer to nature.'* The rustics are full of common-sense; but they are neither intellectuals nor do they believe in the so-called moral inhibitions; they are sensual creatures, who take pains and pleasures of life with equal thanks and in this animal acceptance of things, their affinity with nature and natural world is proclaimed. They assume a stoic status by their philosophical acceptance of the events as they happen to or around them.

David Cecil observes, 'Indeed, these characters — it is their most important function — are necessary to set Hardy's and serious drama in perspective with human life as a whole. The chorus is the symbol of the great majority of humdrum mortals, who go on living through their uneventful day, whatever catastrophe may overtake the finer spirits placed among them.'

Edwin Muir comments on these down-to-earth characters of Hardy, 'The peasants who form a chorus to the novels are the final expression of this endurance, which has become so native to them that it has been transformed into a kind of humour. They are too low to fear a fall. They are in the position where the universe wants to have them; therefore beyond the reach of tragedy : the speakers of the epilogue to every action.'

The peasants of Hardy flow with the tide, there is no friction between them and their fate. They calmly accept what befalls them. They do not have any strong ambitions and plans in life. This is why they never think of struggling against their destiny. The rustic characters of Hardy do not suffer from what the Greeks called hubris [excessive pride, which enraged and provoked the gods to punish mankind] and this is why tragedy does not strike them.

Although Hardy has not given individuality to his rustic characters, yet he has certainly drawn them well as a realistic group. David Cecil asserts, 'Taken individually, they may seem exaggerated, but taken — as they are meant to be taken — in a corporate mass, they build up a picture of average making in its rural manifestation that is carved out of the bedrock of life.'

6. Choric Groups of Rustics in Tess

In *Tess of the d'Urbervilles* Hardy uses the group of chorus very effectively, though not for humorous purpose. Hence it is usually thought that he uses the rustic delineation sparsely in his later novels. In *Tess*, there are three major choric groups of rustics, who comment on the situation from various standpoints. Usually Hardy's practice was to present a single choric judgement on the situation, but here he employs a multiple and complex reaction from several choric groups :

[i] Victorian/Moralist chorus

[ii] Hedonistic chorus of drinkers

[iii] Chorus of dairymaids

[i] *Victorian/Moralist Chorus* : The strict moralist chorus is represented by the painter of signs. In his opinion pre-marital sex is a sin and it deserves heavenly wrath and punishment in hell-fire. In this category of Victorian moralists also come the villagers of Marlott, who compel Tess's family to migrate after Jack Durbeyfield's death. They are offended by her stained past. The hypocrisy of their action is highlighted as they themselves are not blameless in their conduct; they are equally guilty of promiscuity, but they are passing judgement on a young girl for a sin to which she was not a party. Tess and her family have to vacate the place 'if only in the interests of morality... The father, and even the mother, had got drunk at times, the younger children seldom had gone to church, and the eldest daughter had made queer unions. By some means the village had to be kept pure' [Chapter 51].

[ii] *Hedonistic chorus of drinkers* : The second chorus in *Tess* is the hedonistic chorus, which gets drunk, dancing late in the

nights and indulging in amatory pleasures whenever it got a chance. In this group we find the drunken, rough characters who frequent Rolliver's bar and one of the rustics unwittingly predicts Tess's future mishap, when he reacts to Joan's babble : 'Tess is a fine figure o' fun, as I said to myself to-day when I zeed her vamping round parish with the rest,' observed one of the elderly boozers in an undertone. 'But Joan Durbeyfield must mind that she don't get green malt in floor.' The warning is about seduction and it comes true. In the same group come the Queen of Diamonds and Queen of Spades. The whole of Trantridge is permeated with hedonistic impulse, and Hardy takes pains to thrust this point home : 'The levity of some of the younger women in and about Trantridge was marked...The place had also a more abiding defect; it drank hard' [Chapter 10].

It is the drink and dance combination of this chorus group which delay Tess's departure from the fair and the ensuing quarrel is due to their intoxicated condition which precipitates a quarrel and causes Tess's crisis. When Tess jumps on Alec's horse, the apt comment of the chorus is spoken through dark Car's mother, "Out of the frying-pan into the fire!" [Chapter 10]. This group in particular has been Hardy's favourite chorus group. In the eyes of this chorus, sexual lapses are casual happenings; morality counts little and fatalism is the ultimately religion. Hardy uses striking mythological imagery while describing this group *e.g.*, 'satyrs clasping nymphs — a multiplicity of Pans whirling a multiplicity of Syrinxes; Lotis attempting to elude Priapus, and always failing' [chapter 10]. Car's body is shown as shining in the moonlight, 'as luminous and beautiful as some Praxitelean creation' [chapter 10]. By this, Hardy on one hand suggests the uplifting illusion supplied by their intoxication; and on the other insists on their kinship with pagan spirit.

[iii] *Chorus of Dairymaids* : In the third group of chorus characters in *Tess* come the virginal dairymaids, Izz, Retty and Marian. Their function in the novel is to provide parallel and contrast with Tess in her love for Angel. By commenting recurrently on Angel's preference for Tess; they become author's mouthpiece to inform the audience about their developing romance. They provide the norm, from which Tess differs. Izz is ready

to commit sin in accepting Angel's proposal to accompany him to Brazil without marriage. She loves him too much, yet she cannot deceive him by belittling her friend Tess's love. She says that she can die for him, but cannot love him more than Tess, because nobody can love anybody more than Tess does Angel. Significantly it is they who inform Angel by writing a short letter and their letter is important if seen in the light of their choric function. They inform Angel that 'a woman should not be try'd beyond her strength, and continual dropping will wear away a Stone — ay, more — a Diamond.' In their choric function, they indirectly hint to the audience that Tess's return to Alec was natural when she was placed in such precarious circumstances and hence she should not be blamed for her adultery.

Although we find that Hardy has used the chorus of rustics sparingly in *Tess*, he uses it extremely well by repeating the same chorus at Flintcomb Ash. There, the hedonistic chorus becomes subdued because the environment is not congenial for the fun-loving spirit. The virginal chorus of the dairy-maids is shown in pathetic light, even in its decadence in this bleak, rough setting.

Izz, Retty and Marian are seen in interaction with each other, with Tess, with Angel, with Dairyman Crick and his wife. They too are real and functional. They stand in contradistinction to Tess, since they are milkmaids and field-women without the spiritual, imaginative or sexual qualities possessed by Tess. They love Angel and herein lies their functional role. The functional role of both the Queens is simply this that they are the previous beloveds of Alec, who do not mind the sexual promiscuity. They are contrasted with Tess in that Tess does mind the sexual promiscuity and is not satisfied to remain as his kept mistress.

Besides them, Mr. & Mrs. Crick also sometimes serve the choric function, as when Mrs. Crick observes, 'She's not quite like the proud young bride of a well-be-doing man.' This observation is the choric comment on her appearance; the same can be said about the appearance of Groby on Christmas Eve, or the man who reports the behaviour of Izz, Retty and Marian on Tess's wedding day. The brothers of Angel form an intellectual chorus to Angel's situation. They are simply caricatures and their function in the novel is simply to be contrasted with Angel. Mercy Chant, their neighbour, can be seen as a contrast to Tess.

7. Use of Dialect

Hardy is a truthful recorder of the Wessex dialect. His employment of dialect is never excessive; always judicious. David Cecil asserts, "The only mode of speech which Hardy can vividly reproduce to us is that of the Wessex countrymen." His mastery of dialect is such that he uses it with artistic reticence. It must not obscure meaning, but it must reflect characters, locality and tradition. The speech of Hardy's rural characters is normally caught in the form of dialect. It is a sort of chorus commentary on events, particularly those affecting the heroine. One critic comments, 'Sometimes these rural characters are merely witnesses to her situations, but their words are generally charged with significance within the artistic structure of the novel. They have the natural colloquial and dialect usages of their place and time, and their realism makes the texture of Tess at once satisfying and complete. Their speech is the major part of their individual and local reality.' The colloquial and dialect usage helps establishing the novel on the footing of a realistic representation of a rustic society. The realism and naturalness are the salient features of Hardy's dialect. Dialect in Hardy is a major part of the individual and local reality of his characters as well as setting.

Tess herself speaks two variations of language; when she returns home she is apt to use dialect and when she is elsewhere, she uses standard language. Besides Tess, her mother and father use dialect profusely especially in the earlier part of the novel. At Talbothays, dialect is spoken by the Dairyman Crick and at times by the three friendly girls. In Tess Hardy keeps rustic characters in the background and hence dialect is also kept to a minimum.

To illustrate the dialect-usage, we find that Sir John speaks '*wold*' [for *gold*], '*ees*' [for '*yes*'], '*hwome*' [for *home*], and Joan speaks '*shadder*' [for *shadow*], and '*projic*' [for *project*].

The boozer at Rolliver's speaks about Tess, 'I zeed her vamping round' and 'mind that she don't get green malt in floor.' In the first instance the use of 'zeed' instead of 'saw' and in the second, the use of the local phrase are dialectical.

8. Rustic Humour

The rustic characters provide comic relief and rich humour. David Cecil comments, "This chorus provides also the chief occasion for Hardy's humour. Humour is not the quality that one might expect to find in him, so grant and so gloomy as he is. But it is there all right. Nor is it incongruous with the rest of his achievement. It is rustic, it is elemental, it is grotesque, it is Gothic, it is traditional. Like the characters who are its subject, it descends directly from Shakespeare and the Elizabethans."

At Rolliver's Inn, the atmosphere is gay. The most humorous sentence, however, is not spoken by any drinkers; but by the landlady, 'Being a few private friends I've asked in to keep up club-walking at my own expense.' She speaks it every time she hears the sound of footsteps. She has to do it, because she is selling booze illegally.

The next funny thing happens to Car, Queen of Spades; the bottle of teracle is broken and the syrup stains her gown. Tess also laughs at it, and later on suffers for it too. Then, there is the humorous story about the bull which kneeled after hearing the Nativity Hymn. The humour in Tess, however, is more verbal than related to incident. The rustic characters of Hardy like the rustics of Shakespeare, supply ample comic relief and even such a bleak novel as *Tess* offers evidence.

18

Hardy's Heroines with Special Reference to *Tess*

That Hardy had an in-depth knowledge of the female heart goes without saying as can be seen through his various realistic portrayals. The long list includes Elfride, Bathsheba, Eustacia, Fancy Day, Thomasin, Elizabeth-Jane, Marty, Ethelberta, Sue, Tess and so on. There are the patient devoted forgiving women — Tess, Marty, Elizabeth-Jane; the wilful capricious but fundamentally good-hearted — Bathsheba, Grace, Fancy, Anne etc., there is the passion-tormented romantic enchantresses — Eustacia, Mrs. Charmond, Lucetta, Lady Constantine etc. Sue and Tess are totally different.

Eustacia, Lucetta, Ethelberta, Bathsheba, Vivelta, Felice, Elfride and some of the noble names, how admirable is the contrast between these and Anne, Faith, Grace, Elizabeth-Jane, Thomasin, Charlotte, Marty South; upon the one side, all shades and lights of passion, petulance, perversity; upon the other, of reticence, patience, and restraint. The violent or ambitious natures are more opulent and prodigal in their demeanour. Mood follows mood, they are always in a state of revolution against themselves : the quiet or constant natures are more refined and proud in their bearing; they suffer but in silence and with strength. Not one of them is a copy of any other.

Hardy's men and women are most vividly actualised. The clarity and intensity of interest is far greater in the conception and realisation of the women characters. He is at his best in creating what Charlotte Bronte calls '*The Stormy Sisterhood.*'

Albert J. Guerard differentiates the various types of women and finds an evolutionary pattern. He distinguishes seven types :

1. **The Vain & Fickle**
   Cytherea
   Fancy Day
   Elfride
   The Early Bathsheba
   The Early Ethelberta
2. **The Ingenues**
   Picotee
   Thomasin
   Anne
   Tabitha
   Margery
3. **The Average Intelligent Women**
   Cytherea
   Paula
   Vivette
   Elizabeth
   Grace
4. **The Hedonists tending to Neurosis**
   Eustacia
   Lucetta
   Felice
   Marcia
   Sue
5. **The Highly Sexed**
   Eustacia
   Suke
   Tess
   Arabella
6. **The Resourceful & Enduring**
   The later Bathsheba
   The later Ethelberta

Marty
Tess
Arabella

7. Two Pure Women

Marty
Tess

A survey of Hardy's novels reveals the extraordinary knowledge Hardy had of female heart, its girlish coquetries and mannerisms, motives and feelings. Though tempted to generalise about women, his women show a marked variety as is clear from the chart given earlier.

Elfride, in *A Pair of Blue Eyes* is gentle, confiding and innocent by nature but her personality reveals traits of evasiveness. It is a trick of nerves that throws her into Knight's arms, again it is her nervous nature that would not let her confess her sins.

Bathsheba Everdene, a vain and highly amusing tease, later becomes a figure of resourcefulness and endurance. Sue shows great strength of character in facing the difficulties that prove too much for her. Her character undergoes a drastic change as the story proceeds. She is the first of Hardy's heroines to face life squarely. In Sue Bridehead character and personality combine, her nervous disorders are revealed through her bird-like mannerisms and mobile features.

Cytherea's inability to choose the right partner becomes fickleness in Fancy Day and Elfride inherits her pride and fickleness and becomes evasive, and her evasiveness is of tragic consequence. Elfride is endowed with intelligence and so evasiveness in her does not lead to tragic consequence. Bathsheba exhibits courage and her power of endurance and resourcefulness brings her closer to Tess, Marty and Arabella.

Tess takes a lot from Marty and Sue and foreshadows Arabella through her overt sexuality. Marty and Tess are the two pure women, hardworking and enduring adversities, they show a great strength of character.

Both Tess and Arabella have overt sexuality, though Tess remains initially oblivious of it and later tries to wilfully destroy it by nipping her eyebrows to evade attention. Hardy presents various facets of Tess's personality from a mere child/untinctured with experience/'a vessel of emotion' to 'a visionary essence of a woman' Tess passes various stages. Hardy's women, in spite of their absurdities remain convincing and real. They remain radically feminine in all of their responses. Not one of them is devoid of life or vitality.

Lionel Johnson in *The Art* of Thomas Hardy says, "of the women, whose characters and fortunes are portrayed by Hardy, the most varied opinions may be held. Some have a winning audacity and the charm of strength that marks great ladies, some are alternately 'cautelous' and 'temerarious'.....some have a distant likeness to Miss Austen's great characters, some almost incur from Dr. Johnson the charge of flirtation." Adroitness and dexterity have gone into their composition.

To Hardy women are fascinating; their sensuous charm, their femininity is effectively evoked in his novels. Here is Eustacia unclosing her lips in a laugh 'so that the sun shone into her mouth as into a tulip and lent it a similar scarlet fire.' Hardy says she is a goddess in her power and capriciousness and a Titaness in her rebelliousness, a witch in her solitude and mystery, a femme fatale in her power to arouse passion in others, a Cleopatra in her pride, her passion and her scorn of consequences. This creates an awe-inspiring portrait of Eustacia. Considering her age, her frivolity and her power, she appears to be a kind of enigma. Silhouetted against the sky and standing on the grave, Eustacia is both elevated and fatally placed. She looks tragic and acts tragic. The fantastic nature of her passion is self-destructive and causes her downfall. In fact all of Hardy's tragic characters have a self-destructive instinct.

The Mayor of Casterbridge is nearest to Greek tragedy. It is the story of Michael Henchard and the women that come into his life are given a subordinate position. Susan, his wife and Lucetta, his beloved and Elizabeth-Jane his supposed daughter, all are relegated to the secondary position. Susan Henchard is a meek submissive woman. Lucetta, of course, has the cunning of her trade and belongs to the group of hedonists tending to neurosis.

Her bored restlessness and her aura of unmoral glamour, her vivacity link her to Eustacia and Sue.

Elizabeth-Jane is the gentle, kind-hearted, forgiving type of woman. She is linked with Grace and Tess and Marty in her endurance. Tess and Sue and Arabella are vividly realised both as a consciousness and as a presence. We see Tess, a mere girl at the age of sixteen untinctured by experience, a mere 'vessel of emotion.' We can sometimes see her "twelfth year from her eyes, yet she has a luxuriance of aspect, a fullness of growth, which made her appear more of a woman than she really was." The 'mobile peony mouth,' her sparkling eyes with a thousand hues, create a very fascinating picture. She matures right before our eyes. The maiden phase of her life is one of innocence & purity; the girl who returns from Trantridge is wiser but of what use is her knowledge. The birth of Sorrow and his death again bring knowledge and in Baptism Scene we her gradually gaining strength. The scenes at the Talbothays Farm show her blossoming into a full-grown woman. Hardy presents her in a new light, here she is the enchantress, Eve after the fall. Hardy accumulates serpentine images around her. The red interior of her mouth looks as if it had been of a snake's, her hair are 'coiled up.' After the marriage with Angel, the jewels she wears on her neck give 'a sinister wink like a toad's.'

At the Flintcomb Ash — with her eyebrows nipped and a handkerchief tied round her face and wearing the most faded gown, she looks a field woman, pure and simple. She is all dressed up at the Sandbourne like a pet, and when she lies on the sacrificial stone at the Stonehenge, her breathing is fast like a 'lower animal.' Thus, Tess presents a changed personality at each phase of her life. Her strength of character and her power of endurance elevate her to great tragic heights. The time covered may only be a few years, four or five years at the most but Tess has matured from a mere 'vessel of emotion' to a towering tragic figure right before our eyes. The chart also shows her evolving from a highly sexed woman to a resourceful and enduring one and finally proclaims her as one of the two 'pure women' in Hardy's fictional world.

Marty is another pure woman in Hardy's fictional world. She is a child of the soil and is betrayed only in the sense that Giles never appreciates her worth and her fidelity. Hardy's women never lose their feminine mannerisms. The group of women in Hardy's fiction is a charming one. They are more interesting than men and evoke our sympathy and love. In Tess the temptations of Sue, the endurance of Marty, the troubled consciousness of Gracê come together. Tess has no need of any contrast or parallel. The novel is structured entirely on the sexual and marital history of Tess. In Sue the fickleness and capriciousness of Bathsheba and Eustacia combine with the intelligence of Elizabeth-Jane and Grace and others to give us a picture of the modern, emancipated, intelligent woman. Thus, there is an evolutionary aspect in Hardy's women.

Trapped and captured by masculine gaze each is enmeshed in a conflict of perception, a complex vision of herself. Her vanity, her capriciousness, her desire to be mastered, her weakness, her womanliness are all manifestations of the unfathomable mystery of her essential otherness. Tess and Sue bring two extremes. Tess is an embodiment of Hardy's humanism and Sue of his concept of the modern intellectual woman in whom sexuality is extremely repressed. Tess provides for us the 'standard of what is right and essential for human beings to demand from life,' says Irving Howe.

19

Tess of the D'Urbervilles : A Pure Woman

Hardy had deliberately appended the subtitle to the novel, with the comment that it was "...the estimate left in a candid mind, of the heroine's character — an estimate that nobody would be likely to dispute" [Preface, 1912 edition].

Now candid means "frank, open, impartial" and by using this word Hardy had tried to ensure public approval of his opinion, but this didn't happen. The novel's greatest controversy arose from this statement. The readers and reviewers attacked the novel ruthlessly on this very ground.

Was Hardy thinking of woman as an essence while emphasising on the purity of Tess or was he simply speaking from a naturalistic point of view? For what is "pure?" Is it ethereal or sexual?

Hardy's term as applied to Tess was clearly a deliberate assault on the moral attitudes of the Victorian reader. Their concept of purity could not include an adulteress and a murderess in its compass. Hardy was conscious of this attitude of his readers goes without doubt. The novel is full of such references which emphasise the conventional view. As also we find references catering to his viewpoint scattered throughout the novel. This is, perhaps, intentional; Hardy wanted such ambiguity to exist, and the purity of Tess, thus has become an enigma for the readers and critics alike. In order to work out this ambiguity of Tess we must try to analyse Hardy's concept of Tess, how she originates and how she finally figures out through the pages of this extremely fascinating novel.

We meet Tess at the village of Marlott, all dressed up [in the white virginal frock] engaged in the May-Day dance celebrations, carrying in her hands white flowers and a peeled willow wand. White we always associate with purity, virginity, but she is not all white, she displays a red ribbon [only she has it in the whole group] in her hair — a prized article, no doubt but, its colour links it with another important aspect of Tess, "passion." Red is the colour of blood, colour of passion and here we find both aspects of Tess converging; her passionate as well as her virginal aspect existing side by side. We have two persons too, who see these separate sides existing in isolation. To one she is the 'temptress,' to the other 'the visionary essence,' woman devoid of her womanliness or we can say, her 'sexuality.'

Next Hardy focuses on her innocence, inexperience and childish quality. "...for all her bouncing, handsome womanliness, you could sometimes see her twelfth year in her cheeks or her ninth sparkling from her eyes; and even her fifth would flit over the curves of her mouth..." Mind it, Hardy doesn't see the thirteenth or the fourteenth or the fifteenth year; for that would make his heroine a teenager and thus spoil his thesis.

Again, we see Hardy defending her by saying, "It was a luxuriance of aspect, a fullness of growth, which made her appear more of a woman than she really was." Also we see Tess herself referring to this childish quality, "I was a child when I left." Another way to look at this question is from the Tess-Alec relationship viewpoint, for Tess is 'a pure woman' only as imagined by Hardy.

Tess's relationship with Alec is wrong only because she didn't love him [socially because even after 'IT' she wouldn't marry him, any other girl, says her mother, would do it but not Tess]. She was only "temporarily blinded by his ardent manners, had been stirred to confused surrender a while, had suddenly despised and disliked him, and had run away." Ideological fetters bind her to Alec. With Angel the case is different. Theirs is a completely 'unsexed' relationship, he is an 'intelligence' and she is 'a visionary essence.'

In fact, the greatest factor about Tess is her passivity. She assumes the shape that her tormentors would like to see her in. Her sexuality is aroused when Alec perceives her and it is her innate purity that comes to surface when she is with Angel. As George Wotton says, "The material, physical relationship is replaced by a spiritual, idealised relationship." Hardy tries his level best to force the idea that Tess is a victim of Alec, and the scene at The Chase is purposefully described in such an ambiguous manner. Hardy has to give her the image of Eve both before and after the fall. The innocence, he harps at again and again conforms to the image of Eve before the fall. We even have Alec as a tempter in the famous Strawberry scene. The moment she accepts eating the fruit from Alec's hand, her fate is sealed. Alec too refers to the temptation scene of Eve in Milton's *Paradise Lost.* He even calls himself the 'other one' or the 'older one.'

Tess is rendered innocent in a double sense, first as lacking in knowledge and secondly, as an unwilling victim to the sexual act. The references to Tess's guardian angel and the visitation of the sins of fathers upon children further try to corroborate Hardy's argument. *'A little more than persuading had to do wi' the coming o't'*, along with the references to someone heard crying in The Chase is further added to clarify; for, in order to maintain Tess's purity, blackening of Alec is a must. In Alec Hardy presents a prefect villain, with *'a swarthy complexion, with full lips, badly moulded,' 'a well-groomed moustache,' 'touches of barbarism'* and '*a bold rolling eye.'* Hardy never describes Angel in such a manner.

Then Hardy takes up the naturalistic point of view. He speaks of the Darwinist nature of amoral instinct and the 'inherent will to enjoy' running parallel to the naturalistic view of sexuality. It is Tess alone who feels the tragedy, to no one else it seems to have any effect.

Alec emerges a thief, who has stolen Tess's virginity and Angel appears as a hypocrite who would not see the similarity in their faults and condemns Tess for the sin that he has himself committed and which Tess has already forgiven.

Tess as the '*Innocent one*' and Tess as the "*Temptress*" are the two aspects that get muddled up in the novel. Though Hardy harps on her innocence he can't disregard her sexuality. The '*luxuriance of aspect*' which he refers to speaks of the 'erotic' nature of Tess. She is also 'a fresh and virginal daughter of nature.' Her weakness lies in her overwhelming sexuality, a trait she has inherited from her mother — and she being only a milkmaid.

Tess is also the ballad heroine, an innocent milkmaid who murders her seducer. The weakness is the result of her heredity. She is the victim of *'a conventional idea of morality.'* It is her nobility and strength of character, that Hardy wants to emphasise upon. Heredity, economic forces, time, chance and consequence shape her career and cause her downfall. Hardy puts the blame at times on chance and at times on her ancestry and never speaks of her weakness. His universe is one of missed chances, where the *'call seldom produces the comer'* and where 'the two halves of a perfect whole' do not confront each other at the right moment. Here the guardian angel lies drunk or goes on a holiday and nature doesn't say "See!" to her poor creatures. Here delays, anxieties, disappointments, shocks, catastrophes form the norm and happiness is a rare event.

Tess's fault, Hardy seems to say, lay in her inexperience, her innocence and her simple faith in the providence, before her fall and after the fall in the 'conventional aspect.' It was she who looked upon herself as a 'figure of Guilt' and '...no law known to the environment in which she fancied herself such an anomaly.' To Hardy she was almost a 'standard woman, but for the slight incautiousness of character inherited from her race.'

Now one may ask what is this 'slight incautiousness of character' belonging to the race of woman as such. Is it not characteristic inherited from Eve, the first woman — the temptress as well as the tempted one, the victim as well as the victimiser.

In terms of nature philosophy these experiences were "simply a liberal education." Further Hardy says that Tess 'might be happy in some nook which had no memories.' If past could be forgotten, Tess wouldn't feel the hurt so much. She asks herself — "Was once lost always lost really true of chastity?" Nature's recuperative power is for all its creatures. Why should it be denied to womanhood alone?

Arguments against her purity

1. She eats the strawberries from Alec's hands voluntarily and let him put roses in her bosom. It is extraordinary that at the first casual meeting in such unfavourable circumstances she feels tipsy and hypnotised by Alec's personality. In their very first meeting Tess seems to be dazzled by Alec and she mutely responds to his advances.
2. Why did she choose to stay at The Chase when she knew that Alec harbours sexual designs on her? While driving he has already planted a kiss of mastery on her cheeks, and she must have returned to her home even then. When she knew that Alec wrote the letter, that Alec is the real master there, she should not have stayed there. Her choice of staying there was like playing with the fire. It shows that she must have felt somewhat excited about his advances and perhaps wanted to enjoy the experience in her heart.
3. That she sleeps on the fateful night smacks of coincidence; even if we condone Tess for her sleeping in such dangerous circumstances, the crucial fact remains that she stays with Alec as his mistress for a few days even after the seduction. Why does she stay with him, if she dislikes him and if she is not a willing victim to Alec's sexual assault. Even she accepts that she has been dazzled by his ardent manners and she admits her willingness.
4. In her later phase of life she agrees to stay as Alec's mistress, which is even more objectionable than her first fling. Previously, she was guilty of pre-marital sex, now she is guilty of adultery as well. Hardy provides her an excuse in her shouldering of the family responsibility, but it seems a lame excuse. Had she humbly sought help from her in-laws, she would easily have got it, but she chooses

the easy way out and consents to sell her body for the sake of her family.

Somehow, it appears we have muddled up so many issues. Chastity and morality, ethics and convention, personal opinion and social opinion. If we are thinking only of the 'essence' or 'soul,' then the concept of 'purity' can be easily understood. But when one thinks of the heroine's conduct and the epithet of 'pure' affixed to it, it becomes an altogether different issue. For Hardy has not been able to generate the same concern and partial sympathy that he has for her. The reader cannot condone Tess's mistakes which make her morally culpable. To maintain the novel's unity such a view has to be disregarded. Tess, though loved by her readers doesn't deserve the readers' full sympathy in the end. The question regarding Alec's fault and 'undeserved' murder comes up in our exoneration of the heroine. Even the brief period for which she stayed with Alec after the seduction makes her look guilty. She doesn't love Alec, she makes it quite clear, then what keeps her there? Then she herself speaks of her 'weakness' and Hardy too, though he generalises it, speaks of the 'weakness of her sex.' The two weeks after seduction when she stays obviously as Alec's mistress can't simply be forgotten. The initial temptation scene when she 'desultorily...eating in a half-pleased, half-reluctant state whatever d'Urberville offered her' speaks of her later relationship with Alec she tolerates him as long she likes than simply turns him out. Hardy's imagery also changes. He uses serpentine images in describing her now, "the red interior of her mouth" is like 'a snake's.' Alec calls her 'temptress.' The reference to *Paradise Lost* with Alec as the 'Other old one'. further illustrates the point. Moreover, the image of Liza-Lu, without Tess's faults, walking hand-in-hand with Angel further corroborates the ambiguous relationship.

Tess is fascinating, Tess is enchanting, she keeps our interest and faith alive for she is a human being, with weakness as well as strength and she is a woman; the question of 'purity' and 'morality' should be laid aside for this is not a didactic novel. We love her for her beauty, for her strength and also for her weakness for that is what makes her a 'liveable' as well as a 'loveable' character. The subtitle then is a deliberate overwriting of the traditional 'fallen woman atones' story. The subtitle destabilises the notion of 'purity' and builds a thesis that goes contrary to its established 'norms.'

20

Tess : More Sinned against than Sinning

This phrase 'more sinned against than sinning' from Shakespeare's *King Lear* reflect upon the calamities befalling Lear due to one little error of judgement *i.e.*, the misproportion of the deed and its tragic consequence. Something similar comes to our mind when we view the whole tragic consequences of Tess's little mistake. Is Tess the sinner or is she more sinned against? No matter what our answer may be, what is important is that the author doesn't hold Tess guilty of any crime whatsoever. To him the blame may lie in Tess's ancestry or her inheritance or the slight aberration in her physical growth or even in the scheme of things in this world, but certainly it doesn't lie in the character of the heroine.

A close study of the novel shows certain anomalies within the text itself. Many of the events are vividly described but on two issues Hardy is purposefully elusive : The Chase sequence and the events that led to the final persuasion of Tess to go back to Alec. In the early version entitled "Saturday Night in Arcady" Hardy made use of a beverage which the man makes the girl drink before leaving her for a while and so the whole blame is shifted on the man, but in the novel no such excuse is given. Tess is only referred to as a '*pale nebulousness*' at Alec's feet; 'everything else was blackness.' In this primeval jungle, where nature itself was mysterious, what happens is a mystery. Hardy takes recourse to some indirect commentary on the unavailability of Tess's guardian angel [a subtle ironical allusion to *Angel* Clare as well] or the scheme of things "— Why was it that upon this beautiful feminine tissue sensitive as gossamer and practically blank as snow as yet, there should have been traced such a coarse pattern as it was doomed to receive..." or upon the sins of her ancestors — "Doubtless some of Tess d'Urberville's mailed ancestors rollicking home from a fray had dealt the same measure even more ruthlessly towards peasant girls of their time", and lastly because 'it was to be.'

Later he tries to give some more excuses when the people around her say "a little more than persuading has gone into the coming of it" [the child] or that they heard someone crying in the woods. But what Tess herself tells Alec about it puts the case in a totally different light, "My eyes were dazed by you for a little and that was all...." Hardy's comment is also noteworthy, "She had dreaded him, winced before him, succumbed to adroit advantages he took of her helplessness; then, temporarily blinded by ardent manners, had been stirred to confused surrender awhile, had suddenly despised and disliked him, and had run away" [Chapter 12].

But apart from all this is the naturalistic view given by Hardy. It was only Tess who considered herself guilty but 'no law known to the environment in which she fancied herself such an anomaly' and that it was but 'a liberal education' and 'most of the misery had been generated by her conventional aspect.' It is the conventional world opinion that is the root cause of Tess's misery. She has herself adopted this conventional attitude and herein lies her tragedy.

But another potent cause of Tess's misery is the economic aspect, which had first driven Tess to Trantridge to claim kinship. It is also the main cause that takes her back to Alec at Sandbourne. The gradual degradation of the landless labourers is very deftly shown by Hardy. Great families have been reduced to the status of labourers; they have neither fixed destination nor fixed jobs. Seasonal migration is a common feature. One who is familiar with the agricultural life knows the value of land and the misery incurred at being driven out of one's native place. The tragedy of being uprooted from one's ancestral land was viewed with pain by Hardy.

Tess's trouble being over, she moves out of Marlott in a new spirit a few years later to the Talbothays Dairy. It is her experience with Angel that gives her pain as well as fulfilment. She learns the meaning of love and her passion for Angel sets the romantic tone of the Talbothays period. Her passion is deftly differentiated from that of the other milkmaids, through its loftiness and sublimity. It culminates in marriage — a social institution where social norms and conventions have to be followed. The Rally fails and the marriage can't bring the two souls together and now Tess has to suffer the economic as well as the social burden of a deserted woman. Not only this but the spiritual and psychological oppression is also added to her other woes.

Hardy deftly depicts the burdens of a landless class. The shifting jobs, and economic hardships wouldn't let them have a sense of belonging to any place. Moreover, women labour was cheap and so lots of women were employed. There was, however, no relaxation in their work. They had to perform the same tasks that the men performed.

Tess at Flintcomb Ash is an isolated figure. Her trouble with Angel had not broken her spirits. She could 'contemptuously' denounce the religious texts of the painter of signs but now "the hard, logical deposit, like a vein of metal" in Angel had left her completely broken. The hope that lightens every heart, is extinguished and that makes her totally desolate. "There is no sign of young passion in her now," says Hardy. Inside her, 'there was the record of a pulsing life which had learnt too well, for its years, of dust and ashes of things, of the cruelty of lust and the fragility of love.' Patience sustained her now and she is merely reduced to a working woman and this forlorn aspect she bears without questioning the justice or injustice of her lot. What has she done to deserve this? She bears the hardships of swede-hacking patiently, even when she is put to work on the threshing machine, which bodily shakes her from head to foot continually. It is the relentless pestering of Alec and the economic hardship of her family that ultimately leads to her breakdown. Also her appeal for help has not been answered by Angel and she loses all hopes of his ever returning back to her. Her rationalistic mind convinces her that she is in reality [in the physical sense] Alec's wife. All these factors take her back to Alec.

Angel's desertion had caused a kind of dichotomy in Tess's body and soul. She had started disregarding her body and did not care what happened to it. This is a case of complete depersonalisation. She did regard her body not as her own. So, if by living with Alec, her family's needs are satisfied and her mother is not rendered homeless, then let the body live with Alec. This is what Angel notices when he sees her nicely attired in fashionable clothes at Sandbourne. In order to integrate her body and soul, she had to make herself 'whole.' This could only be done by removing the stain or stigma of sin from her body. She does it by the only course left to her *i.e.* by stabbing Alec. The stain of passion and blood could only be removed through blood. It is almost similar to her earlier act of wiping her cheeks after Alec kissed her. The act frees her conscience of the guilt, if not the sin.

Now ecstatic and free from every blemish, Tess can run after Angel, sure of regaining the place once forcefully deprived of. Now the cause of the stain is no more, and hence the stain is no more the tormenting force as it was in the past. It is not for nothing that the final chapter is entitled "The Fulfilment." Tess inwardly succeeds in overpowering and defeating designs of the Omnipotent Fate. The repeated pattern of the Tess-Angel relationship, through the woods, the deserted house, the happy union simply serve to stress this ultimate feeling of joy. Tess is quite ready for the consequences she has to face. The sin of murder has to be atoned by hanging, the convention demands it, but for Tess it is immaterial. She has achieved in life what she wanted and what was plausible in the given circumstances.

We may feel the end to be dismal and bleak but this is justice, not only the justice of the President of the Immortals but the justice of this world. A fine and noble life fell to the dismal designs of a malignant fate but the struggle she put forward was heroic and this is the triumph of man. Though feeble and inconspicuous he can rise to great heights and attempt great things in the face of adversity.

21

Tess : As a Symbol of Agricultural Community in its Moment of Ruin

John Holloway agrees with this comment of Douglas Brown and says that Tess belongs to the old order. As a protagonist, who incarnates the older order and whose decline is linked with an inner misdirection, an inner weakness, Tess has a weakness that can be linked to her heredity. The race is in decline, there is a self-destroying streak in Tess.

Tess embodies Hardy's essential humanism and her struggle is a war against man's inhumanity to man. She is a d'Urberville, and the d'Urbervilles are on a decline; are almost an extinct family of rank. Their name has also degenerated into Durbeyfields — a family that ironically owns no fields. They do have an old rickety horse, ironically called The Prince, their sole breadwinner, whose death finally brings them to the status of wage-labourers.

Alec d'Urberville has made money through business and bought landed property; he has also earned the right to borrow or steal an extinct title of rank; he has everything — money, property, rank. While the Durbeyfield have even forgotten their inheritance, though they have a 'seal' and a 'spoon' bearing the 'insignia;' they neither have money, nor property, nor rank. Their hopes and aspirations are raised through the knowledge of their 'rank' and Mrs. Durbeyfield even starts thinking of a plan to raise their economic as well as social position through their 'prized possession,' their eldest daughter 'Tess,' whose beautiful face and 'luxuriance of aspect' is her trump card. The 'Family Fortune-

Teller' too predicts a bright future and marriage with a gentleman for her!

The knowledge of the great inheritance drives the already tipsy John Durbeyfield to the Rolliver's Inn for more liquor and makes him totally unfit to go to the weekly market to sell their hives. The burden thus falls on Tess, their eldest child, to take the ride to the market on the old horse along with her brother.

The day being the day of May-Day Dance, associated with festivities and celebrations for the agricultural community, but the Durbeyfields are only labourers, and on this day they have to work in order to live.

Tess, tired after the festivities falls asleep and meets with an accident. The mail cart with its noiseless wheels pierces the Prince's heart with its shaft and draws out its life & blood. The mail cart is a product of the world of machines; just as the reaping and the threshing machines are, ruining and destroying the rural life, though in their efficiency and economy they also bring great profit to their owners. Intense machinisation has led to the disappearance of the relatively independent and intermediate class of various types of artisans and only the owners and the labourers have remained.

> "Cottagers who were not directly employed on the land were looked upon with disfavour, and the trade of the others, who were thus obliged to follow. These families, who had formed the backbone of the village life in the past, who were the depositories of the village tradition, had to seek refuge in the large centres; the process, humorously designated by statisticians as 'the tendency of the rural population towards the large towns'; being really the tendency of water to flow uphill when forced by machinery."

Thus, the careers of the traditional village culture were expelled from the village to lead a life of non-entity and economic hardship in the cities. Hardy himself belonged to this relatively independent and intermediate class and he did not welcome this change.

Tess, apart from being the descendent of the d'Urbervilles is the daughter of a haggler, or small trader, with only a horse as his capital. The death of the horse, then drives them to the labour class. The life tenure of their cottage is lost on John Durbeyfield's death which renders them homeless also. Tess begins at the lowest and weakest point of this struggling middle class and is pushed further back to dairy and to the heavy work on the fields through economic pressures. Being a woman and a beautiful and the most 'comeliest' one, she is also exposed to seduction, marriage, desertion, kept-mistress position through her exposure to the economic market. The limits and pressures of her class become an intrinsic part of her history.

In the story of Tess, thus, Hardy presents the decline, the extinction and the flattening of the 'intermediate-independent class' the bearers of culture and tradition and a prominent sector of village economy. Hardy's essay on the '*Dorsetshire Labourer*' makes the position clearer :

> "Every one of these banished people imbibes a sworn enmity to the existing order of things and not a few of them, far from being honest Radicals, degenerate into Anarchists, Waiters on Chance..."

The new situation evolved a theme of mobility through education. It was taken up in *Two on a Tower*, briefly hinted at in *Tess of the d'Urbervilles* and is taken as a central problem in *Jude the Obscure*. It could effect a class change. In Angel's brothers, Hardy reflects a dull and false congruity with a dichotomy in learning, moral purpose and a teaching on one hand and social and financial betterment on another.

In Hardy the working people are always positive characters and those who are waiters on Providence are negative and disruptive.

The landless labourer was subjected to the seasonal change of employment. The '*Our Lady Day*' migrations were a sad reality, "the Egypt of one family was the land of promise to the family who saw it from a distance, till by residence there it became in turn their Egypt also; and so they changed and changed."

It is a case of depopulation. The village with its agricultural labourer, the intermediate independent class of the artisans, was a compact unit. Now with the intermediate class gone, forced to take refuge in large centres, a prominent part of rural life was simply obliterated from the rural scene.

Another factor of importancc was the presence and absence of the owner at the site of occupation. The working people at the Talbothays shared a congenial relationship with the owners. At the Flintcomb Ash the owner-labourer relationship has changed. They no longer work as a family. They work on day-to-day contract and not seasonal contract. Daily labour and daily wages, no matter how difficult and hazardous the conditions.

In Tess, Hardy is at pains to stress that among country folks, degeneration of old stock is a common feature. The Dairyman Crick reports Angel's views on great families,

> '...Old families have done their spurt of work in past days and can't have anything left in 'em now.'

He refers to the Billetts, the Drenkhards, the Grays, the St. Quintius, the Hardys, the Goulds and so on, who owned lands for miles but are now reduced to the state of wage-labourers. Even the conditions of labour differ. The life at Talbothays and the life at Flintcomb Ash is presented as a contrast. Apart from the weakness of the traditional rural order, Hardy wants to hint at something else. There is a drab and harsh element in the rural life. Harshness is intrinsic. The elemental calamities that Tess faces at the Flintcomb Ash are natural. Nature is neither friendly nor antagonistic but is indifferent to Man. Human species wilts out of its natural habitat like all other animals or plants. Human nature does not possess the strength to transform the waste land into a fertile one. The earth is the main factor of causation. It provides dramatic motivation and assumes a character of its own by promoting or clogging action. In *The Return of the Native* it is present as an important character in the form of Egdon Heath. In *Tess*, too, it acts as the Final Cause — mysterious and fathomless. Added to this harshness of Nature is the indifference and the harshness of the machine world, which is fast overtaking the place of man in rural areas.

The village of Marlott has only one reaper but at Flintcomb Ash we have an itinerant steam-threshing machine that not only threatens the labourers but also consumes the identity of its operator.

Hardy had a thorough knowledge of the rural life and his sensuous apprehension of its decay and gradual disintegration provides his novels their unique charm. He is both an educated observer as well as the passionate participant of this dying world. He viewed the life of these landless labourers closely, some of them being descendants of families of rank. On Lady Day these annual migrations took place. Change was a part of their education. By losing their rank and property, they were also losing their class and gradually the humorous simplicity of men and the unsophisticated modesty of women was also lost. Tess, swede-farming at the Flintcomb Ash farm, is just a field woman. The women were generally preferred owing to the low wages and the steadfastness of character. The life at Dairies and harvest fields was easier but swede farming and turnip harking was difficult. Working on the threshing machine was something all women hated. The dust, the din, the sustained exertion was a coarse job. The spinning of the machine and the continuous exertion made them dizzy. Thus, depopulation and the occupational hazards led to the disappearance of many trades and a substantial part of village life was lost for ever, Hardy viewed it with regret and in *Tess* we see these various stages in the phases of her life. In the banishment of Tess's family from Marlott on the moral pretext Hardy saw a common feature of his days. This led to over-population in cities as well as the problem of unemployment.

The regret of those who have been forced to migrate can only be understood by those who have either faced or witnessed it themselves. The phases of Tess's life find a parallel in the ruin of a way life prominent in this part of England. Intense machinisation led to the employment of lesser and lesser people, who were then forced to seek employment elsewhere, especially in urban areas where they led nondescript life and died an obscure death, away from the land of their forefathers.

22

Irony and Humour in *Tess*

1. Irony as Literary Device

Irony is 'the use of words to express something other than and esp. the opposite of the literal meaning.' Irony signifies duality and dichotomy, and hence it is an intellectual device which is related to mental perception. Irony demands reflection and detachment. Irony has been a common literary device in English literature, right from Chaucer's *Prologue to Canterbury Tales* till date. Irony can be classified into several categories but the main divisions of Irony in *Tess of the d'Urbervilles* are Verbal Irony, Irony of Situation and Cosmic Irony.

2. Cosmic Irony in Tess

Cosmic irony is a term which is usually associated with Hardy. Cosmic irony can also be termed as the irony of fate. Hardy's novels are not only about this world, they portray the whole cosmos. There is a strong feeling of a hostile deus ex machina in Hardy's novels. The Irony of Fate refers to those literary works in which Fate assumes the shape of an active participant in the drama of human life and becomes a part of the dramatis personae. In *Tess*, there are several instances of this type of irony. M. H. Abrams explains, "Cosmic Irony or the irony of fate exists, when God, or destiny, or the universal process, is represented as though deliberately manipulating events to frustrate and mock the protagonist. This is a favourite structural device of Thomas Hardy. In his Tess of the d'Urbervilles, the heroine, having lost her virtue because of her innocence, then loses her happiness because of her honesty, finds it again only by murder, and having been briefly happy, is hanged."

The Cosmic Irony is apparently and most strikingly visible in his ironical reference to Christianity, God or gods. Hardy refers to Scriptures in an ironical manner. The ease with which Alec is converted and then retracts are symptomatic of the failure of Christianity to make any real impact on the modern, mercantile world. After Tess's seduction Hardy asks ironically, 'Where was Tess's guardian angel? Where was the Providence of her simple faith? Perhaps, like that other god of whom the ironical Tishbite spoke, he was talking, or he was pursuing, or he was in a journey, or he was sleeping and not to be awaked' [Chapter 11].

Hardy in his description says about 'her own long family of waiters on Providence' and comments on the Biblical knowledge of village girls, 'Like all village girls she was well grounded in the Holy Scriptures' [Chapter 14], but also adds ironically that these village-girls have 'far more of the pagan fantasy of their remote forefathers than of the systematized religion taught their race of later date' [Chapter 16]. The village folk treat the sacred Sunday as the chosen day for fashionable frivolity, "but on this day of vanity, this Sun's day, when flesh went forth to coquet with flesh while hypocritically affecting business with spiritual things" [Chapter 23].

Hardy also refers to the basic irony of human life : the dichotomy of stern moralistic expectations and the limited choice in a hostile environment. He makes it quite plain when he says, "She — and how many more — might have ironically said to God : with Saint Augustine, 'Thou has counselled a better course than Thou hast permitted.' "

> Edward Bright asserts, 'Too much machinery is employed in *Tess* to bring about the catastrophe; and in the latter part of the tale especially, disaster follows disaster in so close and yet disconnected a manner that all sense of verisimilitude is destroyed.'

3. Irony of Structure/Circumstances

The greatest irony of structure in Tess lies in its sub-title 'A Pure Woman.' In the very first chapter, she becomes a 'fallen' woman due to her innate sexuality and half-reluctant complicity in the so-called seduction. Later on, she also chooses to commit adultery rather than seeking help from her in-laws who would most surely have helped her, had she met them. If we look at our heroine without sympathy, we find that she is a party to the pre-marital sex, that she commits adultery, that she is guilty of murder; and yet Hardy chooses to call her 'pure' which is paradoxically ironic.

The structural irony is also found in the conversion of Alec by Angel's father and de-conversion of Alec by Angel's own ideas, 'That clever fellow little thought that, be telling her those things, he might be paving my way back to her!' [Chapter 46].

In his explanatory note Hardy quotes St. Jerome, who is 'the most unlikely defender of sexual growth' according to John Goode. This interlinking of a sinner to a saint is in itself ironic, which goes deeper when we compare the words of St. Jerome in their original context.

In Hardy's philosophy, Irony of circumstance holds an important position. In every novel, this irony is present. This irony has two features; when a person desires one thing and the outcome is opposite and when a person marries, he usually makes a mismarriage. The novel is based on the irony of circumstance; the d'Urbervilles residing at The Chase are not the true d'Urbervilles. Had the parson told this to the father Tess, her tragedy could have been averted. Tess expects help from the d'Urbervilles of The Chase, but ironically she gets troubles. The right man Angel comes first, but he does not pay much attention to her at the May dance and the wrong man enters her life. Angel asks forgiveness for pre-marital affair, but is unable to forgive Tess for the same reason. Tess goes to Alec as she does not expect Angel to return and forgive her, but ironically he returns to forgive her. Tess and Angel are opposites in nature; Tess and Alec belong to the 'pagan' creed and had Tess married Alec, all would have been right but ironically this does not happen. In the seduction-scene, Tess sleeps when Alec returns, and her act causes her deflowering. At the crucial time, Queen of Diamond starts fighting Tess and Alec gets the opportunity of getting Tess on the horseback.

4. Verbal Irony

'A profound irony shadows Hardy's figures,' David Cecil comments. The irony in *Tess* lies at every level : at times it assumes the shape of profoundly religious irony, at times it becomes an indignant jab at the hypocritical society; it is created often by allusions and quotations; sometimes it is structural, but mostly it is verbal and circumstantial. Hardy searched for the *mot juste* to convey his meaning and in particular he revised Tess again and again to get the expression right.

'What a fresh and virginal daughter of Nature that milkmaid is' [Chapter 18], observes Clare on seeing Tess at Talbothays. Now this is a revised expression, on which Hardy worked after the serial publication. Originally Clare simply observes, 'What a genuine daughter of nature?' The change in the adjectives creates an increased ironical effect. *'Genuine,'* which was used originally, is a simple and true assessment of the heroine; on the other hand *'fresh and virginal'* is ironic as Tess is no longer fresh or virginal; she has already been seduced and become a mother. Hardy indulges in this sort of verbal irony around the *'purity'* theme. When she deliberately violates her beauty, Hardy ironically calls her 'a fieldwoman pure and simple.' Then again, verbal irony is thrust in the Clare family's references to Tess after the Angel-Tess separation of which they are unaware. The mother speaks to Angel, 'Since she is pure and chaste she would have been refined enough for me' [Chapter 39] and again she observes, 'There are few purer things in nature than an unsullied country maid' [Chapter 39]. The insistence of Angel's mother on Tess's purity and chastity is found to be ironical by Angel as well as the readers. The mother again speaks to Angel, 'My dear son, your father has decided to read us the chapter in Proverbs in the praise of a virtuous wife. We shall not need to be reminded to apply the words to the absent one' [Chapter 39]. This is an instance of incremental irony, a continual ironic assessment of the heroine and the fate which befalls her.

Just before her confession, Angel ruminates, 'And shall I ever neglect her, or hurt her, or even forget to consider her? God forbid such a crime!' [Chapter 34]. Soon after this he is going to hurt and neglect her and seen in this light the words are full of irony.

Another instance of verbal irony occurs when Alec accuses Tess of tempting him, 'Put your hand upon that stone hand, and swear that you will never tempt me — by your charms or ways' [Chapter 45]. We know that Tess never tempts Alec consciously and hence the words are ironic when seen in the background of the previous seduction. That a seducer is accusing an innocent woman of tempting him is ironic to a great extent. The shifting of responsibility from the male aggressor to the female victim is also apparent.

The heredity theme also produces verbal irony again and again; in fact Hardy leaves no stone unturned to create a deep ironic effect in Tess, up to the final ironical reference to a god who plays with human beings instead of protecting and caring for them.

5. Humour in Hardy

In spite of the gloomy and pessimistic picture of life presented by Hardy in his novels he is not completely devoid of humour. Hardy's humour is mainly provided for by his minor characters who are simple country-folk, and whose part in his novel is that of the chorus. However, in Tess there are no rustic characters per se. the chorus exists in Tess for the sake of parallel and contrast rather than for the sake of providing humour. The novel is far too severe in tone to allow the interludes of gay humour. There is no carefree, bohemian background of Egdon Heath, as is found in the Book First of *The Return of the Native*, no company of the fun-loving rustics and ruffians as we find in *The Mayor of Casterbridge*. Tess and Jude, Hardy's last two novels are also his most humourless novels. They are more ironical than humorous; because their appeal is more calculated to educate our intellect, rather than satiate our instinct.

Hardy's humour in Tess is mostly verbal though occasionally he also resorts to humorous details of circumstance. Lord David Cecil comments, 'In the first place, it is not satirical. Hardy does not make us laugh by the brilliant penetratio9novel with which he exposes his characters' foibles and follies. His are the jokes and anecdotes that enliven the evenings in cottage and village inn, and like theirs his primary aim is simply to make us laugh. The mood which inspires them is simple, genial enjoyment — the countryman's slow relish of the absurd for its own sake. The main themes are the themes of most country humours...Hardy's mode of conveying this humour is also Elizabethan. It is leisurely — there is nothing sharp or slick about it.'

The instances of leisurely rustic humour in Tess are limited, because the novel is too deeply ironical to permit a substantial amount of humour. The theme is so serious and severe and exalted, that laughter should be kept away from the atmosphere. Compton-Rickett comments, 'Save when dealing with his rustic characters, Hardy's humour usually takes the form of irony.'

6. Rustic Humour in Tess

The rustic characters provide comic relief and rich humour. David Cecil comments, "This chorus provides also the chief occasion for Hardy's humour. Humour is not the quality that one might expect to find in him, so grant and so gloomy as he is. But it is there all right. Nor is it incongruous with the rest of his achievement. It is rustic, it is elemental, it is grotesque, it is Gothic, it is traditional. Like the characters who are its subject, it descends directly from Shakespeare and the Elizabethans."

At Rolliver's Inn, the atmosphere is gay. The most humorous sentence, however, is not spoken by any drinkers; but by the landlady, 'Being a few private friends I've asked in to keep up club-walking at my own expense.' She speaks it every time she hears the sound of footsteps. She has to do it, because she is selling booze illegally.

The next funny thing happens to Car, Queen of Spades; the bottle of teracle is broken and the syrup stains her gown. Tess also laughs at it, and later on suffers for it too. Then, there is the humorous story about the bull which kneeled after hearing the Nativity Hymn. The humour in Tess however is more verbal than related to incident. The rustic characters of Hardy like the rustics of Shakespeare, supply ample comic relief and even such a bleak novel as Tess offers evidence.

7. Stylistic/Verbal Humour

David Cecil observes, 'another quality of Hardy's humour — perhaps its most distinctive quality. It is verbal humour, dependent for its effect upon the particular words he uses.' For instance in Chapter 24 Hardy writes, 'Old Pretty by this time had looked round, puzzled; and seeing two people crouching under her where, by immemorial custom there should have been one.' The reference is to Angel's embrace and proposal to Tess at the milking-time.

The verbal humour is also used in describing the two Clare brothers, "They were both somewhat short-sighted, and when it was the custom to wear a single eyeglass and string they wore a single eyeglass and string; when it was the custom to wear a double glass they wore a double glass; when it was the custom to wear spectacles they wore spectacles straightway, all without reference to the particular variety of defect in their own vision. When Wordsworth was enthroned they carried pocket copies; and when Shelley was belittled they allowed him to grow dusty on their shelves" [Chapter 25]. This is pure humour, which exists outside the main frame of the story, which is not related to any incidents, which does not refer or allude to protagonists for the sake of parallel or contrast. The same type of humour is found in the limerick of Chapter 17,

> '*Dairyman Dick*
> All the Week :
> On Sundays Mister Richard Crick'

Hardy's verbal humour is expressed grimly, even ironically in the title-selling episode of Sir John,

> 'Yes, twenty pound — that's the lowest. Dammy, family honour is family honour, and I won't take a penny less' [Chapter 7].

He reduces the amount from a thousand pounds to mere bathetic amount of twenty pound and even when he thinks of selling the title for such a paltry sum, he talks of family honour, which is creating a pathetic irony.

Thus we find that irony constructs the main pattern in Tess, with patches of humour here and there. The irony begins with the sub-title itself and ends with the final Aeschylean phrase of the novel. Nowhere else has Hardy used irony so consistently and recurrently as he does in Tess; this is why the novel is such a palatable food for thought and a feast for intellect.

23

Hardy's Style

1. Introduction

Hardy's style is uneven; at times brilliant and at times incongruous. What is most striking about his style is its individuality. As David Cecil remarks, "His style is capable of greater effects than those of far more competent writers... you could never mistake a paragraph of Hardy by anybody else... He has discovered the 'mot juste,' the single word which can alone express the shade of meaning he has in mind. His words do more than clothe his conception — they are its embodiment". Hardy's style is different from the style of other Victorian novelists; they write about society, Hardy writes about cosmos; they write about the socially expected themes, Hardy about the socially objectionable hypothesis. The universality of the theme is also reflected in the heavily Latinized style of Hardy. Hardy writes about serious things, hence his style is weighty and serious; he finds the Victorian morality hypocritical, hence his style is deeply ironic; he admires the rustic countryside and therefore his style is extremely pictorial; he loves as well as doubts the Bible, so his style is full of Biblical echoes. Thus his style is a cumulative conglomeration of variegated influences : Darwinian, Biblical, social as well as personal and this is why his is the most distinctive style and the most individual.

2. Heavily Latinized Style

'Though the most exclusively and natively English of all the great writers of the Victorian age, he is in point of diction the most Latinical writer we have had since Dryden and Milton,' observes Edmund Blunden. Curiously enough, Hardy's novels are mostly set in the rural Wessex; yet his style is Latinized and herein lies the dichotomy of expression. Normally Hardy uses Old English words or words of Anglo-Saxon roots in the dialect-speeches of rustics or of low-class people. However, in the third person authorial narrative he uses a different type of style which abounds with words of Latin and Greek roots. In the conversation of the intellectuals also, Hardy uses the heavier style. Thus we find that Hardy uses two styles in his novels : one is dialectical and another is Latinized. His infatuation with the Latinized and Greek expression is due to the fact that he learnt these languages after great labour and personal effort. His learning was achieved by hard work and he tries hard to show his learning. In his novels he uses the twin styles effectively, though in *Tess of the d'Urbervilles*, rustic style is not prominently placed and the emphasis here falls clearly on the Latinized expression.

3. Poetic and Pictorial Style

Hardy's style is neither melodious, nor lyrical; yet it is highly poetic as well as essentially pictorial. According to Allen, "Poetry is the constant attendant of Hardy's tragic characters. It is not an intellectual poetry, like Meredith's; it is much more primitive and magical, and always it heightens the significance of the characters and the reader's consciousness of their tragic stature." The poetic element is strong in Hardy, because he considered himself primarily a poet and his sensibility was essentially poetic. There are two types of sensibilities in Hardy: the prosy and the poetic. Through the prosy sensibility are generated all his ideas, philosophy, preaching, propaganda etc. and from the poetic sensibility come the memorable images, the cinematic description, the pictorial narration, the concern for 'mot juste,' the reliance on similes and allusions.

David Cecil comments on the poetic element in Hardy's style, "Hardy seizes every opportunity that his subjects afford for poetic treatment; gets every ounce of picturesque value from that country life which is its subject — from its natural beauty or its historic traditions and association. And, so far as his material has a romantic element in it, Hardy emphasises that romantic element. The life at the dairy where Tess meets Angel, as described by

Hardy, is as much an essay in pastoral poetry as an idyll of Theocritus."

Baker comments on Hardy's pictorial quality in *Tess* and finds that *Tess* is his most pictorial novel, 'Nowhere was Hardy's pictorial mode of narration more finely exercised; the contour of his sentences, also is peculiarly noble and shapely especially when, as often in this novel, he is in a classic mood.' David Cecil observes, 'We are always told what we are looking at. His technique, oddly enough, is that of the modern director of films. We watch the story.... One clear picture succeeds another. When the plot rises to its crisis, Hardy's visualising power burns all the brighter. Once more like a film producer, he often makes his climax a silent one. The dramatic moment expresses itself in action rather than words.' In chapter 19, we get this famous picture : "She went stealthily as a cat through this profusion of growth, gathering cuckoo-spittle on her skirts, cracking snails that were underfoot, staining her hands with thistle-milk and slug-slime, and rubbing off upon her naked arms sticky blights which, though snow-white on the apple-tree trunks, made madder stains on her skin." The sentence begins with a simile, Tess compared to a cat and then her movements are traced. The pictures follow one after another in quick succession. Tess stealthily creeping like a cat [visual], her skirt stained [colour], snails are trodden by her feet [aural/related to sound], then her hands are stained [stain of premarital motherhood/stain of Alec's future murder symbolically represented], then her arms and then her skin — everything is visually sketched and the stain aspect is emphasised throughout the passage. Thus here we find that the description is in the mode of pictures or cinematic frames. The concreteness of the description is also boosted by the frequent use of proper nouns. However, the proper nouns are helpful in providing pictures, although they are impediments in the lyrical flow. The hard-sounding words like 'cuckoo-spittle,' 'thistle-milk,' 'slug-slime' are all compound words producing a jarring note.

David Cecil comments on the visual excellence of Hardy's style, 'No other English novelist has so great a power of visualisation : it is Hardy's most important weapon, and it is the basis of his whole method. He constructs his book in a series of scenes... Hardy's novels are visual novels. It is in his ability to make us "see" that his greatest strength lies.'

4. Sentence-Construction

Hardy's sentence-construction is an important feature of his style. He is fond of compound and complex sentences, this is why there is an excess of relative and co-ordinate clauses in his novels. Take this example from chapter 33,

> 'This condition of mind, wherein she felt glorified by an irradiation not her own, like the angel whom St.John saw in the sun, lasted till the sound of the church bells had died away, and the emotions of the wedding-service had calmed down.'

There are four clauses in this sentence, and the sentences like this are not easy to comprehend while reading fast; but Hardy never wrote his novels for fast reading. The sentence-structure of Hardy is at times repetitive; the repetition intensifying the thought. The antithesis and contrast also feature in his sentences, which shows a strong Biblical influence on his style. Some examples are :

> 'Her journey back was rather a meander than a march' [chapter 44].
>
> 'It was less a reform than a transfiguration' [chapter 45].
>
> 'He was in the agricultural world, but not of it' [chapter 47].
>
> 'Let me come at once, or at once come to me' [chapter 48].
>
> The biblical influence is strongly felt in his shorter sentences; in his longer sentences his learning from classics gets reflected.
>
> The sentence-structure of Hardy is at times repetitive, the repetition of the structure intensifying and highlighting the content :
>
> 'Some dream, some affection, some hobby' [chapter 2].
>
> 'what long-suffering it guaranteed, what honesty, what endurance, what good faith' [chapter 33].
>
> 'I am a bad fellow — a damn bad fellow. I was born bad,

> and I have lived bad, and I shall die bad in all probability' [chapter 12].
>
> 'So pale, so breathless, so quivering' [chapter 57].

Another characteristic feature of Hardy's style is the disjunctive, broken sentence. At the time of powerful emotion, Hardy's characters convey their emotional turmoil and mental turbulence through broken sentences and repetitive phrases or words. When Angel proposes, his dialogue is on this pattern, with several dashes to indicate the shift or strain in the flow of thought :

> 'That I — love you dearly and truly I need not say. But I — it shall go no further now — it distresses you—I am as surprised as you are' [chapter 24].

When Tess narrates his marital mishap in front of her mother she also conveys her anguish and breakdown through broken sentences and repetitive structure.

> 'I know it — I know — I know... If — if — it were to be done again — I should do the same. I could not — I dared not — to sin — against him' [chapter 38].

After her confession to Angel, her pent-up misery is reflected in the disjunctive dialogue :

'I thought — I thought....Believe me—believe me.. yet I believed, without a doubt that you could cast me off if you were determined, and didn't love me at — at — all' [chapter 36].

The broken sentence is a structural device to suggest the shattering of normal grammatical structure under undue mental duress. Browning has also used it with remarkable frequency and facility in his dramatic monologue, and Hardy uses it remarkable well in *Tess of the d'Urbervilles*, as in these heart-rending words of Izz, "O—how can I bear it—how can I—how can I" [chapter 40].

David Cecil observes, 'His words do go beyond his logical meaning to suggest all the subtleties and overtones of the mood in which he regarded it.'

5. Use of Dialect

Hardy is a truthful recorder of the Wessex dialect. His employment of dialect is never excessive; always judicious. David

Cecil asserts, "The only mode of speech which Hardy can vividly reproduce to us is that of the Wessex countrymen." His mastery of dialect is such that he uses it with artistic reticence. It must not obscure meaning, but it must reflect characters, locality and tradition. The speech of Hardy's rural characters is normally caught in the form of dialect. It is a sort of chorus commentary on events, particularly those affecting the heroine. One critic comments, 'Sometimes these rural characters are merely witnesses to her situations, but their words are generally charged with significance within the artistic structure of the novel. They have the natural colloquial and dialect usages of their place and time, and their realism makes the texture of Tess at once satisfying and complete. Their speech is the major part of their individual and local reality' The colloquial and dialect usage helps establishing the novel on the footing of a realistic representation of a rustic society. The realism and naturalness are the salient features of Hardy's dialect. Dialect in Hardy is a major part of the individual and local reality of his characters as well as setting.

Tess herself speaks two variations of language; when she returns home she is apt to use dialect and when she is elsewhere, she uses standard language. Besides Tess, her mother and father use dialect profusely especially in the earlier part of the novel. At Talbothays, dialect is spoken by the Dairyman Crick and at times by the three friendly girls. In *Tess* Hardy keeps rustic characters in the background and hence dialect is also kept to a minimum.

To illustrate the dialect-usage, we find that Sir John speaks '*wold*' [for *gold*], '*ees*' [for '*yes*'], '*hwome*' [for *home*], and Joan speaks '*shadder*' [for *shadow*], and '*projic*' [for *project*].

6. Cluster of Nouns/Adjectives

Hardy is fond of using a cluster of nouns or adjective or verbs. He usually employs a pair of three synonymous words to convey the impression. In this, he has learnt from Shakespeare who also gives us a pair of two synonymous words — one of Anglo-Saxon root and another of Latin/Greek root. The pair of three has been a favourite structural device in prose; in antithetical sentences as in Bacon's famous sentence 'Some books are to be tasted...' Hardy usually uses the pair of three, but at times he exceeds the number. For example,

'...Who are true, and honest, and just, and pure, and lovely' [chapter 31].

'doubt, fear, moodiness, care, shame' [chapter 31].

'arguing, preaching, quarrelling, sobbing, groaning, praying, and cursing' [chapter 32].

'I have been hoping, longing, praying' [chapter 35].

'propensities, tendencies, habits, were as dead leaves' [chapter 36].

'O Tess—you are too, too —childish—unformed—crude.'

'It would anger him, grieve him, stultify him' [chapter 37].

'all his schemes and words and ways' [chapter 39].

'contrasting scenes and notions and habits' [chapter 39].

Hardy also tends to repeat a word or phrase for increasing the emotional tempo.

'No, no, no!' [chapter 42].

'Dead, dead, dead' [chapter 37].

'Too late, too late!' [chapter 55].

'Yes—O, yes, yes!' [chapter 55].

'O — O — O!......... O — O — O!' [chapter 56].

'Drip, drip, drip' [chapter 56].

'Why didn't you stay and love me ..... why didn't you, why didn't you?' [chapter 31].

'He was becoming ill with thinking, eaten out with thinking, withered by thinking' [chapter 36].

7. Startling Similes

C. Thompson comments, "Hardy works predominantly with similes, which he clusters around moments of fantasising or intense emotion." David Cecil observes, "He makes extensive use of arresting similes...Hardy's Gothic fancy does always run to strangeness, and it is the strangeness that makes it so vivid."

'An immense rope of hair like a ship's cable' [chapter 39]. and 'The evening Sun was now ugly to her, like a great inflamed wound in the sky' [chapter 21], 'Two girls crawling...like flies' [chapter 43], 'who had been caught...like a bird in a springe' [chapter 31], 'a dawn that was ashy and furtive, as though associated with crime' [chapter 36].

The startling simile of Hardy can be called a conceit, which he learnt from metaphysical school and which in modern age became a significant poetic tool, particularly employed by T.S. Eliot among others.

8. Sensuous Note

Hardy's style is highly sensuous, showing a strong influence of Keats and the pre-Raphaelite school. In his description, this sensuous side helps in the painting of scenes; the sensuous note generating a pictorial quality. The senses of sight, sound, touch, smell and taste come frequently; however the emphasis in Hardy is on the senses of sight and sound.

'Drip, drip, drip' is related to sound, as is 'cracking snails that were underfoot.' Hardy is especially fond of adjectives; he dislikes to leave his nouns bare. This fondness for epithets and adjectives contributes to the pictorial quality of his style, because an adjective defines and particularises a noun. The adjective also contributes to the sensuous description. Church comments on sensuousness in Hardy's style, "Yet it remains the prose of a poet in close contact with things, a creature of tangibilities even in the imaginative handling of abstract ideas. There is indeed a Keats-like quality in Hardy. His soul doth ache, with physical as well as spiritual longings, and in his evocation of scenes and persons, his senses bring into play a verbal incantation that relates him to the Pre-Raphaelites [as Meredith was] but through the sensual side, and thus directly to Keats, the progenitor of that school." Critics have pointed out the luxurious, mossy, redolent sensuousness of Hardy's phrases and neologisms.

9. Style with Overtones

Hardy's style is fraught with overtones, not only in case of incidents such as the strawberry scene or the baptism scene, but also in case of words and phrases. As a conscious artist, he always paid attention to the overtones of the individual words and he carefully repeats the significant words at proper situation to give them a meaning beyond their dictionary meaning. An example from chapter 14 may be discussed in this respect, 'Perhaps one reason why she seduces casual attention is that she never courts it.... holding the corn in an embrace like that of a lover. .....A bit of her naked arm is visible...and as the day wears on its feminine smoothness becomes sacrificed by the stubble and bleeds.'

Here Hardy is overtly describing the reaping of corn by Tess after her seduction. However, it is more than a simple description. The use of word 'seduces' means more than 'draws;' it reminds us of her seduction, which she never 'courted' or sought. She holds the corn 'in an embrace;' which again reminds us of Alec embracing her. 'Naked' takes us to her nakedness in the seduction scene. The word 'feminine' has previously been used in a significant phrase of chapter 11 of the seduction scene {'feminine tissue'} and here he again uses the adjective to reinforce the idea of feminine fate and weakness. She has bled in the seduction by a pointed phallus and here stubble has pricked her. Thus Hardy subtly fills his description with overtones.

In *The Rally* Hardy uses '*pilgrimage*' to signify Tess's journey to Talbothays 'that was the aim and end of her day's pilgrimage.' Two pages later he again says, 'the dairy of her pilgrimage.' Now pilgrimage has been used instead of journey, which is a strange word as it carries with it religious connotations. Pilgrimage is related to penance for past sins as well as to some holy spot. Here at Talbothays she will expiate for her pre-marital sin after her marriage with Angel, whom she has always seen as her '*Apollo*' or '*God.*' Thus, we find that Hardy uses individual words with overtones to convey a deeper meaning.

10. Defects

[i] *Not a Good Style* : In conventional terms, Hardy does not have a good style — he tends to use long words where shorter ones would be more direct and effective; his sentences are often clumsily put together. At one time in his life he made a deliberate attempt to improve his style by reading authors, who possessed model or ideal style. It is not difficult to find passages where clumsy pomposity gets in the way of what he is trying to say. David Cecil comments, 'In order to improve his style,

he made a study of Addison, Burke, Gibbon, Lamb, Defoe — and "*The Times*" newspaper.... He is always getting tied up in his phrases.... He often cannot manage the ordinary syntax and grammar of the English language. He finds it hard to make a plain statement plainly.'

[ii] Difficult Words : Hardy was a self-made scholar and he, consciously or unconsciously, flaunted his learning. This factor is responsible for the intrusion of difficult or obsolete words in his novels. Even in his life-time, this tendency was criticised by critics. *The Athenaeum* [1892] commented, 'his use of scientific and ecclesiastical terminology grows excessive.' Andrew Lang [Feb. 1892] asks about his style, 'Why should people who are drinking beer be said to "seek vinous bliss?"'

Richard le Gallienne in *Star* [23 Dec. 1891] criticises Hardy's fondness for scientific and philosophical terminology *e.g.*, '*photosphere,' 'concatenation,' 'prestidigitation,' 'dolorifuge,' 'heliolatries' and 'the horrid verb 'extasize.'* Some of the other difficult words used unnecessarily are '*lucubrations', 'purlieus', 'integument', 'convenances' and 'terraqueous.'* Hardy also uses foreign words, and the best example is the three-line quotation of Pascal in French. The difficult or bizarre words are as inseparable a part of Hardy's style, as are the numerous literary allusions and biblical references in his novels.

David Cecil comments, 'His Gothic taste shows itself in his choice of words as much as in his choice of subject. He has a perverse pleasure in crabbedness for its own sake — he loves to employ words that most people would avoid; "domicile" for house, for example, or "congelation" for freezing, or "habiliments" for clothes.' In his long sentences, Hardy uses more clauses than are easily comprehended. At times, the twisted order of ideas causes difficulty to the readers.

[iii] *Incongruity between words and speaker's character* : At times, Hardy's style suffers from the incongruity between words and the speaker's character. His characters seem to be speaking a language which they cannot speak, but which Hardy speaks. Examples are numerous; Tess herself speaks unnaturally at times especially in *The Rally* and *The Consequence*. In chapter 19, we find Tess speaking "Because what's the use of learning that I

am one of a long row only.... The best is not to remember that your nature and your past doings have been just like thousands' and thousands,' and that your coming life and doings'll be like thousands' and thousands.'" In her dialogue with her brother Abraham on the fatal night of Prince's death we find her speaking about the earth as a 'blighted' star. David Cecil comments about the dialogue, "Here is no unsophisticated country-girl speaking. Through her lips comes the voice of a middle-aged novelist, brooding in gloomy mood on the riddle of the painful earth."

The other characters also speak unnaturally, for example, when Alec quotes Milton in his biblical references or when Mrs. Durbeyfield thinks in chapter 3. The incongruity is between the mediocre character and the philosophical or intellectual dialogue, which the character is incapable of speaking realistically.

24

Symbolism in *Tess*

Hardy is a conscious symbolist; he not only uses conventional symbols, but also develops private or personal symbols. Hardy uses symbolism in *Tess* very skillfully. At times Hardy's symbolism is too deep to be missed at first reading. In the novel he has used Edenic symbols, colour symbolism, symbol of changing seasons, symbolism from flora and fauna. Hardy has also used events in a symbolic manner; the events are more than mere events as they foreshadow and foretell other events. The major symbols or symbolic events in *Tess* are :

1. Symbol of Names

In the Victorian novels, names were part of characterization-technique. The names of characters used to be tell-tale. Hardy also chooses names of his characters meaningfully and symbolically. The name of Tess is an abridged form of her full name 'Teresa' meaning 'of the earth' [from the root 'terra', earth]. By the name itself she represents daughter of the soil, which is a major theme in the novel. Thus the name of Tess is not simply a name, but a symbol. The name of Angel is also symbolic of his elevated nature, more intellectual than others, more sky-ward, more heavenly, but also not like human beings. He represents 'cold intellectuality and high-flown idealism' which is inherent in the name itself. Angel's name suggests his spiritual nature — but it also suggests something which is not 'human.' Even the name of Alec is taken from the book of Job, where Alec is a fallen angel and hence it is an appropriate symbolic name for the sensual seducer. Thus, we find that Hardy has made the names of three major characters symbolic of their nature and behavioral pattern.

2. Edenic Symbolism

The novel is rich in Biblical quotations and references. One symbol of Bible used recurrently is the Adam-Eve-Satan parallel to Angel-Tess-Alec. It is easy to allegorically interpret the novel in the light of this symbolism. Satan tempts Eve in floral background and in the similar fashion Tess is tempted by Alec. Eve later on goes to Adam and in the same way Tess goes to Angel in an Edenic atmosphere. Satan is the villain of the piece, as he is responsible for bringing sex and death to Adam and Eve. From the very outset, this Edenic symbolism becomes manifest. Alec-Tess first meeting takes place in the context of an Edenic bower where there is a profusion of fruits and flowers. When Tess accepts to eat strawberries fed by Alec 'in a slight distress she parted her lips and took it in,' we understand Tess as the Eve who yields to the temptation of eating the Fruit of Knowledge. Alec later on refers to this Edenic parallel himself,

> *'A jester might say this is just like paradise. You are Eve, and I am the old Other One come to tempt you in the disguise of an inferior animal.'*

Later on, when she rushes through the 'apple-tree' garden to hear Clare's music, we are once more reminded of Eden and the story of the Original Sin related with the eating of the Forbidden Fruit. Hardy himself explicitly gives them the Edenic parallel, 'The spectral, half-compounded, aqueous light which pervaded the open mead, impressed them with a feeling of isolation, as if they were Adam and Eve' [Chapter 20]. The parallel of Eden is not very systematically or consistently developed, but it is nevertheless present in the background of the love-story.

3. The Death of Prince

The death of Prince, the horse means a great financial setback to the d'urbervilles family. However, it also symbolizes or foretells another major event — the seduction of Tess. The linguistic and image-associations in the death-scene of Prince are noteworthy. 'The pointed shaft of the cart had entered the breast of the unhappy Prince like a sword, and form the wound his life's blood was spouting in a stream.... In her despair Tess sprang forward and put her hand upon the hold, with the only result that she became splashed from face to skirt with the crimson drops' [p. 95]. The 'pointed shaft,' 'entered,' 'life's blood,' 'hole' and 'skirt' all can be symbolically related to the seduction-scene. The death-scene of Prince adumbrates the loss of her virginity, for she, too, will be brutally pierced on a darkened road far from home.

4. Symbol of Dying Pheasants

Dying pheasants were suffering due to the hunting of men. A shooting party was responsible for the sad plight of the dead and the dying pheasants . Hardy comments on 'a blood-thirsty light in their eyes,' and also digresses further, 'they ran amuck, and made it their purpose to destroy life — in this case harmless feathered creatures, brought into being by artificial means solely to gratify these propensities — at once so unmannerly and so unchivalorous towards their weaker fellows in Nature's teeming family' [Chapter 41]. Pheasants somehow become a symbol of the hunted, while the shooting party represents the hunters. Symbolically, Tess also belongs to the hunted class and this is why the symbol of dying pheasants is closely related with Tess's lot as she is also being hunted by a malevolent Destiny.

5. Colour Symbolism

Colour symbolism is a recurrent motif [see the note on *The Recurrent Motifs in Tess*]. The white colour signifies purity, and the red colour signifies violence, death, passion, or sex. In Tess Hardy carefully uses the red colour symbol, as this novel is about sexual passion as well as murder. When Tess goes to meet Mrs. d'Urberville, her house is of 'rich red colour.' This red colour is symbolic of Alec's sexual designs on Tess. When Tess meets Alec for the first time, he decks her with roses [flowers of red colour] and forces strawberries into her mouth [fruits of red colour]. The predominance of the red colour confirms the sexual connotations of the situation, and it has to be kept in mind that the Original Sin was also connected with a *red* fruit. It is significant that in the seduction scene, Tess is a 'white muslin figure,' for till then her body is untainted and pure. The association of white colour to virginity is manifest in May dance where every girl is wearing white to denote the dance of the virgins. Dull colours like brown and grey signify dull, hard lives and this is why these dull colours are prominently used in Flintcomb-Ash period.

6. Symbol of Harvester

In the novel we find that harvesting machines are twice brought in focus, first time at Marlott and another time at Flintcomb-Ash. The reaping machine which comes at Marlott becomes responsible for the death of 'rabbits, hares, snakes, rats, mice' [Chapter 14]. Hardy had an ambivalent attitude towards machines and in Tess the reaping machine or harvester has become a symbol of modernity encroaching upon rustic settings and destroying rural life. At Flintcomb Ash, the harvester is called 'the red tyrant' and 'plutonic master' which dehumanizes its engineer by reducing him to an apathetic mechanic; 'He was in the agricultural world, but not of it' [Chapter 47]. Once again we find that the natural inhabitants of the soil, *viz*. Animals get killed by the touch of the machine, 'the time for the rat-catching arrived at last' [Chapter 48]. The strain of working on the machine makes Tess also 'as weak as a bled calf' [Chapter 48]. The machines were town-made and hence alien to the setting. Hardy makes them symbols of modern scientific progress of his age but still has an skeptic attitude towards their influence on rustic humanity.

7. Capture at Stonehenge

Tess's capture at Stonehenge is not the simple apprehending of a murderer by policemen. It signifies more than that. Stonehenge is the heathen temple, where in ancient times sacrifices were done to the Sun-god. The pre-Christian pagan belief is adhered to by the novel's heroine and she upholds the heathen temple as her own. Still more significant is the fact that policemen let her sleep and wait till sunrise to capture her. Only at sunrise, the sacrifice can take place and hence the capture in night will not be symbolic. This is why Tess is caught after the sun rises and hanged after sunrise as well. The ritual of capture is actually the ritual of sacrifice made by human beings to the Sun-god.

8. Strawberry Symbol

Strawberry is as common a fruit as an apple, but it can also become as potent a symbol as apple has become of 'the forbidden fruit.' When Tess chooses to eat strawberries from Alec's hands, she symbolically surrenders to his sexual advances. It is significant that 'she obeyed like one in a dream'/according to Laura Claridge, "Tess accedes to Alec's demand that he feed her the strawberry himself : 'in a slight distress she parted her lips and took it in' [p. 64]. It is precisely our sense that Tess chooses her sexual initiation — that she knows what she is about — that makes this scene highly erotic.... After Tess 'takes in' Alec's offering, she wanders 'desultorily...eating in a half-pleased, half-reluctant state whatever d'Urberville offered her' [p. 64]. Her willingness to sate her appetite before leaving anticipates her reaction to her 'seduction' later on : thus she will stay with d'Urberville two weeks beyond the initial liaison, her eyes 'dazed' a little." The subtexts of both the strawberry scene and the seduction scene have to be studied as symbolic complements of each other.

9. Symbol of Seasons

Seasonal symbolism is a significant feature of Tess. It has been used to heighten the emotional response to Tess's fluctuating fortunes and her vicissitudes in her life's journeys [Symbolism of seasons has been dealt with elsewhere].

25

Imagery in *Tess*

Introduction

Hardy creates the kinship of his heroine with Nature principally by the subtle employment of imagery and suggestion. Hardy compares her to flora and fauna, to plants and animals. This brings into focus on one hand the passivity of Tess when pitted against the savage human assaults, and on the other hand the instinctive and emotional temperament of Tess which are not so sophisticated and artificial as those of society people. One of the subtlest techniques Hardy uses in *Tess* is that of creating atmosphere through connected images and corresponding verbal details, which work sometimes overtly, sometimes subtly.

Images from the Plant World

The schematic association of Tess with Nature is enforced by insistent allusions, literal and figurative, to the plant life. She is the 'daughter of the soil,' as all plants are. Early in the novel she appears with 'roses at her breast; roses in her hat; roses and strawberries in her basket to the brim' [chapter 6]. Her hair is 'earth-coloured' [chapter 5], and her mouth 'flower-like' [chapter 14]. she is compared to a 'plant' [chapter 27] and a 'sapling' [chapter 20]; the dew falls on her as naturally as on the grass [chapter 20] "Her physical appearance finds its metaphorical equivalents in the vegetable world," says David Lodge.

Animal Imagery

The behaviour, actions and sufferings of Tess are compared

to that of animals. Out pity of Tess is increased as we are made aware of how she is a victim, as all animal creation is, of external and uncomprehended forces. Allen comments, "Hardy describes Tess as having been 'caught during her days of immaturity like a bird in a springe'. . . When Tess was seduced at night in the wood, her experience really was like that of 'an animal caught in a trap as might have happened in the very same place.' The image goes to the heart of Tess's situation. She is caught in tragedy because she is animal; but if she had been merely animal, or if she had been Retty Priddle or Izz Huett, there would have been no tragedy."

[i] *Imagery of Animal Death* : Imagery of animal-death is a recurring pattern in Tess beginning with the death of prince, the horse. Then 'rabbits, hares, snakes, rats, mice. . . were every one put to death by the sticks and stones of the harvesters' [chapter 14]. Later on, Tess finds several pheasants 'writhing in agony' and to relieve their suffering 'her tears running down as she killed the birds tenderly' [Chapter 41]. The birds which have been killed so mercilessly symbolize Tess's feeling of being hunted and foreshadow the time when she will be run to death at Stonehenge. The death of prince also foreshadows the loss of virginity of Tess. The pointed shaft of the cart had entered the breast of the unhappy Prince like a sword, and from the wound his life's blood was spouting in a stream. It adumbrates the loss of her virginity, for she, too, will be brutally pierced on a darkened road far from home. The death of pheasants due to inadvertent shooting by hunters is also significant, because Tess belongs to their category as she is also hunted by men and by the President of the Immortals.

[ii] *Animals in the background* : Throughout her wandering career, Tess works in the animal background. When she goes to Trantridge, she tends fowls 'as supervisor, purveyor, nurse, surgeon and friend' [Chapter 9]. She whistles to the fowls and takes care of them. Even when she is seduced we find animal imagery in the background, 'gentle roosting birds... hopping rabbits and hares' [Chapter 11]. Later on, she goes to Talbothays and works as a dairymaid. There she milks cows and her affection for and affiliation with the cows is traced by Hardy,

'Tess went and bade all her favourite cows good-bye, touching each of them with her hand' [Chapter 37]. At Flintcomb Ash we find the migrating birds in the background, 'strange birds from behind the North Pole began to arrive' [Chapter 43]. Even when Angel proposes to Tess, the event takes place in the animal background. Tess is milking a cow and suddenly Angel embraces Tess, surprising Tess and the cow to a great degree. In the background we also find the story of the mad bull who kneels after listening to the Nativity tune. In the animal background, the omen of the cock crowing in the noon is also lurking. The animal background is also significant in Angel-Tess wooing. "Clare persistently wooed her in undertones like that of the purling milk — at the cow's side, at skimmings, at butter-makings, at cheese-makings, among broody poultry, and among farrowing pigs — as no milkmaid was ever wooed before by such a man." [Chapter 29]. Penny Boumehlha comments, "the broody hens and farrowing pigs of Talbothays, the stir of germination and the 'hiss of fertilization' give a context of impersonal biological process to the equally impersonal instinct that torments the women dairy-workers."

[iii] *Animal comparsion* : Tess has been compared to animals continuously, 'it moved her, as it moved the wild animals' [Chapter 15]. she 'wears the look of a wary animal.' [chapter 31]. she is as unresponsive to sarcasm as a 'dog or cat' [chapter 35]. She listens to Angel's harp like a 'fascinated bird,' and moves through the garden as 'stealthily as a cat' [chapter 19]. After sleep 'she was as warm as a sunned cat' [chapter 27]. Before the confession of Tess, 'she was surcharged with emotion, and winced like a wounded animal' [Chapter 34]. When she is happy, her tread is like 'the skim of a bird which has not quite alighted' [chapter 31]. She faces d'Urberville with 'the hopeless defiance of the sparrow's gaze before its captor twists its neck' [chapter 47]. When Tess overworks on the harvester, Alec says, 'You are as weak as a bled calf' [Chapter 48]. Even when she is finally captured, 'her breathing now was quick and small, like that of a lesser creature than a woman.' When Alec teases Tess, we find 'her large eyes staring at him like those of a wild animal.' Even the enemies of Tess are

compared to animals, 'they were waiting like wolves' [Chapter 31].

[iv] *Fly imagery* : Hardy uses fly imagery only thrice in the novel, but it is nonetheless significant. Although fly imagery should have come in the category of the animal imagery itself, yet it is so significant that it deserves separate category. The first fly-image comes when Tess goes to Talbothays, 'Not quite sure of her direction Tess stood still upon the hemmed expanse of verdant flatness, like a fly on a billiard-table of indefinite length, and of no more consequence to the surroundings than that fly' [Chapter 16]. The second image is at the stream-side where, Angel 'stood looking at the entrapped flies and butterflies.' The next fly-image is to be found at Flintcomb-Ash, when standing between the earth and the sky we find 'the two girls crawling over the surface of the former like flies.' Now this reduction of the heroine to the size of a fly implies a vertical, bird's eye picture; the looking down of Providence from a great height. The fly imagery is not a simple phenomenon, but carries pessimistic overtones by alluding to Shakespeare's most pessimistic play *King Lear.* Hardy himself quotes in his Preface to the fifth and later editions,

> As flies to wanton boys are we to the gods;
> They kills us for their sport.

In the view of the President of the Immortals human beings are as insignificant as flies are to human beings, and hence He does not pay any heed or attention to their prayers or pleas for mercy. The fly imagery is a powerful symbol of Hardy's pessimism. It also comments on the puny stature of mankind when pitted against the vast spectacle of Nature and deities as underlined by the fly imagery.

[v] *Significance of Animal imagery* : Animal imagery provides an animated but dehumanized background to human beings. Usually, it serves the writer to trace the degradation of human beings, their reduction from humanity to the level of animals. When human beings are devoid of intelligence, reason and speech [all of which separate men from animals]; and when they care merely for food, sleep and sex [which are associated with

animals]; they stoop to the animal state. Hardy has used animal imagery to indicate that Tess's kinship with nature is as strong as an animal's, that Tess is as emotional and sensuous as an animal, that she is neither so intellectual as Angel nor so perverted as Alec, that she resembles animals in her pagan and instinctive behaviour. The comparison of Tess with animal life also brings her into the category of 'the hunted.' Human beings hunt and shoot [at dead pheasants]. and kill [rats, snakes] animals for their pleasure. In the same manner, human beings [Angel and Alec in particular] have played with Tess and caused suffering to her and more importantly, the President of the Immortals has sported with her. Throughout the novel she runs away like an animal, pursued by a malevolent destiny like a hunter; and in the end she, being tired, gives up the struggle. The whole novel can be interpreted in terms of animal imagery, where Providence plays with her as a cat plays with a helpless and hapless mouse.

As the passion of Tess grows, the images grow richer and fuller. The images increase in proportion to the increase in the romance. The images become more detailed, more mythological, more intense. The paucity of natural images mark the neutral days of Tess's life. When Tess reveals to Clare her past sin, the images stop, die as rapidly as the love dies in Angel's heart. It is on the road to Flintcomb Ash that the images return. But they are very different now from the rich images of Talbothays. At Flintcomb Ash, she disfigures herself and the images are grim and grey, as in 'a hard black frost,' 'the whole field was in colour a desolate drab,' 'sticking into them like glass splinters,' 'the wide acreage of blank agricultural brownness.'

26

Hardy's Contribution to the Novel

1. Freed the novel from shackles of 18th century realism
2. Introduced the philosophical content
3. Brought epic grandeur to the novel
4. Portrayed man-woman relationship naturally without inhibitions and constraints
5. He is traditional as well as modern and hence bridges the gap between tradition and modernity
6. Has immortalised Wessex — the southernmost region of England.

Hardy has created for himself a permanent niche in the realm of English fiction. Though he stumbled, fumbled and erred again and again, he remains the most popular novelist of the Victorian era. The kind of fiction Hardy tried to explore had no parallel in the English literary world. His imagination was coloured by his upbringing in the southern most tradition-bound rural region of England. Here fiction was a tale told or song. Music was in his blood. He conceived his novel as a 'told' or 'sung' story — as an extension of a traditional ballad or an oral tale. The kind of climate he builds in his novels is where superstition, fate, chance and coincidence are given a full play. Here extraordinary events are given a local habitation and a name. It is the world of balladry where the extraordinary and the unseen have taken the place of the supernatural. Hardy does not write the chronicle novel or the biographical novel. He does not accumulate circumstantial details too. He loves country stories, where 'love' is the main focus, passion the main motivational force and 'death' the natural calamity. The logic of his fiction is not the logic of the modern fiction, here the improbable and the unpredictable is not only welcome but is essential. "A story has to be exceptional enough," said Hardy. The events had to be extraordinary but the characters should never be 'abnormal' or 'incredible' for that would at once strike a false note.

Perhaps the one reason for his extreme popularity is that he caters to the infinite urge of humanity to hear strange tales of love and passion. The ills and woes to which lovers are subjected to, in their progress towards happiness and consummation of 'love' have fascinated man from times immemorial. Hardy's world is peopled with simple, inarticulate, rustic people whose literary accomplishments amount to a study of Bible and technical skill to the common village occupations. Their simplicity, steadfastness, elemental passions forged a strange relationship with the reader which could not be broken. Hardy's faults are many, yet his admirers love him.

Within the circumscribed limits of Wessex, Hardy created many characters who dance, sing, make love and die, doing at times desperate things like murder and suicide, adultery and moral cheating. Their manner, their speech may be outdated but they have something that surpasses the limits of time and place and makes them of all places and all times.

Richard Church, in The Growth of English Novel says, 'Hardy, therefore, is important in the history of English novel, because he brought it back to its full authority of poetry. I spoke of Aeschylus; here is what Hardy did. He used the novel in English as that ancient father of Greek drama used the stage and the religious grove. He kept the novel in the centre of life's road with no eccentric turn to right or left, of verbal foppery or intellectual trope. He was essentially humble-minded and that is a base which in the long run affords the firmest of all human perspectives against which to pose the story of man-in-passing.'

What marks Hardy is his deep love and sympathy for man. He makes his characters infinitely enchanting. We see them, hear them, feel for them without realising that theirs is a world, conjured up by a fine artist whose heart rendering presentation has created a verisimilitude of life seen in its myriad colours. We wake up to the realities of our existence when the novel ends.

Hardy's fictional output is of uniform consistency. Never before had a region been so comprehensively celebrated as in these books. It is a world of lush meadows and vernal woods, as well as the harsh upland of the Flintcomb Ash. The stubborn soil and the rough conditions of weather make labour extremely difficult here. The desolate and drab condition is described by Hardy as a 'complexion without features,' the 'white vacuity of countenance with the lineaments gone.' Here nature existed in all its ferocity and scantiness, exacting hard labour from man, who helpless and defenceless, stands in antagonism to the harsh earth. Human isolation is best exemplified here in the vast swede-fields where the upper half of each turnip had been eaten off by livestock and the lower half had to be hacked for consumption.

Hardy is not only alive to the harsh conditions of the earth, he also brings live the dehumanising impact of machine on man. The Threshing machine and the Reaping machine are good examples. Not only men but small animals like rats, rabbits, snakes etc., also stand in subjugation to the machine.

What strikes us most in Hardy's realistic portrayal of the aspects of Nature is their precision. Hardy is like Keats in this aspect. All the senses are receptive to the slightest change in nature. His appraisal of the world of Nature is direct and, therefore, so engaging and realistic. Intellectually Hardy was a man of his age and his novels, though written in the conventional form raise the issues prevalent in the modern world. His taste in story-telling, his love of rustic life, his chronological story-pattern, puts him into the category of the traditional novelists; but the frank delineation of the issues regarding religion, marriage, love, sex etc., reveal his modern concern.

Concerned with the deep forces that govern our lives, Hardy says, "My art is to intensify the expression of things so that the heart and inner meaning is made vividly visible." He finds discord in the nature of existence, Man is working to one end, Destiny to another. These ends may or may not coincide. Either way it is Destiny who decides what shall happen. The past is kept like a hostage, and the greatest ransom is asked by Destiny at the most crucial moment of one's life. Through this pattern he conveys the impact of the hidden forces that shape our life.

What man thirsts for is happiness and, the happiness promised by 'love' is as Fielding says, 'the greatest felicity attainable upon earth.' But 'love' in Hardy is 'the Lord of terrible aspect' — a blind irresistible power that more often than not brings ruin and catastrophe.

We are shown here, says David Cecil, "life in its fundamental elements." In their fight against destiny these simple, rustic folks exhibit a great strength of character and reach great tragic heights. They fall, as is inevitable for their enemy is too powerful, yet their fall exhibits the limits to which human beings can aspire. Man is a victim of the supernatural forces, yet his fight is noble. Man, said Hardy, had outraced his own gods and was now to be seen turning and attempting to civilise the gods, with disastrous results.

Hardy's imaginative range covers the struggle of man with destiny and thus his scale is as vast as his setting is confined or localised. His imagination combined the fantastic and the real in a strange mixture; the result was a most moving vivid picture of life firmly rooted in the common soil of the fundamental truths that make for our existence upon this earth. No other English novelist has such a fine power of visualisation. He builds up his novels upon a series of most vividly realised scenes. As the novel proceeds to its climax, the scenes become clearer and get firmly rooted in the memory of the reader, entertaining our minds, we never get bored. Like Shakespeare he uses the tools of the popular writer to the best of his advantage. His works entertain us, thrill us and also make us a sadder and wiser person.

His characters are life-like. Their passions, their actions, their speech never enter the realm of the improbable or unnatural. They have a family likeness. We share their joys and sorrows. There are the simple, staunch, tender-hearted selfless characters like Gabriel Oak, Giles Winterbourne, Diggory Venn; the dashing, fickle, heart-broken — Troy, Wildeve, Fitzpiers, d'Urberville etc. There are the patient devoted forgiving women — Tess, Marty,

Elizabeth-Jane; the wilful capricious but fundamentally good-hearted — Bathsheba, Grace, Fancy, Anne etc. There is the passion-tormented romantic enchantress — Eustacia, Mrs. Charmond, Lucetta, Lady Constantine etc. There are also modern intellectual modern men like Knight, Angel etc. and so on. In a harsh world, Hardy sees man thirsting for happiness which 'love' can bestow. Thus not only the range but even the emotions are to some extent limited. Hardy's sensibility to 'feminine charm' has been widely acclaimed. The heroines of most other novelists appear like wax dolls before these wonderfully realistic, life-like portraits, who live in our memory for ever.

David Cecil calls Hardy the master of the dying fall, the Miltonic close in calm of mind, all passions spent, the fading echoing music, that, when soft voices die, vibrate in our memory. His novels present a defiant despairing cry against the injustice of it all, so many fine lives are lost due to the injustice of gods and men. As one of the characters in Tess says, it is always the 'comeliest ones' who meet with such drastic fate, the defiant ones, who dare to rise against 'It', that are trampled upon by 'Destiny,' for "happiness was but the occasional episode in a general drama of pain."

Humour, character, landscape, vividly depicted scenes, tales brilliantly opened and eloquently ended are the tools with which Hardy casts his spell upon us. Behind them lies the emotional force which makes his canvas as vast as the universe scaling the depths of black despair as well as the ecstatic joy. He is a dreamer and his dreamworld is full of men and women who reach great heights in their most tragic moments. Their passions are ineffectual in curbing their destiny.

Hardy was the last lonely representative of an ancient race. Endowed with Elizabethan imagination, he found himself, by some accident of Destiny, into the alien world of the later nineteenth century. He didn't find man to be a noble piece but found him to be the late and transient product of some automatic principle of life, cast in a universe of which he knew nothing and to whom he was nothing. There was no benign spirit behind him and there was no promise of a 'heaven' in front of him. It was all bleak, dark and dismal. But as he himself says, some natures become vocal in 'tragedy.' His is the world of a man 'in whose soul the iron has entered.' We go to him again and again for these tales of woes and passions.

Glossary

Cerealia	:	Festivities held in the honour of Ceres from April 12-19. The goddess Cerelia was identified with Demeter.
Satyrs	:	In Greek mythology, attendants of Dionysus, spirits of the woods & hills. They were lustful and fond of revelry. Connected with fertility, they are represented as grotesque creatures.
Nymphs	:	In Greek mythology female personifications of various natural objects, rivers, trees, mountains; Vague beings represented as young and beautiful, fond of music and dancing, long-lived but not immortal. Those of trees are called Dryads, of mountains Oreads, of rivers and springs Naiads.
Pan	:	Greek god of flocks and shepherds, son of Hermes or of Zeus, represented as partly goat-like in form. He invented the musical pipe of seven reeds named Syrinx. Romans identified him with Fannus. In another version, Pan the lustful god pursued Syrinx a nymph who was changed into a reed by other gods who took pity on her.
Lotis	:	A nymph who was changed into a plant while running from a base pursuer.
Priapus	:	God of fertility, of gardens and herds; son of Aphrodite and Dionysus.
Selene	:	In Greek mythology, the moon daughter of Hyperion and Theia and sister of Sun, sometimes identified with Artemis.

Artemis	:	Identified with Diana, in Greek mythology, daughter of Zeus and Lelo and sister of Apollo. Goddess of wild life, a virgin huntress, also a goddess of childbirth and of all very young things, also identified with moon.
Demeter	:	Daughter of Cronus and Rhea and sister of Zeus; goddess of corn and patroness of agriculture in general, identified with Ceres by the Romans; mother of Persephone.
Adam	:	The first man and Eve his wife — the first woman created out of his ribs.
Norman Conquest	:	The defeat of Harold, the king of England. At Senlac in 1066 by William the Conqueror from Normandy is called Normandy is called Norman conquest.
King Stephen	:	King of England from 1135 to 1154.
King John	:	King of England from 1199 to 1216.
Charles II	:	Son of Charles I, ascended the throne of England after Cromwell's death in 1660.
Malthus	:	An economist found that population if unchecked goes on growing at a rate higher than the means of substance.
Praxiteles	:	A great Greek sculptor, unrivalled for creating beautiful female figures.
Guardian Angel	:	The Christians believe that every human being has a guardian angel hovering over him to save him from danger. Hardy makes fun of such a notion.
Heliolatries	:	Sun worship, from Helios, Sun.
Monotheism	:	Belief in only one God.
Alexander	:	A great ruler and conqueror of 4th century B.C.
Caesar	:	The first Roman Emperor of 1st Century.
Pharaohs	:	Kings of Egypt.

Low Church	:	The Evangelical wing of the Anglican Church; emphasis on preaching, very plain services.
High Church	:	The branch of the Anglican Church nearest to Roman Catholic, with an emphasis on ritual.
Evangelists	:	Those who emphasise on the special importance of the words of Bible in the Christian life.
Peter the Great	:	The emperor of Russia from 1689 to 1725.
Resurrection Hour	:	The hour when the Christ rose from the dead.
Antinomianism	:	The belief that Christians are emancipated by the gospel from obligation to keep the moral law.
John Wycliff	:	The morning star of Reformation in the medieval age.
Calvin	:	A great reformer, author of Institutes of the Christian religion.
Whitman	:	A great American poet, novelist and short story writer. These lines are from '*Crossing the Brooklyn Ferry.*'
Conversionist	:	A believer in the conscious change of heart impelling the sinner to repent and begin a new life.
Paul of Tarsus	:	St. Paul, Christ's disciple who spread Christianity.
St. John	:	St. John, the apostle, a disciple of St. John the Baptist.
Gospel of St. John	:	The son of God came in flesh to absolve the humanity of its sins.
Saint James	:	Author of a Catholic epistle of the New Testament, based on the Sermon on the Mount for its emphasis on morality.
Schopenhauer	:	A great philosopher, author of *The World as Will and Idea.*

Mead	:	A fermented drink made from honey and water.
Centurions	:	Commanders of a hundred men in army.
Guinevere	:	Wife of King Arthur, the legendary king of Scotland.
Soloman	:	King of Israel in 10th century B.C., mentioned in the Old Testament, much acclaimed for his wisdom.
Scepticism	:	Disbelief in the reality of the transcendental.
Infidel	:	One who rejects Christianity as disbeliveers ın divine revelation.
Faustina	:	Wife of the Emperor Marcus Aurelius.
Druidical Mistletoe	:	The pre-Christian priests, the Druids held Mistletoe to be especially sacred.
Dolorifuge	:	A chaser away of sorrow.
Lotis	:	Daughter of sea-god; she was changed into a lotus when the god of sexuality pursued her.
Ironical Tishbite	:	Elijah, describing Baal, the heathen god.
Aholah and Aboiibah	:	Biblical harlots.
Sorrow, the Undesired	:	Rachael's son was named Ben-Oni, son of my sorrow.
Nature's Holy Plan	:	Wordsworth's Lines written in Early Spring.
Tree of Knowledge	:	The forbidden tree from which Eve ate the apple, which in turn brought about the expulsion of man from Paradise. Bible, Genesis
Olympian	:	The classical gods lived on Mount Olympus.
Valley of Humiliation	:	In Bunyan's The Pilgrim's Progress.
Queen of Sheeba	:	A biblical character, overwhelmed by Solomon's knowledge and wisdom.
Man of Uz—Job	:	The biblical example of extreme suffering.

Peter the Great	:	Emperor of Russia, who studied in foreign shipyards 1697-98 before building his own navy.
Abraham	:	In the Bible, he possessed many animals and servants.
Mary Magdalene	:	One of the first to see the risen Christ— a fallen woman, who had repented.
Holy Thursday	:	The day of Christ's Ascension into Heaven.
Three Leahs to get one Rachel	:	Jacob first married Leah and only then was allowed to work to earn Rachel as his wife. Bible — Genesis.
Thorny Crown	:	Recalling the crown of thorns placed on the head of Christ before his crucifixion.
First Cause	:	Philosophical term for that which sets the universe in motion.
Antinomianism	:	A belief, favoured by evangelical Christians, that belief in Jesus Christ is above the moral law.
Determinism	:	The belief that the way one lives does not affect salvation or damnation in the next life, which is already known to God.
Canons	:	Laws of Church.
Rubric	:	Instruction for the carrying out of services.
Geocentric	:	The old belief that the earth was at the centre of the universe, hell below and heaven above.
Vestal	:	Roman Virgin who tended the temple of Vestal.
Christologist	:	Student of the theology of Christ's life.
Calvinistic	:	Follower of Calvin.
Basnns, licence	:	Before Church wedding, notice must be given by reading out the names of the couple in three weekly services unless a special licence is obtained.
Temerarious	:	Rash.
Friar Lawrence	:	In Shakespeare's Romeo and Juliet.

Prestidigitation	: Conjuring trick.
Agape	: Love-feast
The Nazarene	: Jesus Christ.
Amazonians	: The Amazons were a legendary race of warrior women.
Methodists	: Followers of John Wesley (1703-91) who broke away from the Anglican Church.
Dictionnaire Philosophique	: (1764) by Voltaire.
Witch of Babylon	: The horrendous figure in the Bible.
Weltlust	: [German] delight in the world.
Lucretia	: Virtuous woman raped by Tarquin [534-510 B.C.].
Wife of Uriah	: Bathsheba, seduced by Kind David, who later marries her.
Ixionian Wheel	: In classical mythology Ixion was condemned in Hell to be bound to an ever-turning fiery wheel.
Atlanta	: Legendary woman, who would marry a man who could defeat her in a race.
Antinous	: Beautiful youth loved by Emperor Hadrian.
Aeschylean Phrase	: From famous Greek dramatist Aeschylus' play 'Prometheus Bound.'
Joined hands again	: From Milton's Paradise Lost, where Adam and Eve descend on earth with joined hands.